Other Books and Seri

*1901-1907 Native American Census Seneca,
Ottawa, Peoria, Quapaw, and Wyandotte In(
Territory)*

*1932 Census of The Standing Rock Sioux Reservation with Births /....
1924-1932*

Census of The Blackfeet, Montana, 1897- 1901 Expanded Edition

Eastern Cherokee by Blood, 1906-1910, Volumes I thru XIII

*Choctaw of Mississippi Indian Census 1929-1932 with Births and Deaths 1924-
1931   Volume I
Choctaw of Mississippi Indian Census 1933, 1934 & 1937, Supplemental Rolls to
1934 & 1935 with Births and Deaths 1932-1938, and Marriages 1936-1938
Volume II*

*Eastern Cherokee Census Cherokee, North Carolina 1930-1939
Census 1930-1931 with Births And Deaths 1924-1931 Taken By Agent L. W. Page
Volume I
Eastern Cherokee Census Cherokee, North Carolina 1930-1939
Census 1932-1933 with Births And Deaths 1930-1932 Taken By Agent R. L.
Spalsbury   Volume II
Eastern Cherokee Census Cherokee, North Carolina 1930-1939
Census 1934-1937 with Births and Deaths 1925-1938 and Marriages 1936 & 1938
Taken by Agents R. L. Spalsbury And Harold W. Foght Volume III*

*Seminole of Florida Indian Census, 1930-1940 with Birth and Death
Records, 1930-1938*

Texas Cherokees 1820-1839 A Document For Litigation 1921

Choctaw By Blood Enrollment Cards 1898-1914 Volumes I thru XVII

*Starr Roll 1894   (Cherokee Payment Rolls) Districts: Canadian, Cooweescoowee,
and Delaware Volume One
Starr Roll 1894 (Cherokee Payment Rolls) Districts: Flint, Going Snake, and
Illinois   Volume Two
Starr Roll 1894 (Cherokee Payment Rolls) Districts: Saline, Sequoyah, and
Tahlequah; Including Orphan Roll   Volume Three*

Cherokee Intruder Cases Dockets of Hearings 1901-1909 Volumes I & II

*Indian Wills, 1911-1921 Records of the Bureau of Indian Affairs
Books One thru Seven;
Native American Wills & Probate Records 1911-1921*

Other Books and Series by Jeff Bowen

Turtle Mountain Reservation Chippewa Indians 1932 Census with Births & Deaths, 1924-1932

Chickasaw By Blood Enrollment Cards 1898-1914 Volume I thru V

Cherokee Descendants East An Index to the Guion Miller Applications Volume I
Cherokee Descendants West An Index to the Guion Miller Applications Volume II (A-M)
Cherokee Descendants West An Index to the Guion Miller Applications Volume III (N-Z)

Applications for Enrollment of Seminole Newborn Freedmen, Act of 1905

Eastern Cherokee Census, Cherokee, North Carolina, 1915-1922, Taken by Agent James E. Henderson   *Volume I (1915-1916)*
                                      Volume II (1917-1918)
                                      Volume III (1919-1920)
                                      Volume IV (1921-1922)

Complete Delaware Roll of 1898

Eastern Cherokee Census, Cherokee, North Carolina, 1923-1929, Taken by Agent James E. Henderson   *Volume I (1923-1924)*
                                      Volume II (1925-1926)
                                      Volume III (1927-1929)

Applications for Enrollment of Seminole Newborn Act of 1905 Volumes I & II

North Carolina Eastern Cherokee Indian Census 1898-1899, 1904, 1906, 1909-1912, 1914 Revised and Expanded Edition

1932 Hopi and Navajo Native American Census with Birth & Death Rolls (1925-1931) Volume 1 - Hopi
1932 Hopi and Navajo Native American Census with Birth & Death Rolls (1930-1932) Volume 2 - Navajo

Western Navajo Reservation Navajo, Hopi and Paiute 1933 Census with Birth & Death Rolls 1925-1933

Cherokee Citizenship Commission Dockets 1880-1884 and 1887-1889 Volumes I & II

Visit our website at **www.nativestudy.com** to learn more about these
and other books and series by Jeff Bowen

CHEROKEE CITIZENSHIP COMMISSION DOCKETS 1880-1884 AND 1887-1889
VOLUME III

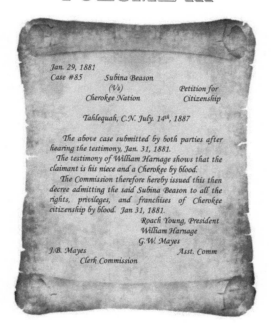

Jan. 29, 1881
Case #85   Subina Beason
                   (Vs)   Petition for
              Cherokee Nation   Citizenship

Tahlequah, C.N. July. 14ᵗʰ, 1887

    The above case submitted by both parties after hearing the testimony, Jan. 31, 1881.
    The testimony of William Harnage shows that the claimant is his niece and a Cherokee by blood.
    The Commission therefore hereby issued this then decree admitting the said Subina Beason to all the rights, privileges, and franchises of Cherokee citizenship by blood. Jan 31, 1881.
               Roach Young, President
               William Harnage
               G. W. Mayes
J.B. Mayes   Asst. Comm
     Clerk Commission

TRANSCRIBED BY
JEFF BOWEN

NATIVE STUDY
Gallipolis, Ohio
USA

Originally published:
Baltimore, Maryland
2011

Reprinted by:

Native Study LLC
Gallipolis, OH
www.nativestudy.com
2020

Library of Congress Control Number: 2020916859

ISBN: 978-1-64968-060-0

Made in the United States of America.

INTRODUCTION

This publication was previously published by another publisher in 2009 and has now been reproduced by Native Study LLC. There are five volumes in this series concerning the Cherokee Citizenship Commission Dockets 1880 to 1889. This is material that was never before transcribed containing 2,288 Cherokee docket decisions.

This is somewhat of an explanation concerning the reasoning behind the proceedings that led the Cherokee tribal courts to take charge of these docket hearings.

The Cherokee relied upon their leaders to guide them but they ended up hanging in the balance after the Civil War, with their loyalties split worse than ever and their country ravished. Fathers and brothers were off fighting a war that didn't even concern them. By the time the war was over the Cherokee people had lost any form of stability. The men fighting the war came back to the same old political hatreds and in-fighting. The Nation was being over run with many that claimed they were Cherokee, hoping to benefit from false claims of citizenship. These people, known as intruders, did nothing but make it more difficult for the Cherokees because of the pressures from the Government to control their boundaries. The blood Cherokees that were seeking their homeland were again in question as to who they were. They found nothing but scrutiny and distrust, the war had made them choose a side, and the U.S. Government didn't care for the choice of the majority.

Intruder after intruder was encroaching on Cherokee land and what was to seem like a never ending battle. Many Cherokee citizens had lost their rights while intruders that didn't belong stayed using up what little resources there were. The government was telling the Cherokee leaders to settle their own intruder problems or else they would have to intercede. In an effort to clarify who were true Cherokee citizens and who were not, or who had been wrongfully taken off of the rolls, was a problem.

There were part-bloods, full-bloods, and no bloods along with mass confusion, prejudice, vendettas, and deceptions. The intruders wanted a free ride and were willing to use the confusion as a camouflage to achieve their purpose and greed.

This was a situation where the government was threatening to come in and turn the Cherokee Nation into a Federal Territory because it appeared to them that the Tribal Council would not be able to organize an effort to control the problem. But this wasn't the issue at hand as far as the Cherokee were concerned. They felt as if, according to their treaty stipulations, the United States was responsible for intruder removal. They felt as if the United States had let things get out of hand and that the government had not lived up to its contractual agreement. According to treaty stipulations this was true, but, they were told to either come up with a solution or lose their rights as a sovereign nation.

From William G. McLoughlin's book , *After the Trail of Tears, The Cherokees Struggle for Sovereignty 1839-1880,* it references on page 354, "Still, the Nation remained very uneasy about the fundamental question of its right to define who were its own citizens and its right to expect the United States to remove those who the Nation judged were not. Ever since 1872, federal agents had refused to expel from the Nation those former slaves whom the Nation considered 'aliens' and since 1874, federal agents had been under instructions from the Bureau of Indian Affairs to compile their own list of black or white persons who, in their opinion, had some claim to citizenship despite previous rulings of the Cherokee Courts on their claims."

On page 355-356, "On the basis of the affidavits and reports submitted, the Secretary of Interior, Zachariah Chandler, sent E.C. Watkins to the Nation in 1875, to investigate the citizenship problem and gather information that Chandler could use to ask Congress to take action on behalf of these 'men without a country'. Watkins reported in February, 1876, that many of those on Ingall's list were 'clearly entitled' to Cherokee citizenship. Oochalata denied it. He counter charged that Ingalls was meddling in Cherokee affairs and wrote to the Bureau of Indian Affairs to complain. Receiving no satisfactory response, he wrote directly to President Grant on November 13, 1876, enclosing a petition from the Cherokees Cooweescoowee District, complaining that the agent had not removed thousands of intruders in their area though ordered to do so by the Council. Some of these intruders were former slaves from the Deep South, but most were white U.S. citizens from Kansas, Missouri, and Arkansas.

Grant referred this letter to Commissioner J.Q. Smith. Annoyed that Oochalata had gone over the head of the Interior Department to the President, on December 8, Smith wrote Oochalata a long, assertive, and highly provocative letter outlining for the first time the department's position on this question. Smith said that from the evidence he had received, both from various federal agents and from the investigations of E.C. Watkins, the Cherokee Nation had failed to deal consistently and impartially with the problems of former slaves and others who claimed Cherokee citizenship. Therefore, the Bureau of Indian Affairs would continue to compile its own list of those who had 'prima facie' evidence for citizenship [whether the Cherokee courts had acted negatively on their claims or not], and it would take no action to remove them until the Cherokees carried four stipulations to resolve the issue. First, the Council must establish a clear, legal procedure providing due process for adjudicating all prima facie claims. Second, the rules by which such cases were decided must be approved by the Secretary of the Interior to ensure their impartiality. Third, he suggested that the Cherokee Circuit Courts be designated as the appropriate bodies for such hearings. Finally, claimants' appeals of the decisions of the Cherokee Circuit Courts must be forwarded to the Secretary of the Interior, and no claimant for citizenship should be removed from the Nation until the Secretary had made his own ruling. In effect, Smith asserted the right of the Bureau of Indian Affairs to decide who was and was not a Cherokee citizen. A crucial decision concerning the issue of the sovereignty of Indian nations was about to be reached.

Oochalata was stunned and wrote a 139-page letter to Smith explaining why this procedure was totally unacceptable and contrary to law, treaties, precedent, and the U.S. Constitution."

On page 357, "Acting on instructions from Oochalata, the Cherokee Delegation sent another letter to President Grant on Jan. 9, 1877, insisting that treaty rights, the Trade and Intercourse Act, and precedent gave the Nation the right 'to determine the question as to who are and who are not intruders.' The president referred their letter to Secretary of the Interior, Carl Schurz, who, on April 21, 1877, told the delegation that he supported Smith's four stipulations for settling the matter. Oochalata ignored this response and in August, 1877, sent to the new Commissioner of Indian Affairs, Ezra A. Hayt, a list of all the intruders whom the Cherokees wished to be immediately removed. On Nov. 7, Hayt replied flatly that the Bureau of Indian Affairs would not do so: 'while the department reserves to itself the right to finally determine who are and are not intruders under the law, **it expects the Cherokee Nation Council to enact some general and uniform law by which the Cherokee courts shall hear and determine the rights of claimants to citizenship,** subject only to the review of the Secretary of Interior after a final adjudication has been reached.'"

On page 358-9, "The department's claim that it had the right to judge intruders was, in Oochalata's opinion, 'a new doctrine for construing treaty or contracts in writing, to add to it verbally, a new clause, after the expiration of 92 years from date of that compact or treaty and without the consent of [one] party. . . . It is a dangerous doctrine to which I can never agree.'

While he urged the Council to send a protest through its delegation, Oochalata also asked it to enact a law that would establish a court to decide citizenship claims in a legal and uniform manner. The Council complied on Dec. 5, 1877, but the compromise was fatally weakened by the Council's failure to address two aspects of the law governing the Citizenship Court's actions.

First, the law provided no guidelines for deciding cases that would meet the demands of the Bureau of Indian Affairs, and consequently, in cases involving former slaves, the Citizenship Court relied, as the Cherokee Supreme Court had in 1870-71, simply on the wording in the Treaty of 1866. Second, the Council explicitly refused to allow the right of the Secretary of the Interior to review the decisions of the Court, stating that the Cherokee Citizenship Court was 'a tribunal of last resort'. The three persons appointed to the court, were John Chambers, O.P. Brewer, and George Downing. Also referred to as the Chamber's Commission, the Court began to hold hearings early in 1878. All persons claiming to have grounds for citizenship were required to present them or be declared intruders."

On pages 359-360, McLoughlin continues, "By the end of 1878, Oochalata struggling to find some new approach to the problem. On Dec. 3, he went over the head of the Bureau of Indian Affairs again, and wrote to Pres. Rutherford B. Hayes, forwarding a complete account of all of the cases adjudicated by the Citizenship Court and asking him to order the expulsion of those rejected and all other intruders. He told Hayes that the Cherokee Nation had an 'inherent national right' to define its own citizens, while the United States had a well-established obligation to expel non-citizens. Suspecting that Hayes would reject this request, Oochalata approached Commissioner Ezra A. Hayt and tried to work out a compromise. He said that the Cherokees would stop confiscating the property of those former slaves judged to be intruders pending the appointment of a joint commission of Cherokees and members of the Bureau to review the rejected claims.   Hayt agreed only on the condition that decisions of this commission must be unanimous or the Bureau would retain the right to make its own decision in each case. Oochalata and the delegation could not accept such a condition, and the negotiations broke down. Finally, as a last resort, the council decided to submit a series of questions to the Secretary of Interior, Carl Schurz, about their right to determine citizenship and the obligation of the United States to accept their determinations. They asked Schurz to present their questions to Attorney General Charles Devens for his opinion. They sent the letter on March 3, 1879, and after Hayt informed Devens of his views on the matter, Devens held hearings at which both sides presented their views.   Realizing the importance of the decision, the Cherokees spent the money necessary to hire the best lawyers they could find to assist them. Hayt said that the status of at least one-thousand persons was at issue, the Council argued that there were over twice that many intruders whom the Department was refusing to move.

Throughout the dispute, the Bureau of Indian Affairs declined to act against intruding squatters from Kansas who made no pretense to citizenship.

"The three questions that the Council asked Devens to answer were: Did the Cherokee Nation have the right to determine its own citizenship? Did the former slaves who were citizens have any share in the use of Cherokee land or in the money derived from the sale of the Cherokee land? Was it, or was it not, the duty of the Federal government to remove intruders under treaty stipulations and Trade and Intercourse Act? By the time Devens sent his reply, the Citizenship Court had heard 416 claims for citizenship and rejected 338."

Devens' opinion was clearly in the negative as far as the Cherokee Nation's sovereignty and decision processes were concerned. On page 364, McLoughlin observes, "Clearly, as since the days of Andrew Jackson, Federal refusal to honor the requirement of removing intruders was to be the means of forcing the Indian nations to do what they did not want to do." Ochalata would not run again as the election of August 1879 neared and Dennis W. Bushyhead became the new chief on August 4, 1879 but in the end it didn't matter who was chief the fight to keep Cherokee sovereignty along with self government was all but lost by 1880. On pages 365-366, McLoughlin wrote, "The turning point was reached in 1887 when Congress passed the Dawes Severalty Act. The act expressed what was now the national consensus among white voters (including Indian reformers, railroad magnates, and entrepreneurs) -that the solution to "'the Indian question'" was to denationalize the tribes in the Indian Territory, survey and allot their land in severalty, and establish a white-dominated territorial government over "'Oklahoma'" the Choctaw word for "'red man.'"

The sovereignty of the Western Cherokee tribe was taken, and to this day they still don't have a true land base as a nation. Even though others were able to take away the land that was promised to remain theirs forever; nobody was able to take away their right and ability to choose who was a true citizen and who was not. The dockets transcribed within this series are exactly as they appeared on the microfilm copies from the original court records involving citizenship during the time periods of 1880-1889.

These dockets were referenced and transcribed from microfilm series; 7RA25-0001 (American Genealogical Lending Library), Cherokee Citizenship Commission Docket Books, 1880-1884 and 1887-1889.

Jeff Bowen
Gallipolis, Ohio
NativeStudy.com

BRYANT

Docket #719

CENSUS ROLLS 1835

APPLICANT FOR CHEROKEE CITIZENSHIP

POST OFFICE: Miland[sic] Tenn		ATTORNEY: C H Taylor	
NO	NAMES	AGE	SEX
1	George W Bryant	52	Male
2	John Bryant	20	"
3	James Bryant	18	"
4	Ouey Bryant	14	female
5	Willie Bryant	10	Male

ANCESTOR: John Bryant

Rejected March 18- 1889

<u>Adverse</u>

Embraced in decission[sic] on page 431
Book B. in the Aaron Bellew case.
Rendered March 18 – 1889.

Will P. Ross
Chairman Com.
John E. Gunter   Com

Office Commission on Citizenship
Tahlequah I.T.   March 18th 1889
D.S. Williams
Clk Com

BRYANT

Docket #720

CENSUS ROLLS 1835

APPLICANT FOR CHEROKEE CITIZENSHIP

POST OFFICE: Miland[sic] Tenn		ATTORNEY: C H Taylor	
NO	NAMES	AGE	SEX
1	Charles Bryant	26	Male

ANCESTOR: John Bryant

Rejected March 18 – 1889

Cherokee Citizenship Commission Docket Books
(1880-84, 1887-89) Volume III
Tahlequah, Cherokee Nation

<u>Adverse</u>
Embraced in decission[sic] on page 431
Book B. in the Aaron Bellew case.
Rendered March 18 – 1889.

Will P. Ross
Chairman Com.
John E. Gunter   Com

Office Commission
on Citizenship
Tahlequah I.T.
March 18 – 1889

D.S. Williams
Clk Com

Commission on Citizenship.

CHEROKEE NATION, IND. TER.

Tahlequah,   March 18 – 1889

Familys	Charles Bryant	aged	26	years	male
"	W.R. Bryant	"			
"	Lillian Bryant	"	16	"	Female
"	John Bryant	"	14	"	Male
"	Ethel Bryant	"	12	"	Female
"	Eugena Bryant	"	10	"	Male
"	Stella Bryant	"	8	"	Female
"	Agnes Bryant	"	6	"	"
"	Sybyl Bryant	"	4	"	"
"	William C. Bryant	"	21	"	Male
"	Brinkley Bryant	"	23	"	"
"	Hannah Cannan	"	21	"	Female
"	Tennessee Carter	"	30	"	"
"	Sallie Carter	"	6	"	"
"	Vinnie Lee Carter	"	4	"	"
"	Mary E. Baird	"	41	"	"
"	W.M. Baird	"	19	"	Male
"	M.D.L. Baird	"	17	"	"

"	G.M. Baird	"	14	"	"
"	G A Baird	"	10	"	Female
"	Z.V. Coley	"	35	"	"
"	Maud Coley	"	14	"	"
"	Robert Coley	"	12	"	Male
"	Neva Coley	"	10	"	Female

DS Williams
Clk. Com

BAIRD

Docket #721
CENSUS ROLLS 1835

APPLICANT FOR CHEREOKEE CITIZENSHIP

POST OFFICE: Chelsea IT.		ATTORNEY: C H Taylor	
NO	**NAMES**	**AGE**	**SEX**
1	Mary C Baird	41	female
2	W M Baird	19	Male
3	M D L Baird	17	"
4	G.M. Baird	14	"
5	J A Baird	10	female

ANCESTOR: John Bryant
Rejected March 18 – 1889

<u>Adverse</u>
Embraced in decission[sic] on page 431
Book B. in the Aaron Bellew case.
Rendered March 18 – 1889.

Will P. Ross
Chairman Com.
John E. Gunter   Com

Office Commission
on Citizenship
Tahlequah I.T.
March 18 – 1889

D.S. Williams
Clk Com

3

BRYANT

Docket #722
CENSUS ROLLS 1835

APPLICANT FOR CHEROKEE CITIZENSHIP

POST OFFICE: Chauteau Ind Tery		ATTORNEY: C H Taylor	
NO	NAMES	AGE	SEX
1	David Boyd Bryant	32	Male
2	Audery Bryant	12	female
3	Julian Bryant	10	Male

ANCESTOR: John Bryant

Rejected March 18 – 1889

Adverse

Embraced in decission[sic] on page 431
Book B. in the Aaron Bellew case.
Rendered March 18 – 1889.

Will P. Ross
Chairman Com.
John E. Gunter   Com

Office Commission
on Citizenship
Tahlequah I.T.
March 18 – 1889

D.S. Williams
Clk Com

BRYANT

Docket #723
CENSUS ROLLS 1835

APPLICANT FOR CHEROKEE CITIZENSHIP

POST OFFICE: Miland[sic] Tenn		ATTORNEY: C H Taylor	
NO	NAMES	AGE	SEX
1	Zack Bryant	69	Male

ANCESTOR: John Bryant

Rejected March 18 – 1889

<u>Adverse</u>
Embraced in decission[sic] on page 431
Book B. in the Aaron Bellew case.
Rendered March 18 – 1889.

Will P. Ross
Chairman Com.
John E. Gunter   Com

Office Commission
on Citizenship
Tahlequah I.T.
March 18 – 1889

D.S. Williams
Clk Com

BELEW

Docket #724
CENSUS ROLLS

APPLICANT FOR CHEROKEE CITIZENSHIP

POST OFFICE: Chelso Ind Ter		ATTORNEY: C.H. Taylor	
NO	NAMES	AGE	SEX
1	Governor Belew	54	Male
2	M.C. Belew	12	

ANCESTOR: John Bryant

Rejected March 18 – 1889

<u>Adverse</u>
Embraced in decission[sic] on page 431
Book B. in the Aaron Bellew case.
Rendered March 18 – 1889.

Office Commission on Citizenship   Will P. Ross
Tahlequah I.T. March 18 – 1889   Chairman Com
                                                    John E. Gunter   Com

D.S. Williams
Clk Com

BARNETT

Docket #725

CENSUS ROLLS 1835/52

APPLICANT FOR CHEROKEE CITIZENSHIP

POST OFFICE: Bloomfield Ark		ATTORNEY: James M Bell	
NO	NAMES	AGE	SEX
1	Jessie Barnett	40	Male

ANCESTOR: Nancy Lucus

Office Commission on Citizenship
Tahlequah CN June 13th 1889

There being no evidence in support of the above named case the Commission decide that Jessie Barnett age 40 years is not a Cherokee by blood and are[sic[not entitled to Citizenship in the Cherokee Nation. Post Office address, Bloomfield Ark.

Will P. Ross

Chairman

Attest   John E. Gunter   Com

E.G. Ross
Clk. Com.

BARNETT

Docket #726

CENSUS ROLLS 1835/52

APPLICANT FOR CHEROKEE CITIZENSHIP

POST OFFICE: Bloomfield Ark		ATTORNEY: James M Bell	
NO	NAMES	AGE	SEX
1	James Barnett	35	Male

ANCESTOR: Nancy Lucus

Rejected June 13th 1889

Office Commission on Citizenship
Tahlequah CN June 13th 1889

There being no evidence in support of the above named case the Commission decide that James Barnett age 35 years is not of Cherokee blood. Post Office address, Bloomfield Ark.

Cherokee Citizenship Commission Docket Books
(1880-84, 1887-89) Volume III
Tahlequah, Cherokee Nation

Will P. Ross

Chairman

Attest

J. E. Gunter   Com

DS Williams
Asst. Clk. Com.

BETHEL

Docket #727
CENSUS ROLLS 1835/52

APPLICANT FOR CHEROKEE CITIZENSHIP

POST OFFICE: Farmer Ark		ATTORNEY: Boudinot & R[sic]	
NO	**NAMES**	**AGE**	**SEX**
1	James Bethel	34	Male
2	Louisa L Bethel	4	female
3	Marshall Bethel	2	Male

ANCESTOR: Leah Reeves

Office Commission on Citizenship
Tahlequah CN June 13th 1889

There being no evidence in support of the above named case the Commission decide that James Bethel age 34 years and the following named children Louisa L Bethel aged 4 years and Marshall Bethel aged 2 years are not of Cherokee blood. Post Office address Farmer Ark.

Attest

Will P. Ross

E.G. Ross

Chairman

Clerk Commission

John E. Gunter   Com

BETHEL

Docket #728
CENSUS ROLLS 1835/52

APPLICANT FOR CHEROKEE CITIZENSHIP

POST OFFICE: Farmer Ark		ATTORNEY: Boudinot & R[sic]	
NO	**NAMES**	**AGE**	**SEX**
1	W M Bethel	36	Male
2	Ada Bethel	14	female

3	David F Bethel	12	Male
4	Ella G Bethel	10	female
5	Louisa M Bethel	8	"
6	Minnie M Bethel	6	"
7	James W Bethel	5	Male
8	Benj F Bethel	4	"
9	Laura L Bethel	1	female

ANCESTOR: Leah Reeves

Rejected June 13th 1889

Office Commission on Citizenship
Cherokee Nation Ind. Ter.
Tahlequah June 13th 1889

There being no evidence filed in support of applicants of Cherokee blood & in view of this fact we are of the opinion & so decide that applicant W.M. Bethel and his children Ada age 14 yrs, David F. aged 12 yrs, Ella G. aged 10 yrs, Louisa M aged 8 yrs. Minnie M. aged 6 yrs, James W aged 5 yrs, Benj F. aged 4 yrs. and Laura L. Bethel aged 1 year, are not Cherokee by blood & not entitled to Citizenship in the Cherokee Nation.

Will. P. Ross

Chairman

Attest

R. Bunch   Com

DS Williams
Asst. Clk. Com.

BOYETT

Docket #729

CENSUS ROLLS 1835/52

APPLICANT FOR CHEROKEE CITIZENSHIP

POST OFFICE: Shavin Ark		ATTORNEY: Boudinot & R[sic]	
NO	**NAMES**	**AGE**	**SEX**
1	Tennessee Boyett	28	female

ANCESTOR: Nancy Lewis

Cherokee Citizenship Commission Docket Books
(1880-84, 1887-89) Volume III
Tahlequah, Cherokee Nation

Office Commission on Citizenship
Tahlequah CN June 14th 1889

There being no evidence in support of the above named case the Commission decide that Tennessee Boyett age 28 years is not of Cherokee blood. Post Office address Salisaw[sic] I.T.

Will P. Ross

Chairman

Attest   R. Bunch   Com
        E G Ross   John E. Gunter   Com
        Clerk Commission

BENNET

Docket #730
CENSUS ROLLS /35

APPLICANT FOR CHEROKEE CITIZENSHIP

POST OFFICE: Siloam Springs		ATTORNEY: Ivey & Welch	
NO	NAMES	AGE	SEX
1	Amos Bennet	53	Male
2	Elizabeth Bennet	44	female
3	Joseph Bennet	20	Male
4	Fannie Bennet	17	female
5	Dora Bennet	14	"
6	Ode M Bennet	12	"
7	Washington Bennet	1	Male

ANCESTOR: Oo-yah-sir-tah

Office Commission on Citizenship
Tahlequah CN June 14th 1889

There being no evidence filed in support of applicants claim of Cherokee blood & in view of this fact we are of the opinion & so decide that applicant W.M. Bethel and his children Ada age 14 yrs, David F. aged 12 yrs, Ella G. aged 10 yrs, Louisa M aged 8 yrs. Minnie M. aged 6 yrs, James W aged 5 yrs, Benj F. aged 4 yrs. and Laura L. Bethel aged 1 year, are not Cherokee by blood & not entitled to Citizenship in the Cherokee Nation.

9

Will. P. Ross
Chairman

Attest
R. Bunch   Com

DS Williams
Asst. Clk. Com.

BOWLIN

Docket #731

CENSUS ROLLS /35

APPLICANT FOR CHEROKEE CITIZENSHIP

POST OFFICE: Salisaw[sic] Ind Terry		ATTORNEY: Ivey & Welch	
NO	NAMES	AGE	SEX
1	Jane Bowlin	34	female
2	Lori T Bowlin	13	"
3	Earley Bowlin	2	Male
4	Levi Bowlin	9	"

ANCESTOR: Oo-yah-sir-tah

Rejected June 14th 1889

Office Commission on Citizenship
Cherokee Nation Ind Ter
Tahlequah CN June 14th 1889

There being no evidence submitted in the above named case the commission are of the opinion and so decide that Jane Bowlin age 34 years and the following named children Lou T. Female age 13 years, Levi male age 9 years, and Earley Bowlin male age 2 years, are not of[sic] Cherokee by blood. Post Office address Sallisaw Ind. Ter.

Will. P. Ross

Attest
Chairman

DS Williams
R. Bunch   Com

Asst Clk Com
John E. Gunter   Com

BRACKET

Docket #732
CENSUS ROLLS

APPLICANT FOR CHEROKEE CITIZENSHIP

POST OFFICE: Carlisle		ATTORNEY: A E Ivey	
NO	NAMES	AGE	SEX
1	Bailis Bracket	50	Male
2	Midge Bracket	16	"
3	William Bracket	14	"
4	Ada Bracket	11	female
5	Augustus Bracket	9	Male
4[sic]	Francis Bracket	7	female
5[sic]	Charles A Bracket	4	"

ANCESTOR: Bracket

Readmitted August 6th 1889

Office Commission on Citizenship
Cherokee Nation Ind. Ter.
Tahlequah Aug. 16th 1889

The evidence shows that Bolin Brackett the applicant named is now deceased but that he was the son of Mige Brackett and Cynthia Brackett nee Cynthia Hubbard and grand son of Nellie Wilkerson from whom he derived his Cherokee blood and whose name is found on the Siler Roll of Cherokees taken in 1852. The children of Balis Brackett identified as Midge Brackett age 16 yrs, William Brackett 14 yrs, Augustus Brackett 11[sic] yrs and Ada Brackett (daughter) 11yrs and they are therefore adjudged by the Commission to be of Cherokee blood and entitled to readmission to Citizenship in the Cherokee Nation. See evidence in case of Benj. J. Brackett, Docket 666, Book B. Page 381.

Will. P. Ross

Chairman

Attest

DS Williams
Asst Clk Com

R. Bunch   Com
John E. Gunter   Com

BYASS

Docket #733

CENSUS ROLLS 1851

APPLICANT FOR CHEROKEE CITIZENSHIP

POST OFFICE: Ellijay Ga		ATTORNEY: A E Ivey	
NO	NAMES	AGE	SEX
1	William B Byass	31	Male
2	Bluford Byass	7	"
3	Sarah Byass	4	"[sic]

ANCESTOR: *(Illegible)* Byas[sic]

Office Commission on Citizenship
Tahlequah Cherokee Nation
June 14th 1889

There being no evidence in support of the above named case the Commission decide that William B Byass age 31 years and the following named children Blueford[sic] male age 7 years and Sarah Byass Female age 4 years are not of Cherokee blood. Post Office Ellejay[sic] Ga.

Will. P. Ross

Attest   Chairman

    E G Ross   R. Bunch   Com

    Clerk Commission   John E. Gunter   Com

BRACKETT

Docket #734

CENSUS ROLLS 1851

APPLICANT FOR CHEROKEE CITIZENSHIP

POST OFFICE: Carlisle Ga		ATTORNEY: A E Ivey	
NO	NAMES	AGE	SEX
1	Bradford W Brackett	46	Male
2	Lucinda L Brackett	31	Female
3	Laura Brackett	12	Male[sic]
4	John W Bracket[sic]	18[sic]	"
5	Catharine Bracket[sic]	7	female
6	Mary J Bracket[sic]	6	"
7	Arthur Brackett	1	Male

ANCESTOR: Smitha Hubbard

Re-admitted Aug. 16th 1889

Office Commission on Citizenship
Cherokee Nation Ind. Ter.
Tahlequah Aug. 16th 1889

The evidence in the above named case shows that the applicant is the son of Midge Brackett and Cynthia Brackett nee Cynthia Hubbard and grand son of Nellie Wilkerson from whom he derives his Cherokee blood. The name of ancestor are[sic] found on the census rolls of Cherokees by blood taken and made in the year 1852 by the United States. The Commission therefore decide that Bradford W Brackett age 41 and children Laura Brackett age 12 yrs, John W age 8 yrs, Catherine 7 yrs, Mary age 6 yrs & Authur[sic] Brackett age 1 yr are of Cherokee blood and entitled to re-admission to Citizenship in the Cherokee Nation. See Docket 666 Book B, Page 381. P.O. Carlisle Georgia

Will. P. Ross
Chairman
Attest   John E. Gunter   Com
    DS Williams
    Asst Clk Com

BARRETT

Docket #735
CENSUS ROLLS 1835/52

APPLICANT FOR CHEROKEE CITIZENSHIP

POST OFFICE: Camp Creek IT		ATTORNEY: A E Ivey	
NO	NAMES	AGE	SEX
1	Susan J Barrett	26	female
2	Robb Barrett	10	Male
3	Georgia Barrett	8	female
4	Thomas M Barrett	6	male
5	Isaac C Barrett	2	"

ANCESTOR: Liddia Wofford

13

Office Commission on Citizenship
Tahlequah Cherokee Nation
June 14th 1889

There being no evidence in support of the above named case the Commission decide that Sarah J Barrett age 26 years and the following named children Robert male age 10 years, Georgia A Female age 8 years, Thomas M male age 6 years, Isac[sic] C male age 2 years are not of Cherokee blood. Post Office address Camp Creek IT.

Will. P. Ross

Attest   Chairman
    E G Ross   R. Bunch   Com
    Clk Com   John E. Gunter   Com

BRASWELL

Docket #736

CENSUS ROLLS 1835/52

APPLICANT FOR CHEROKEE CITIZENSHIP

POST OFFICE: Van Buren Ark		ATTORNEY: A E Ivey	
NO	**NAMES**	**AGE**	**SEX**
1	Mary F Braswell	50	female
2	Jeremiah Braswell	15	male
3	Alfred Braswell	12	"

ANCESTOR: Herbert Harris

Office Commission on Citizenship
Tahlequah CN
June 14th 1889

There being no evidence in support of the above named case the Commission decide that Mary F Braswell age 50 years and the following named children Jeremiah male age 15 years and Alfred Braswell male age 12 years are not of Cherokee blood. Post Office address Van Buren Ark.

Will. P. Ross

Attest   Chairman
    E G Ross   R. Bunch   Com
        Clerk Commission   John E. Gunter   Com

14

BRYANT

Docket #737

CENSUS ROLLS 1835/52

APPLICANT FOR CHEROKEE CITIZENSHIP

POST OFFICE: Miland[sic] Tenn		ATTORNEY: C H Taylor	
NO	NAMES	AGE	SEX
1	W R Bryant		male
2	Lillian Bryant	16	female
3	John Bryant	14	male
4	Ethel Bryant	12	female
5	Eugenia Bryant	10	"
6	Stella Bryant	8	"
7	Agnes Bryant	6	"
8	Sybile Bryant	4	male

ANCESTOR: John Bryant

Rejected March 18 – 1889

<u>Adverse</u>

Embraced [sic] decission[sic] on page 431
Book B. in the Aaron Bellew case
Rendered March 18 – 1889.

Will P. Ross
Chairman Com.
John E. Gunter   Com

Office Commission
on Citizenship
Tahlequah I.T.
March 18 – 1889

D.S. Williams
Clk Com

BRYANT

Docket #738

CENSUS ROLLS 1835/52

APPLICANT FOR CHEROKEE CITIZENSHIP

POST OFFICE: Chocoville Ark		ATTORNEY: Boudinot & R[sic]	
NO	NAMES	AGE	SEX
1	Mary E Bryant	46	female

ANCESTOR: Andrew Miller

Cherokee Citizenship Commission Docket Books
(1880-84, 1887-89) Volume III
Tahlequah, Cherokee Nation

Commission on Citizenship
Tahlequah May 14th 1889

Now on this day the above case coming on for final hearing, The application was filed on the 5th day of October 1887. After examining the papers we fail to find any evidence in support of the application. The applicant alleges that one Andrew Miller was his[sic] ancestor. We have examined the census rolls but fail to find the name of applicant's ancestor Andrew Miller. In view of these facts the Commission is of the opinion and so declare the applicant Mary E Bryant, aged 46 years, Post Office Chocoville Ark, is not a Cherokee by blood and are[sic] not entitled to Cherokee Citizenship in the Cherokee Nation.

	Will. P. Ross	Chairman
E.G. Ross	J.E. Gunter	Com
Clk Commission		

McBROOM

Docket #739

CENSUS ROLLS 1835

APPLICANT FOR CHEROKEE CITIZENSHIP

POST OFFICE: Siloam Spg Ark		ATTORNEY: L.S. Sanders	
NO	NAMES	AGE	SEX
1	Thomas J McBroom	39	male
2	Rachael Cora Broom	16	female
3	John Ira McBroom	14	male
4	Effie Dorf McBroom	18	female
5	*(Blank on microfilm)*		female

ANCESTOR: McAfee

Office Commission on Citizenship
Cherokee Nation Ind. Ter.
Tahlequah June 19th 1889

In the above named case the applicant alleges that he is the blood kin of the McAfee. The evidence in the case is exparte affidavits taken before a Notary Public in Benton County Arkansan[sic] and represents that the applicant is the son of Edward J. McBroom and Rachel McBroom nee Rachel McAffee who claimed to be a Cherokee Indian by blood of Blount County Tennessee. These statements fail to show that Elizabeth McAffee was of Cherokee blood and as her name is not found on the census rolls of Cherokees refered[sic] to the Commission decide that Thomas J. McBroom aged 39 years, and Rachel Cora McBroom aged 16 years, John Ira McBroom aged 14 years and daughter Effie Mrs. George Spencer 18 years and her daughter Mamie Spencer, are not of Cherokee blood and not entitled to Citizenship in the Cherokee Nation. Post Office Siloam Springs, Arkansas.

Will P. Ross

Attest   Chairman

EG Ross   J.E. Gunter   Com

Clerk Commission

BARNES

Docket #740

CENSUS ROLLS 1835

APPLICANT FOR CHEROKEE CITIZENSHIP

POST OFFICE: Unionville Ark		ATTORNEY: John E Welch	
NO	NAMES	AGE	SEX
1	Jennie Barnes	41	Female
2	Louisa Boulden		"
3	Robert Boulden		Male
4	Sarah Boulden	17	female
5	Mary M Bolden[sic]	14	"
6	John Bolden	12	Male
7	Tum Bolden	9	"
8	Samuel Bolden	4	"
9	Minnie Boulden	2	female

ANCESTOR: Chas Boulden

Office Commission on Citizenship
Tahlequah June 14th 1889

There being no evidence in support of the above named application the Commission decide that Jennie Barnes age 41 years and the following names children Louisa, Robert age 20 years, Sarah age 17 years, Mary M age 14 years, John age 12 years, Tum age 9 years, Samuel age 4 years, Minnie Boulden age 2 years are not of Cherokee blood. Post Office Unionville Ark.

Cherokee Citizenship Commission Docket Books
(1880-84, 1887-89) Volume III
Tahlequah, Cherokee Nation

Will. P. Ross

Attest   Chairman

    E G Ross   R. Bunch   Com

        Clerk Commission   John E. Gunter   Com

BERRY

Docket #740[sic]
CENSUS ROLLS 1835 to 52

APPLICANT FOR CHEROKEE CITIZENSHIP

POST OFFICE: Red River Station		ATTORNEY: W A Thompson	
NO	NAMES	AGE	SEX
1	Josephine H Berry	20	female
2	Minnie L Berry	2	"
3	Hettie P Berry	4 mo	"

ANCESTOR: Jack McGarrah

Office Commission on Citizenship
Cherokee Nation I.T.
Tahlequah June 26, 1889

The above case having been submitted by the Attorney without evidence the Commission decide that Josephine H. Berry aged 20 years, and her daughters Minnie L. Berry aged 2 years, Hettie P. Berry aged 4 months of Red River Station Montague County Texas, are not of Cherokee blood.

Will. P. Ross

Attest   Chairman

    E G Ross   R. Bunch   Com

        Clerk Commission   John E. Gunter   Com

BOATRIGHT

Docket #742
CENSUS ROLLS 1835/52

APPLICANT FOR CHEROKEE CITIZENSHIP

POST OFFICE: Van Buren Ark		ATTORNEY: L S Sanders	
NO	NAMES	AGE	SEX
1	Wm N Boatright	30	Male
2	Mary E Boatright		female

3	Wm V Boatright	Male
4	Lillie M Boatright	female
5	Othello Boatright	male
6	Alonzo Boatright	"
7	Carlton Boatright	"

ANCESTOR: Emaline Boatright

Office Commission on Citizenship
Tahlequah May 14, 1889

Now comes the above case for final hearing which was filed on the 3rd day of Oct 1887 the same having been submitted by Attorneys without any evidence to sustain the application. Therefore the Commission decide that Wm N. Boatright age 30 years and his children, to wit: Mary E. Boatright Female aged 12 years, Wm V. Boatright male aged 10 years, Lillie M Boatright Female aged 7 years, Othello Boatright male aged 5 years, Alonzo Boatright aged 3 years male, and Carlton Boatright male aged 1 year, are not of Cherokee blood and <u>not</u> entitled to Citizenship or to any of the privileges as such within the limits of the Cherokee Nation. Post Office Van Buren Ark.

Will. P. Ross

Attest   Chairman

E G Ross   J E Gunter   Com

Clerk Commission

BRACKETT

Docket #743
CENSUS ROLLS 1851

APPLICANT FOR CHEROKEE CITIZENSHIP

POST OFFICE: Carlisle Ga		ATTORNEY: A E Ivey	
NO	**NAMES**	**AGE**	**SEX**
1	Daniel Brackett	42	male
2	Sarah C Brackett	36	female
3	Emily M Brackett	17	"
4	Willy H Brackett	16	male
5	Susan J Brackett	14	female
6	Martha S Brackett	12	male[sic]

ANCESTOR: Carlile Ga[sic]

Re-admitted Aug 16th 1889

Office Commission on Citizenship
Cherokee Nation Ind. Ter.
Tahlequah August 16th 1889

The applicant for re-admission to Citizenship in the Cherokee Nation is the son of Mige Brackett and Cynthia Brackett nee Cynthia Hubbard, and grand son of Nellie Wilkerson from whom he derives his Cherokee blood. The names of Mige Brackett and Cynthia are found on the Census rolls of Cherokees by blood taken in the year 1852, by the United States. The Commission therefore decide that Daniel Brackett and his children to wit, Emily M. Brackett age 17 yrs, Susan J. Brackett 14 yrs, Martha S. Brackett 12 yrs, and William H. Brackett 16 yrs. are of Cherokee blood and entitled to re-admission to Citizenship in the Cherokee Nation. The testimony *(illegible)* is not sufficient to show that Sarah C. Brackett wife of applicant is of Cherokee blood as alleged. P.O. Carlisle, Georgia.

See case Benj J. Brackett D.666, B.B.P.381.

Will. P. Ross

Attest   Chairman
    D.S. Williams   John E Gunter   Com
    Asst Clerk Commission

BOGAN

Docket #744
CENSUS ROLLS

APPLICANT FOR CHEROKEE CITIZENSHIP

POST OFFICE: Spiceland Ind		ATTORNEY: L B Bell	
NO	**NAMES**	**AGE**	**SEX**
1	Sibbie J Bogan	45	Female

ANCESTOR: Martha Sanders

See decision in this case in Book E, Page 29, Docket 2183. The case has been docketed twice.

Will P. Ross
Chairman
Attest   J.E. Gunter   Com
    D.S. Williams
Asst Clk. Com.

BRAND

Docket #745

1835		APPLICANT FOR CHEROKEE CITIZENSHIP	
POST OFFICE: Esi[sic] Kansas		**ATTORNEY:** L.B. Bell	
NO	NAMES	AGE	SEX
1	David Brand		Male

ANCESTOR: David England

Rejected July 2nd 1889

> Office Commission on Citizenship
> Cherokee Nation Ind. Ter.
> Tahlequah July 2nd 1889

There being no evidence in support of this case the Commission decide that David Brand age 50 years is not a Cherokee by blood.
Post Office Esi Kansas.

Attest

    D.S. Williams

Asst Clerk Commission

      Will. P. Ross

         Chairman

    John E. Gunter   Com

BRAND

Docket #746

CENSUS ROLLS 1835

		APPLICANT FOR CHEROKEE CITIZENSHIP	
POST OFFICE: Easton Kansas		**ATTORNEY:** L B Bell	
NO	NAMES	AGE	SEX
1	N.V. Brand	46	Male
2	Sarah Brand		female

ANCESTOR: Wm T England

> Commission on Citizenship
> Tahlequah C.N. June 25, 1889

The above application was filed the 5th day of October 1887 and this day submitted by Attorneys without evidence in its support. The Commission therefore decide that N.V. Brand age 46 years of Eureka Springs Arkansas is not of Cherokee blood and not entitled to Citizenship in the Cherokee Nation.

21

Cherokee Citizenship Commission Docket Books
(1880-84, 1887-89) Volume III
Tahlequah, Cherokee Nation

Will. P. Ross   Chairman

Attest

    E.G. Ross   R. Bunch   Com

        Clerk Commission

BROWN

Docket #747

CENSUS ROLLS 1835/52

APPLICANT FOR CHEROKEE CITIZENSHIP

POST OFFICE: Carr Mo		ATTORNEY: AE Ivey	
NO	NAMES	AGE	SEX
1	Robt Brown	47	Male
2	May E Brown	26	female
3	Henrietta Brown	25	"
4	Salina Brown	23	"
5	Lillie Brown	19	"
6	John R Brown	14	male
7	Bessie Brown	11	female
8	Eliza W Brown	9	"

ANCESTOR: Thomas Brown

Office Commission on Citizenship
Tahlequah Cherokee Nation
June 15th 1889

There being no evidence in support of the above named case the Commission decide that Robert Brown age 47 years and the following named children May E. Female age 26 years, Henrietta Female age 25 years, Salina Female age 23 years, Lillie Female age 19 years, John R. Male age 14 years, Bessie Female age 11 years, Eliza W. Brown Female age 9 years are not ob Cherokee by blood. Post Office address Carr, Mo.

Attest   Will.P. Ross

    EG Ross   Chairman

        Clerk Commission

           John E. Gunter   Com

SHOEMAKER

Docket #748
CENSUS ROLLS

APPLICANT FOR CHEROKEE CITIZENSHIP

	POST OFFICE:		ATTORNEY: C H Taylor	
NO	NAMES		AGE	SEX
1	Alma L Shoemaker		9	female
2	Lelia Bell Shoemaker		7	
3	Eddy C Shoemaker		4	

ANCESTOR:

(No other information given.)

BOBBITT

Docket #749
CENSUS ROLLS 1835/52

APPLICANT FOR CHEROKEE CITIZENSHIP

	POST OFFICE: Tahlequah CN	B H Stone		
		ATTORNEY: ~~Martin Manny~~		
NO	NAMES		AGE	SEX
1	William C Bobbitt		37	male
2	John A Bobbitt		15	"
3	Chas Bobbitt		13	"
4	James C Bobbitt		11	"
5	Addie E Bobbitt		8	Female
6	Edgar J Bobbitt		6	male

ANCESTOR: Martin Manny

Office Commission on Citizenship
Tahlequah CN June 18th 1889

The applicant in the above named case fails to show that he is the Grand Son of one Martin Many[sic] from whom he claims to have derived his Cherokee blood while the paper purporting to be an Act of the North Carolina band of Cherokees dated July 22nd 1875 and adopted at the Chedah Council Ground in Graham County N.C. is not only a copy without a certificate and inadmissible as evidence but is contradicted by John Ross whose name appears to it as Principal Chief of the Eastern Band of Cherokees who swears positively before the Commission on Citizenship Oct 3rd 1888, that Wm C. Bobbitt and

23

Deshazo (Nancy) failed to establish their rights as Cherokees. The Commission therefore decide that Wm C. Bobbitt aged 37 years, John A Bobbitt aged 15 years, Charles Bobbitt aged 13 years, James C. Bobbitt aged 11 years and Edgar J. Bobbitt aged 9 years, Sons and Addie E Bobbitt aged 8 years daughter of said Wm C Bobbitt are not of Cherokee blood and not entitled to Cherokee Citizenship in the Nation.

Will. P. Ross

Attest   Chairman

    EG Ross

        Clerk Commission   John E. Gunter   Com

BROWN

Docket #750

CENSUS ROLLS 1835/52

APPLICANT FOR CHEROKEE CITIZENSHIP

POST OFFICE: Mt Carmel Ill		ATTORNEY: Boudinot & R[sic]	
NO	NAMES	AGE	SEX
1	Aramantha Brown	33	Female

ANCESTOR: Emaline P Denham

Office Commission on Citizenship
Tahlequah CN June 15, 1889

There being no evidence in support of the above named case the Commission decide that Aramantha Brown age 33 years is not of Cherokee blood. Post Office address Russeville[sic], Ark.

Attest   Will. P. Ross

    EG Ross   Chairman

        Clerk Commission   R Bunch   Commissioner

                      John E. Gunter   Com

ROREX

Docket #751

CENSUS ROLLS 1835 to 1852

APPLICANT FOR CHEROKEE CITIZENSHIP

POST OFFICE: Russellville Ark		ATTORNEY: Boudinot & R[sic]	
NO	**NAMES**	**AGE**	**SEX**
1	Geo L Rorex	19	Male
2	John F Rorex	17	"
3	Samuel J Rorex	15	"
4	Sarah E Rorex	12	female
5	Lee Rorex	6	"
6	Sidney N Rorex	4	male
7	James W Rorex	43	"

ANCESTOR: Polly Keys

Office Commission on Citizenship
Tahlequah CN June 17, 1889

There being no evidence in support of the above named case the
Commission decide that James W. Borex[sic] aged 43 years and the following
named children George S[sic] male aged 19 years, John F. male age 17 years,
Samuel J age 15 years, Sarah E Female age 12 years Lee Female age 6 years and
Sidney N. Borex male age 4 years are not of Cherokee blood. Post Office
address Russeville[sic] Ark.

Will. P. Ross
Chairman
John E. Gunter   Com

Attest
E.G. Ross
Clk Com

BEALER

Docket #752

CENSUS ROLLS 1835

APPLICANT FOR CHEROKEE CITIZENSHIP

POST OFFICE: Saint Louis Mo		ATTORNEY: AE Ivey	
NO	**NAMES**	**AGE**	**SEX**
1	Elizabeth Bealer	35	Female
2	Louisiana Bealer		"

25

3	John Henry Bealer	Male

ANCESTOR: John Lowery

Office Commission on Citizenship
Tahlequah Cherokee Nation
June 15th 1889

There being no evidence in support of the above named case the Commission decide that Elizabeth Bealer age 41[sic] years and the following named children Louisiana Bealer and John Henry Bealer ages not given are not Cherokees by blood and not entitled to Citizenship in the Cherokee Nation.

Attest   Will. P. Ross

    EG Ross   Chairman

    Clerk Commission   R. Bunch   Com

                   John E. Gunter   Com

BAXTER

Docket #753

CENSUS ROLLS 1835

APPLICANT FOR CHEROKEE CITIZENSHIP

POST OFFICE: Decatur Texas		ATTORNEY: C H Taylor	
NO	**NAMES**	**AGE**	**SEX**
1	Nancy E Baxter	36	Female

ANCESTOR: Wm Chisholm

Office Commission on Citizenship
Tahlequah Cherokee Nation IT
June 17th 1889

There being no evidence in support of the above named case the Commission decide Nancy E Baxter age 36 years and the following named children Becky Female age 15 years and Kate Baxter Female age 12 years. Post Office address Decatur, Texas.

                 Will. P. Ross

Attest   Chairman

    EG Ross   R. Bunch   Commissioner

        Clerk Commission   John E. Gunter   Com

Cherokee Citizenship Commission Docket Books
(1880-84, 1887-89) Volume III
Tahlequah, Cherokee Nation

BROWN

Docket #754

CENSUS ROLLS 1835

APPLICANT FOR CHEROKEE CITIZENSHIP

POST OFFICE: Clifty Ark		ATTORNEY: C H Taylor	
NO	NAMES	AGE	SEX
1	Mary F Brown	26	Female
2	S M Brown	5	Male[sic]
3	J C Brown	1	Male

ANCESTOR: *(Illegible)* Vaughn

Rejected July 2nd 1889

Office Commission on Citizenship
Cherokee Nation Ind. Ter.
Tahlequah July 2nd 1889

There being no evidence in support of this the Commission decide that Mary F. Brown age 26 years and the following children S.M. Brown female age 5 years and J.C. male age 1 year are not Cherokees by blood. Post Office Clifty Ark.

Will. P. Ross

Attest   Chairman

DS Williams   John E. Gunter   Com
Asst Clerk Commission

BATTLES

Docket #755

CENSUS ROLLS 1835

APPLICANT FOR CHEROKEE CITIZENSHIP

POST OFFICE: Valley Town NC		ATTORNEY: C H Taylor	
NO	NAMES	AGE	SEX
1	Adda Battles	33	Female
	Florence Battles	15	"
	Forsty Battles	14	"
	Stephen Battles	12	male
	Bruce Battles	10	"
	Dazy Battles	8	female
	Lar Battles	6	male
	Willie Mc Battles	5	"

27

	Laura Battles	1	Female

ANCESTOR: Elizabeth *(Illegible)*

Now on this the 10th day of February 1888 comes the above case case[sic] for a final hearing, and the parties having made application pursuant to the provisions of an Act of the National Council approved December 8th 1886, and all the evidence being duly examined and found to be sufficient and satisfactory to the Commission it is adjudged and determined by the Commission that Addy Battles, Florence Battles, Forsty Battles, Stephen Battles, Bruce Battles, Dazy Battles, Lar Battles, Willie Mc Battles and Laura Battles, are Cherokees by blood and they are hereby re-admitted to all the rights privileges and immunities of Cherokee Citizens by blood.

And a certificate of said decision of the Commission and of re-admission was made and furnished said parties accordingly.

J.T. Adair   Chairman Commission
John E. Gunter   Commissioner
Commissioner

Attest
C.C. Lipe
Clerk Commission

BELL

Docket #756
CENSUS ROLLS 1835

APPLICANT FOR CHEROKEE CITIZENSHIP

POST OFFICE: Coy Mo   **ATTORNEY:** C H Taylor

NO	NAMES	AGE	SEX
1	William M Bell	63	male
2	Martha Bell	39	female
3	Angeline Bell	37	"
4	James B Bell	33	male
5	Cyntha Bell	29	female
6	J.C. Bell	26	male
7	Stella Bell	24	female
8	Jeannia Bell	19	"
9	Elisha Bell	16	male
10	Chas F Bell	15	"

28

11	Henry Bell	13	"

ANCESTOR: Mary S Bell

Rejected April 6th 1889

      The case of Wm M Bell applicant for Citizenship having been submitted on this the 6th day of April 1889 by the Attorney C.H. Taylor, the Commission on examining the application find that William M. Bell alleges that he is the grand son of one Mary S. Bell formerly Lewis whose name would be found on the census roll of Cherokees taken in the year 1835. There being no evidence accompanying the application and the name of Mary S. Bell or Mary S. Lewis not being found on said roll of 1835, the Commission decide and decree that William M. Bell aged 63 years, where his application was filed the 28th September 1887, and his children, Martha Bell aged 39 years, Angeline Bell aged 37 years, James B. Bell aged 33 years, Cytha[sic] Bell aged 29 years, J.C. Bell (son) aged 26 years, Sterling Bell (son) aged 24 years, Jimma Bell (daughter) aged 19 years, Elisha M. Bell aged 17 years, Charles F. Bell aged 15 years, Henry Bell aged 13 years, are not of Cherokee blood and are not entitled to Citizenship in the Cherokee Nation. Post Office address Coy, Missouri.

Will. P. Ross   Chairman
John E. Gunter   Comm

Office Com. on Citizenship Tah. I.T.
April 6th 1889   D.S. Williams Clk. Com.

BURGESS

Docket #757
CENSUS ROLLS 1835/52

APPLICANT FOR CHEROKEE CITIZENSHIP

POST OFFICE: Canadaville I.T.		ATTORNEY: A E Ivey	
NO	**NAMES**	**AGE**	**SEX**
1	Martha J Burgess	60	female
2	J M Robinson	20	male

ANCESTOR: Jones Nealy

Office Commission on Citizenship
Tahlequah Cherokee Nation June ?1, 1889

There being no evidence in support of the above named case the Commission decide that Martha J Burgess age 60 years and her son J.M. Robinson male age 20 years are not of Cherokee blood. Post Office address Canadaville, I.T.

Will. P. Ross

Attest   Chairman

    E.G. Ross   R. Bunch   Commissioner

    Clerk Commission   John E. Gunter   Com

BARTON

Docket #758

CENSUS ROLLS 1835

APPLICANT FOR CHEROKEE CITIZENSHIP

POST OFFICE: Tulsa I.T.		ATTORNEY:	
NO	NAMES	AGE	SEX
1	M J Barton	42	male

ANCESTOR: William R Gourd

Office Commission on Citizenship
Tahlequah C.N. June 17th 1889

There being no evidence in support of the above named case the Commission decide that M.J. Barton age 42 years is not of Cherokee blood. Post Office address Tulsa I.T.

Will. P. Ross

Attest   Chairman

    E.G. Ross   R. Bunch   Commissioner

    Clerk Commission   John E. Gunter   Com

BROWN

Docket #759

CENSUS ROLLS 1835

APPLICANT FOR CHEROKEE CITIZENSHIP

POST OFFICE: Union Town Ark		ATTORNEY: AE Ivey	
NO	NAMES	AGE	SEX
1	Alexander Brown	35	Male

ANCESTOR: Isom Brown

Office Commission on Citizenship
Tahlequah CN June 17th 1889

There being no evidence in support of the above named case the Commission decide that Alexander Brown age 35 years is not of Cherokee blood. Post Office address Union Town Ark.

Attest   Will.P. Ross
    EG Ross   Chairman
    Clerk Commission   R. Bunch   Commissioner
                    John E. Gunter   Com

BLAIR

Docket #760

CENSUS ROLLS 1835/52

APPLICANT FOR CHEROKEE CITIZENSHIP

POST OFFICE: Tahlequah CN		ATTORNEY:	
NO	NAMES	AGE	SEX
1	Geo W. Blair	43	male
2	Dora L Blair	20	female
3	Samuel M Blair	17	male
4	John L Blaire	13	"
5	Theodoshia L Blair	6	female
6	Joseph L Blair	3	male

ANCESTOR: Sam Blair

Rejected Aug 20 1889

Cherokee Citizenship Commission Docket Books
(1880-84, 1887-89) Volume III
Tahlequah, Cherokee Nation

Commission on Citizenship.

CHEROKEE NATION, IND. TER.

Tahlequah, August 20th 1889

George W. Blair
vs
Cherokee Nation

Application for
Cherokee Citizenship

The above application was filed on the 5th day of October 1887. The applicant claims to derive his Cherokee blood from his father, Calvin M. Blair and his mother, Catherine Hughes. In support of the allegations ~~filed~~ in claimant's application he produces *(illegible)* affidavits of persons taken out side of the Nation also the testimony of Calvin Blair, G.W.L. Blair and George W Blair (the applicant) taken before the Commission. He also claims that his ancestor named Samuel Blair & Nancy Hughes should appear upon the census rolls of Cherokees taken in the years 1835 & 1852 – The testimony produced by claimant is conflicting in several points but agree upon one point that applicant was born in Hamilton County Tenn. from here he moved with his relatives to the State of Arkansas ~~who~~ mainly on the line between said State and the Cherokee Nation, about ten years ago, and only in the year 1887 did the applicant avail himself of the opportunity & privilege of making application for his alleged Cherokee Citizenship – And from this fact the name of his ancestor Samuel Blair & Nancy Hughes does not appear upon the census rolls of 1835 & 1852. In view of these facts we are of the opinion & so decide, that applicant George W. Blair age 42 yrs & children Dora L Blair age 20 yrs, Samuel M Blair age 17 yrs, John L Blair age 13 yrs, Theodosa[sic] L Blair age 6 yrs, Joseph L Blair age 3 yrs are not Cherokees by blood & are not entitled to Cherokee Citizenship in the Cherokee Nation – Will.P.Ross Chairman.
Post Office Tahlequah, Ind. Ter. John E. Gunter Com.

BRISTO

Docket #761
CENSUS ROLLS 1835

APPLICANT FOR CHEROKEE CITIZENSHIP

POST OFFICE: Salisaw[sic] C.N.		ATTORNEY: Ivey & Welch	
NO	NAMES	AGE	SEX
1	Nevada Bristo	19	Female

2		Minnie Bristo	6 mo	"

ANCESTOR: Reason Bagley

Office Commission on Citizenship
Tahlequah C.N. June 17, 1889

There being no evidence in support of the above named case the Commission decide that Nevada Bristo age 19 years and her Daughter Minnie Bristo Female age 6 months are not of Cherokee blood.

	Will.P. Ross
Attest	Chairman
E.G. Ross	R. Bunch Commissioner
Clerk Commission	John E. Gunter Com

BREEDLOVE

Docket #762
CENSUS ROLLS 1835/52

APPLICANT FOR CHEROKEE CITIZENSHIP

POST OFFICE: Grapevine Texas		**ATTORNEY:** AE Ivey	
NO	NAMES	AGE	SEX
1	Elizabeth Breedlove	46	Female
2	J A Breedlove	19	male
3	Nellie Breedlove	17	female
4	Hattie Breedlove	16	"
5	Laura Breedlove	15	"

ANCESTOR: Jack Carey

Office Commission on Citizenship
Tahlequah Cherokee Nation June 17th 1889

There being no evidence in support of the above named case the Commission decide that Elizabeth Breedlove age 46 years and the following named children, J.A. Breedlove age 19 years, Nellie Breedlove age 17 years. Hattie Breedlove age 16 years, Laura Breedlove age 15 years are not of Cherokee blood. Post Office address Grapevine Texas.

Attest

Will.P.Ross

E.G. Ross

Chairman

Clerk Commission

R. Bunch   Commissioner

John E. Gunter   Com

BROWN

Docket #763

1835/52		APPLICANT FOR CHEROKEE CITIZENSHIP	
POST OFFICE: Galena Ark		ATTORNEY: John Thimpson[sic]	
NO	NAMES	AGE	SEX
1	Mary J Brown	40	female
2	Riley D Brown		
3	Martha Brown		
4	Tiney Brown		

ANCESTOR: John Thimpson

Office Commission on Citizenship

Tahlequah CN June 17th 1889

There being no evidence in support of the above named case the Commission decide that Mary J Brown age 40 years and the following named children Riley D male age 12 years, Martha Female age 9 years and Tiney Brown Female age 5 years are not of Cherokee blood. Post Office address Galena Ark.

Will.P.Ross

Attest

Chairman

EG Ross

R. Bunch   Commissioner

Clerk Commission

John E. Gunter   Com

BOWLAND

Docket #764

CENSUS ROLLS 1835/52

		APPLICANT FOR CHEROKEE CITIZENSHIP	
POST OFFICE: Little River Tex		ATTORNEY: AE Ivey	
NO	NAMES	AGE	SEX
1	D C Bowland	37	Male

ANCESTOR: James *(Illegible)*

Cherokee Citizenship Commission Docket Books
(1880-84, 1887-89) Volume III
Tahlequah, Cherokee Nation

Office Commission on Citizenship
Tahlequah CN June 17, 1889

There being no evidence in support of the above named case the Commission decide that D.C. Bowland age 37 years is not of Cherokee blood. Post Office address Little River Tex.

Attest
    EG Ross
    Clerk Commission

Will.P.Ross
    Chairman
John E. Gunter Com

BEASLEY

Docket #765
CENSUS ROLLS 1835/52

APPLICANT FOR CHEROKEE CITIZENSHIP

POST OFFICE: White Apple Miss		ATTORNEY: AE Ivey	
NO	NAMES	AGE	SEX
1	W.B. Beasley	36	Female

ANCESTOR: John *(Illegible)*

Office Commission on Citizenship
Cherokee Nation Ind. Ter
Tahlequah June 18, 1889

The above named case having been submitted without evidence the Commission decide that W B Beasley of White Apple Missippi[sic] is not of Cherokee blood and not entitled to Citizenship in the Cherokee Nation.

Attest
    EG Ross
    Clerk Commission

Will.P. Ross
    Chairman
JE Gunter Com

BUSHONG

Docket #766

CENSUS ROLLS 1835/52

APPLICANT FOR CHEROKEE CITIZENSHIP

POST OFFICE: Mountainburg Ark		ATTORNEY:	
NO	NAMES	AGE	SEX
1	Mary Bushong	37	Female
2	William L Bushong	16	Male
3	Mary Elenson Bushong	14	Female
4	Chas Henry Bushong	12	Male
5	James Thomas Bushong	10	"
6	John Aglett Bushong	8	"
7	Rena May Bushong	6	female
8	Robert Anderson Bushong	4	male
9	Arthur Eugene Bushong	2	"

ANCESTOR: Ezekiel Gibson

Commission on Citizenship
Tahlequah CN June 19th 1889

The application in the above case alleges that she is the descendant of Ezekiel Gibson whose name should be found on the census rolls of Cherokees by blood taken in the years 1835, 52. The evidence shows that Mary Bushong commonly known as "Sally" Bushong is the daughter of Joel Gibson and Nancy Gibson and that Joel Gibson was the son of Ezekiel Gibson and his wife Rachel Gibson who were said to be of Cherokee blood and that she was born and raised in the State of Kentucky and has resided for several years in Crawford County Arkansas. Joel Gibson came to Madison County Arkansas when he was about 16 or 17 years old and has resided there for more that thirty years without making an application for Citizenship in the Cherokee Nation. The evidence does not establish the Cherokee blood of Mary Bushong and as the name of neither Joel nor Ezekiel Gibson can be found on the rolls of Cherokees taken in 1835 or 1852 the Commission decide that Mary Bushong or Sally Bushong nee Gibson is not of Cherokee blood. This decision includes the names of the children of the said Sally or Mary Bushong to wit; William Lindsey Bushong a6 years, Charles Henry Bushong 12 years, James Thomas Bushong 10 years, John Aglett Bushong 8 years, Robert Anderson Bushong 4 years, Arthur Eugene Bushong 2 years, males, Mary Elenson Bushong 14 years, and Rena May Bushong 6 years, daughters.

Cherokee Citizenship Commission Docket Books
(1880-84, 1887-89) Volume III
Tahlequah, Cherokee Nation

Will.P.Ross Chairman

Attest J.E. Gunter Com

E.G. Ross
Clk. Com.

BANTLEY

Docket #767
CENSUS ROLLS 1835/52

APPLICANT FOR CHEROKEE CITIZENSHIP

POST OFFICE: *(Illegible)* Mo		ATTORNEY: A E Ivey	
NO	**NAMES**	**AGE**	**SEX**
1	Oscar G Bantley	16	Male
2	Rosa E Bantly[sic]	12	female
3	Berlea E Bantley	10	"
4	Chas H Bantley	8	male

ANCESTOR: Oscar Rogers

Now on this the 12 day of 1887, comes the above case for a final hearing and the parties having made application pursuant to the provisions of an Act of the National Council approved Dec. 8 1886. And all the evidence being duly examined and found to be sufficient & satisfactory to the Commission and the name of the ancestor Oscar Rogers appearing on the rolls of 1835/52, it is adjudged & determined by Commission that Oscar G Brantly[sic], Rosa E Brantly, Berlea E Brantly, Chas H Brantly are Cherokees by blood and are hereby re-admitted to all the rights privileges and immunities of Cherokees by blood. And a certificate of said decission[sic] of the Commission & re-admission was made and furnished to said parties accordingly.

J.T. Adair Chairman Commission
John E. Gunter Commissioner

C.C. Lipe
Clerk Commission

Cherokee Citizenship Commission Docket Books
(1880-84, 1887-89) Volume III
Tahlequah, Cherokee Nation

McDONALD

Docket #768

CENSUS ROLLS 1851/2

APPLICANT FOR CHEROKEE CITIZENSHIP

POST OFFICE: Grape Creek CN		ATTORNEY: CH Taylor	
NO	**NAMES**	**AGE**	**SEX**
1	Catherine McDonald	65	Female

ANCESTOR: Polly Taylor

Now on this the 12 day of Oct. comes the above case for a final hearing. And the parties having made application pursuant to the provisions of an Act of the National Council approved Dec. 8 1886. And all the evidence being duly examined and found to be sufficient and satisfactory to the Commission and the name of the ancestor Polly Taylor appearing on the rolls of 1851/2. It is adjudged and determined by Commission that Catherine McDonald is a Cherokee by blood and are[sic] hereby re-admitted to all the privileges rights and immunities of Cherokees by blood. And a certificate of said decission[sic] of the Commission and re-admission was made and furnished to said parties accordingly.

> J.T. Adair   Chairman Com
> John E. Gunter   Commissioner

C.C. Lipe
Clerk Commission

GRAYBEARD

Docket #769

CENSUS ROLLS 1835

APPLICANT FOR CHEROKEE CITIZENSHIP

POST OFFICE: Marble NC		ATTORNEY: C H Taylor	
NO	**NAMES**	**AGE**	**SEX**
1	Johnson Graybeard	69	Male
2	Zekiel Graybeard	49	"
3	Stacy Graybeard	43	female
4	Eggie Graybeard	41	"
5	Lizzie Graybeard	39	"
6	John Graybeard	35	male
7	Charlie Graybeard	31	"
8	Cah-la-yah Graybeard	65	Female

ANCESTOR: Teck-un-quah-las-ka

38

Cherokee Citizenship Commission Docket Books
(1880-84, 1887-89) Volume III
Tahlequah, Cherokee Nation

Now on this the 11th day of October 1887 comes the above case for a final hearing and the parties having made application pursuant to the provisions of an Act of the National Council approved December 8th 1886. And all the evidence being duly examined and found to be sufficient and satisfactory to the Commission and the name of the ancestor Teck-un-quah-las-ka appearing upon the Rolls 1835. It is adjudged and determined by the Commission that Johnson Graybeard, Zekiel Graybeard, Stacy Graybeard, Eggie Graybeard, Lizzie Graybeard, John Graybeard, Charlie Graybeard and Cah-la-gah Graybeard are Cherokees by blood and are hereby readmitted to all the rights privileges and immunities of Cherokees by blood. And a certificate of said decission[sic] of the Commission and re-admission was made and furnished to said parties accordingly.

	J.T. Adair	Chairman Com
Henry Eiffert	John E. Gunter	Commissioner
Clk Com		Commissioner

BURCHFIELD

Docket #770
CENSUS ROLLS 1835/52

APPLICANT FOR CHEROKEE CITIZENSHIP

POST OFFICE: Union Town Ark		ATTORNEY: A E Ivey	
NO	NAMES	AGE	SEX
1	Martha J Burchfield	29	Female
2	Sarah C Burchfield	9	"
3	John R Burchfield	6	male
4	Lora Lee Burchfield	4	female
5	Isaac N Burchfield	2	male

ANCESTOR: Elizabeth Baker

Office Commission on Citizenship
Cherokee Nation Tahlequah
June 19th 1889

There being no evidence in support of the above named case the Commission decide that Martha J Burchfield aged 29 years and the following named children Sarah C Female aged 9 years, John R Male aged 6 years, Lora Female aged 4 years, Isaac N. Burchfield aged 2 years are not of Cherokee blood.

Attest	Will.P.Ross
E G Ross	Chairman
Clerk Commission	R. Bunch Commissioner

BAKER

Docket #771
CENSUS ROLLS 1835

APPLICANT FOR CHEROKEE CITIZENSHIP

POST OFFICE: Cedar Vale Ark		ATTORNEY: A E Ivey	
NO	NAMES	AGE	SEX
1	Samuel A Baker	57	Male
2	John Baker	28	
3	Sarah E Baker	16	
4	Malissa Baker	14	
5	Emily Baker	10	
6	Silas Baker	8	
7	Laura Ann Baker	6	
8	Polly Ann Baker	4	
9	James Calvin Baker	3	

ANCESTOR: Minnie Edwards

Now on this the 9th day of January comes the above case for a final hearing and the parties having made application pursuant to the provisions of an Act of the National Council approved December 8th 1886. And the evidence being duly examined and found not to be sufficient and satisfactory to the Commission and the name of the ancestor not appearing on the Rolls as claimed in the application.

It is adjudged and determined by the Commission that Samuel A Baker, John Baker, Sarah E Baker, Malissa Baker, Emily Baker, Silas Baker, Laura Ann Baker, Polly Ann Baker, and James Calvin Baker are not Cherokees by blood and are hereby rejected & declared to be intruders.

	J.T. Adair Chairman Commission
Attest	John E. Gunter Commissioner
C.C. Lipe	
Clerk Commission	

BELLEW

Docket #772
CENSUS ROLLS 1835

APPLICANT FOR CHEROKEE CITIZENSHIP

POST OFFICE: Yerdell[sic] Ark		ATTORNEY: AE Ivey	
NO	**NAMES**	**AGE**	**SEX**
1	John M Bellew	44	Male
2	Adda Lee Bellew	9	Female
3	Arthur Eli Bellew	7	Male
4	Lula May Bellew	4	Female

ANCESTOR: Mima Edwards

Now on this the 9th day of January 1888 comes the above case up for final hearing, the applicant having made application pursuant to the provisions of an Act of the National Council approved Dec. 8th 1886, and all the evidence being duly examined in the Mary A Couch case, which was by an agreement of the Attys made a list one, giving all cases claiming a direct ancestry from the same ancestor, Mima Edwards; it is adjudged and determined by the Commission that John M. Bellew, Adda Lee – Arthur Eli – Lula May Bellew are not Cherokees by blood, and in consequence not entitled to the rights of such.

The decision in the Mary A. Couch case found on page 100, Docket A; governs this case.

J.T. Adair   Chairman Commission

Attest   D.W. Lipe Commissioner

C.C. Lipe
Clerk Com

BROWN

Docket #773
CENSUS ROLLS 1835

APPLICANT FOR CHEROKEE CITIZENSHIP

POST OFFICE: Mt Carmel Ill		ATTORNEY: AE Ivey	
NO	**NAMES**	**AGE**	**SEX**
1	Ora Nancy Brown		Female

ANCESTOR: Wm Sevier

Office Commission on Citizenship
Tahlequah CN June 18, 1889

There being no evidence in support of the above named case the Commission decide that Ora Nancy Brown is not of Cherokee blood. Post Office address Mt. Carmel Ill.

Attest   Will.P.Ross
     EG Ross   Chairman
         Clerk Commission   John E. Gunter   Commissioner

BROWN

Docket #774

CENSUS ROLLS 1835

APPLICANT FOR CHEROKEE CITIZENSHIP

POST OFFICE: Bartlesvilles IT		ATTORNEY:	
NO	NAMES	AGE	SEX
1	Vicy J Brown	43	Female

ANCESTOR: James Smith

See decision in this case in that of Margaret A. Puffer in Book "C" page 434 – Adverse to claimant.

Cornell Rogers.
Clk Com on Citizenship

Office Com on Citizenship
Tahlequah I.T. Sept 24th 1888.

BROWN

Docket #775

CENSUS ROLLS 1835

APPLICANT FOR CHEROKEE CITIZENSHIP

POST OFFICE: *(Illegible)* Ga		ATTORNEY: A E Ivey	
NO	NAMES	AGE	SEX
1	Lodskyan Brown	42	Female
2	Nancy Brown	21	"
3	James Brown	17	"
4	Mary J Brown	15	"
5	Josephine Brown	9	"

6	Caroline Brown	7	"

ANCESTOR: John Tidwell

We the Commission on Citizenship after carefully examining the evidence in the above case and also the census rolls of 1851, taken East of the Mississippi River, find that the above applicants are descendents of John Tidwell and are Cherokees by blood and under an Act of the National Council creating this Commission dated Dec. 8th 1886. We the Commission decide that Lodskyan Brown and her five children, viz: Nancy, James, Mary J, Josephine and Caroline Brown are Cherokees by blood, and are hereby re-admitted to all the rights and privileges of Cherokee citizens by blood.

J.T. Adair   Chairman Commission
D.W. Lipe   Commissioner
H.C. Barnes   Commissioner

Office Com on Citizenship
Tahlequah I.T. Sept 21st 1888

BOVENDOO

Docket #776
CENSUS ROLLS 1835/52

APPLICANT FOR CHEROKEE CITIZENSHIP

POST OFFICE: Blue Jacket IT.		ATTORNEY: A E Ivey	
NO	**NAMES**	**AGE**	**SEX**
1	Sarah C Bovendoo	21	Female

ANCESTOR: Isam Sizemore

Office Commission on Citizenship
Tahlequah June 19th 1889

There being no evidence in support of the above named case the Commission decide that Sarah C Bovendoo age 21 years is _not_ of Cherokee blood. Post Office address Blue Jacket I.T.

Attest

    EG Ross
       Clerk Commission

Will.P. Ross
     Chairman
John E. Gunter   Com

BEALER

Docket #777

CENSUS ROLLS 1835/52

APPLICANT FOR CHEROKEE CITIZENSHIP

POST OFFICE: St Louis Mo		ATTORNEY: AE Ivey	
NO	NAMES	AGE	SEX
1	Samuel Bealer	41	Male

ANCESTOR: Richard Bealer

Office Commission on Citizenship
Tahlequah Cherokee Nation I.T.
June 18, 1889

The above named case having been submitted by Attorneys for both parties the Commission decide that Samuel Bealer age 41 years of No 3029 Clay Avenue, West St Louis Mo is not of Cherokee blood and not entitled to Citizenship in the Cherokee Nation.

Attest   Will.P. Ross

     E G Ross   Chairman

        Clerk Commission   JE Gunter   Com

BOX

Docket #778

CENSUS ROLLS 1835/52

APPLICANT FOR CHEROKEE CITIZENSHIP

POST OFFICE: Tucson Arizona		ATTORNEY: Boudinot & R[sic]	
NO	NAMES	AGE	SEX
1	Hannah Box		Female

ANCESTOR:

Office Commission on Citizenship
Cherokee Nation Tahlequah
June 18th 1889

There being no evidence in support of the above named case the Commission decide that Hannah Box is not of Cherokee blood and is not entitled to Citizenship in the Cherokee Nation. Post Office Tucson Arizona.

Cherokee Citizenship Commission Docket Books
(1880-84, 1887-89) Volume III
Tahlequah, Cherokee Nation

Attest   Will.P. Ross

     EG Ross   Chairman

         Clerk Commission   J E Gunter   Com

BUTLER

Docket #779

CENSUS ROLLS 1835/52

APPLICANT FOR CHEROKEE CITIZENSHIP

POST OFFICE: Heico[sic] Ark		ATTORNEY: Geo O Butler	
NO	NAMES	AGE	SEX
1	L Butler	38	Female

ANCESTOR: Mariah Waakins[sic]

Office Commission on Citizenship
Tahlequah C.N. June 18, 1889

There being no evidence in support of the above named case the Commission decide that L. Butler age 38 years is not of Cherokee blood. Post Office Nico, Ark.

                 Will. P. Ross

Attest   Chairman

    E.G. Ross   R. Bunch   Com

       Clerk Commission   John E. Gunter   Com

BROCK

Docket #780

CENSUS ROLLS 1835/52

APPLICANT FOR CHEROKEE CITIZENSHIP

POST OFFICE: Siloam Spgs		ATTORNEY: L.S. Sanders	
NO	NAMES	AGE	SEX
1	W.C.P. Brock	57	Male
2	Mary C Pigeon	38	Female
3	Johanna F. Chandler	34	"
4	Margaret Powell	32	"
5	Virginia Carroll	28	"
6	Anna G. Powell	25	"
7	Perry G. Brock	21	Male
8	Robert L. Brock	18	"

45

9	Octavia Brock	12	"[sic]

ANCESTOR: Brock

Office Commission on Citizenship
Cherokee Nation Tahlequah
June 18th 1889

There being no evidence in support of the above named case the Commission decide that W.C.P. Beck[sic] age 57 years, Mary C. Pigeon, Female age 38 years, Johanna F. Chandler Female age 34 years, Margaret Powell Female age 32 years, Virginia Carroll Female age 28 years, Anna G. Powell Female age 25 years, Perry G. Beck Male age 21 years, Robert L Beck, Male, age 18 years, Octavia Beck Femmale[sic] age 12 years are not of Cherokee blood. Post Office Siloam Springs.

Attest   Will.P. Ross
    E.G. Ross   Chairman
        Clerk Commission   J E Gunter   Com

BELL

Docket #781
CENSUS ROLLS 1835

APPLICANT FOR CHEROKEE CITIZENSHIP

POST OFFICE: Sialom[sic] Spgs		ATTORNEY: L S Sanders	
NO	NAMES	AGE	SEX
1	Callie Bell	19	Female

ANCESTOR: Susan Bell

Office Commission on Citizenship
Cherokee Nation I.T.
Tahlequah June 18th 1889

There being no evidence in support of the above named case the Commission decide that Callie Bell, aged 19 years, is not of Cherokee blood.

Attest   Will.P. Ross
    EG Ross   Chairman
        Clerk Commission   J.E. Gunter   Com

Cherokee Citizenship Commission Docket Books
(1880-84, 1887-89) Volume III
Tahlequah, Cherokee Nation

BUSH

Docket #

CENSUS ROLLS 1835/52

POST OFFICE: Sherman Texas		ATTORNEY: L.B. Bell	
NO	**NAMES**	**AGE**	**SEX**
1	Rosa Bush		Female

APPLICANT FOR CHEROKEE CITIZENSHIP

ANCESTOR: Nancy *(Illegible)*

Rejected Sept. 9th 1889

Office Commission on Citizenship
Cherokee Nation Ind. Ter.
Tahlequah Sept. 9th 1889

Application for Cherokee Citizenship

The above applicant was called 3 times & no answer & there being no evidence on file in support of the application we decide that claimant Rosa Bush is not a Cherokee by blood & his[sic] application is hereby rejected. Post Office Sherman Texas.

Will.P. Ross   Chairman

Attest

D.S. Williams   J.E. Gunter   Com
Asst. Clk. Com.

BRADSHAW

Docket #783

CENSUS ROLLS 1835/52

APPLICANT FOR CHEROKEE CITIZENSHIP

POST OFFICE: Webbers Falls, I.T.		ATTORNEY: W.A. Thompson	
NO	**NAMES**	**AGE**	**SEX**
1	Nancy Bradshaw	72	Female

ANCESTOR: *(Name Illegible)*

Office Commission on Citizenship
Cherokee Nation Tahlequah
June 19th 1889

There being no evidence in support of the above named case the Commission decide that Nancy Bradshaw age 72 years is not a Cherokee by blood. Post Office address Webbers Falls, I.T.

Will.P. Ross
Chairman
J E Gunter   Com

Attest
E.G. Ross
Clk Com.

BROWN

Docket #784
CENSUS ROLLS

APPLICANT FOR CHEROKEE CITIZENSHIP

POST OFFICE:		ATTORNEY: Boudinot & R[sic]		
NO	NAMES		AGE	SEX
1	Harvey F Brown			Male
2	Henry E Brown			Female[sic]
3	Nellie E Brown			Female

ANCESTOR: Sarah Brown

Office Commission on Citizenship
Cherokee Nation I.T.
Tahlequah June 19th 1889

There being no evidence in support of the above named case the Commission decide that Harvey F Brown, Henry E Brown and Nellie E Brown are not of Cherokee blood.

Will.P. Ross
Chairman
J E Gunter   Com

Attest
E.G. Ross
Clerk Com

48

Cherokee Citizenship Commission Docket Books
(1880-84, 1887-89) Volume III
Tahlequah, Cherokee Nation

BABB

Docket #785

CENSUS ROLLS 1835/52

APPLICANT FOR CHEROKEE CITIZENSHIP

POST OFFICE: Blue Grass I.T.		ATTORNEY: W.A. Thompson	
NO	NAMES	AGE	SEX
1	Louisa K Babb	38	Female
2	Chas M Babb	15	Male
3	Rosannah P. Babb	8	Female
4	Eunice Lassiter	42	"

ANCESTOR: John Dunbar

Commission on Citizenship
Tahlequah CN June 25 1889

The application in the above case alleges that the applicant is the Grand daughter of one Elizabeth Dunbar whose name should be found on the rolls of Cherokees by blood taken in 1835 to 51. 2. The name of Elizabeth Dunbar is not so found. She states that she is the daughter of one Jane Lassater of Cherokee Indian blood who was born in North Carolina in 1817 and died in Kansas n June 1886, that Jane Lassater was the reputed daughter of one John Dunbar of Cherokee Indian descent who was born in Virginia in 1794 and died in North Carolina in May 1863, and that he was the son of one Elizabeth Dunbar a half breed Cherokee woman who died in that state in 1815 and she was the reputed daughter of one Joseph Hoskell, a Cherokee Indian who is said to have died in North Carolina in 1829. As the names of none of these persons are found on the census rolls of Cherokees named in the 7th Section of the Act of December 8th 1886, the Commission decide that Louisa K. Babb aged 38 years in 1887 and her children, Charles M. Babb aged 15 years and Rosana P. Babb aged 8 years and Eunice Lassiter an invalid sister age 42 years are not of Cherokee blood. Post Office Blue Grass I.T.

Will.P. Ross   Chairman

Attest

E.G. Ross   John E. Gunter   Com
Clerk Com.

49

Cherokee Citizenship Commission Docket Books
(1880-84, 1887-89) Volume III
Tahlequah, Cherokee Nation

BROWN

Docket #786

CENSUS ROLLS 1835/52

APPLICANT FOR CHEROKEE CITIZENSHIP

POST OFFICE:		ATTORNEY: Boudinot R	
NO	NAMES	AGE	SEX
1	Theodore E. Brown		Male

ANCESTOR: Sarah Brown

Office Commission on Citizenship
Cherokee Nation Tahlequah June 19 1889

There being no evidence in support of the above named case the Commission decide that Theodore E Brown is <u>not</u> a Cherokee by blood.

Attest

    E.G. Ross

        Clerk Commission

Will.P. Ross

        Chairman

J.E. Gunter   Com

BROWN

Docket #787

CENSUS ROLLS 1835/52

APPLICANT FOR CHEROKEE CITIZENSHIP

POST OFFICE:		ATTORNEY: Boudinot & R[sic]	
NO	NAMES	AGE	SEX
1	Mary E Brown		Female

ANCESTOR: Sarah Brown

Office Commission on Citizenship
Tahlequah Cherokee Nation I.T.
June 19th 1889

There being no evidence in support of the above named case the Commission decide that Mary E. Brown is not a Cherokee by blood.

Attest

    E.G. Ross

        Clerk Commission

Will.P. Ross

        Chairman

J.E. Gunter   Com

BROWN

Docket #788

CENSUS ROLLS 1835/52

APPLICANT FOR CHEROKEE CITIZENSHIP

POST OFFICE:		ATTORNEY: Boudinot & R[sic]	
NO	**NAMES**	**AGE**	**SEX**
1	James M. Brown		Male

ANCESTOR: Sarah Brown

Office Commission on Citizenship
Cherokee Nation Tahlequah
June 19th 1889

There being no evidence in support of the above named case the Commission decide that James M. Brown and the following named children Edward Male, Claude Male Avery Male are not Cherokees by blood.

Attest   Will.P. Ross   Chairman

     EG Ross   JE Gunter Com

         Clerk Commission

BROWN

Docket #789

CENSUS ROLLS

APPLICANT FOR CHEROKEE CITIZENSHIP

POST OFFICE:		ATTORNEY: Boudinot & R[sic]	
NO	**NAMES**	**AGE**	**SEX**
1	Sarah J Brown		
2	Azelen[sic] Brown		

ANCESTOR: Sarah Brown

Office Commission on Citizenship
Tahlequah CN June 19th 1889

There being no evidence in support of the above named case the Commission decide that Sarah J Brown and Daughter Angeline Brown are not Cherokees by blood.

\

Attest	Will.P.Ross
EG Ross	Chairman
Clerk Commission	John E. Gunter Com

BROWN

Docket #790

CENSUS ROLLS

APPLICANT FOR CHEROKEE CITIZENSHIP

POST OFFICE: Garden City Kansas		ATTORNEY: Boudinot & R[sic]	
NO	NAMES	AGE	SEX
1	Milton Brown, Jr		Male
2	Chauncey C. Brown		"

ANCESTOR: Sarah Brown

Office Commission on Citizenship
Cherokee Nation I.T.
Tahlequah June 19th 1889

There being no evidence in support of the above named case the Commission decide that Milton Brown Jr and son Chauncy[sic] C. Brown male are <u>not</u> Cherokees by blood. Post Office Garden City, Kansas.

Attest	Will.P. Ross
EG Ross	Chairman
Clerk Commission	J.E. Gunter Com

BROWN

Docket #791

CENSUS ROLLS 1835/52

APPLICANT FOR CHEROKEE CITIZENSHIP

POST OFFICE: Baxter Springs Kas		ATTORNEY: Boudinot & R[sic]	
NO	NAMES	AGE	SEX
1	James Brown	43	Male
2	May Brown	8	Female
3	Mystie Brown	6	"
4	Lillie Brown	4	"
5	Preston Brown	1 mo	Male

ANCESTOR: Louisa Brown

Office Commission on Citizenship
Tahlequah CN June 19th 1889

The applicant in the above case alleges that he is the son of Louisa Brown nee Moss and Grand son of Jerry and Sally Moss. The evidence consists of two affidavits taken in Cherokee County, state of Kansas before Isaac C. Perkins Notary Public on the 23rd day of January 1885 to wit: Reuben Davis swears that he is 61 years old, that he has known claimant from the date of his birth, that he is of Cherokee Indian descent being the son of one Louisa Moss who is said to have been born in Pitman County, Georgia in the year 1823 and died in Spalding County in said state in 1858 and that she was said to be the daughter of one Jerry Moss a Cherokee Indian who it is said was born on the Cherokee Indian reservation East of the Missippi[sic] River in 1796 and died in Putman County Georgia in 18?4. The affidavit of Leander Armstrong 68 years of age is of like import with the preceeding. These statements and ~~from~~ that of the applicant himself is all the evidence which shows that James Brown was of Cherokee blood but they further show that Louisa Moss was 35 years of age at the time of her death in Putman County Georgia in 1858 and that her Father Jerry Moss was born in 1796 and died in 1844. The name of Louisa Moss should therefore appear on the Census Rolls of Cherokees in Georgia taken in the years 1848-52 and that of James Moss on the rolls of 1835, but neither name so appears. The Commission therefore in view of the insufficient character of the evidence as proving the Cherokee descent of James Brown and the names of alleged ancestors do not appear on the census rolls named decide that the said James Brown aged 43 years and his daughters May Brown aged 8 years, Mystie Brown aged 6 years and Lilly Brown aged 4 years and Preston Brown Infant son are not of Cherokee blood and not entitled to Citizenship in the Cherokee Nation.

Attest   Will.P. Ross   Chairman
     E.G. Ross   J.E. Gunter   Com
        Clerk Commission

Cherokee Citizenship Commission Docket Books
(1880-84, 1887-89) Volume III
Tahlequah, Cherokee Nation

BROWN

Docket #792

CENSUS ROLLS 1835

APPLICANT FOR CHEROKEE CITIZENSHIP

POST OFFICE: Alena Ark		ATTORNEY: A E Ivey	
NO	NAMES	AGE	SEX
1	James H. Brown	38	Male
2	Job A Brown	10	"
3	Rehalh[sic] Brown	10	Female
4	Laura Isabella Brown	7	
5	Arthur Oster Brown	3	

ANCESTOR: Isom Brown

Rejected June 19th 1889

Commission on Citizenship
Cherokee Nation Tahlequah
June 19th 1889

The evidence in this case, a statement sworn to by one Isaac Glass before Allen Ross, Clerk of Tahlequah District Cherokee Nation on the 1st day of October 1887 fails to show that he has any knowledge of the applicant further than his own alleged statements made several years ago to him and is insufficient to show that Isom Brown was of Cherokee blood. In addition to this, the name of Isom Brown does not appear on the roll of 1835. The Commission therefore decide that James H. Brown is not of Cherokee blood nor are his children, to wit; Job A Brown 10 years and Arthur Oster Brown 3 years, Sons, and Rehalh Brown 10 years and Louisa Isabel Brown 7 years daughters and that they are not entitled to citizenship in the Cherokee Nation.

Attest

E.G. Ross

Will. P. Ross
Chairman
J.E. Gunter   Com

BROWN

Docket #793

CENSUS ROLLS 1835

APPLICANT FOR CHEROKEE CITIZENSHIP

POST OFFICE: Van Buren Ark		ATTORNEY:	
NO	NAMES	AGE	SEX
1	Isam A Brown	42	Male

2	Louisa Brown	17	Female
3	Isom A Brown	12	Male
4	Harry M Brown	4	"

ANCESTOR: Isam Brown

Rejected June 20th 1889

Office Commission on Citizenship
Cherokee Nation
Tahlequah June 20th 1889

There being no evidence in support of the above named case the Commission decide that Isam A Brown age 42 years, Louisa Female 17, Isom A. male age 12 years and Harry M. Brown male age 4 years are not of Cherokee blood. Post Office address Van Buren Ark.

Will. P. Ross

Attest   Chairman

DW. Williams   R. Bunch   Com

Asst. Clk. Com.   John E Gunter   Com

BOLDEN

Docket #794

CENSUS ROLLS 1835

APPLICANT FOR CHEROKEE CITIZENSHIP

POST OFFICE: Van Buren Ark		ATTORNEY: Ivey & Welch	
NO	NAMES	AGE	SEX
1	Alverder[sic] Bolden	21	Female
2	Baley M Bolden	3	"
3	Asa M Bolden	1	"

ANCESTOR: Isam Brown

Rejected Sept 9th 1889

Office Commission on Citizenship
Cherokee Nation Ind. Ter.
Tahlequah Sept. 9th 1889

Application for Cherokee Citizenship.

The above case was called three several times and no response from applicant or by Atty the Commission after examing[sic] the papers fail to find any evidence in support of application we decide that Alverder Bolden age 21 years and the following children, Baley M Bolden Female 3 yrs, Asa M Bolden Female 1 yr are not Cherokees by blood. Post Office Van Buren Ark.

Attest
    DSWilliams
Asst. Clk Com

Will. P. Ross   Chairman
J.E. Gunter   Com

BROWN

Docket #795

CENSUS ROLLS 1835/52

APPLICANT FOR CHEROKEE CITIZENSHIP

POST OFFICE: Thornfield Mo		ATTORNEY: Ivey & Welch	
NO	NAMES	AGE	SEX
1	Robt Brown	4	Male
2	John A Brown	14	"
3	Bissie Brown	11	Female
4	Eliza Brown	9	"

ANCESTOR: Isam Brown

Rejected June 20th 1889

Office Commission on Citizenship
Cherokee Nation
Tahlequah June 20th 1889

There being no evidence in support of the above named case the Commission decide that Robert Brown age 4 years and the following named John A Male age 14 years, Bissie Female age 11 years, Eliza Female age 9 years are not Cherokees by blood. Post Office address Thornfield Mo.

Attest
    D.S. Williams
    Asst. Clk Com

Will.P. Ross
    Chairman
R. Bunch Com
John E. Gunter   Com

Cherokee Citizenship Commission Docket Books
(1880-84, 1887-89) Volume III
Tahlequah, Cherokee Nation

BROWN

Docket #796

CENSUS ROLLS 1835

APPLICANT FOR CHEROKEE CITIZENSHIP

POST OFFICE: Thornfield Mo		ATTORNEY: Ivey & Welch	
NO	NAMES	AGE	SEX
1	Elijah Brown	49	Male
2	Rufus Brown	18	"
3	Silas Brown	15	

ANCESTOR: Isam Brown

Rejected June 20th 1889

Office Commission on Citizenship
Cherokee Nation
Tahlequah June 20th 1889

There being no evidence in support of the above named case the Commission decide that Elijah Brown age 49 years, Rufus male age 18 years and Silas Brown male age 15 years are not of Cherokee blood. Post Office address Thornfield Mo

Will.P. Ross

Attest   Chairman

DSWilliams   R. Bunch Com

Asst Clk Com   John E. Gunter   Com

BROWN

Docket #797

CENSUS ROLLS 1835

APPLICANT FOR CHEROKEE CITIZENSHIP

POST OFFICE: Ark.		ATTORNEY: AE Ivey	
NO	NAMES	AGE	SEX
1	Daniel E Brown	22	Male

ANCESTOR: Isam Brown

Rejected June 20th 1889

Office Commission on Citizenship
Cherokee Nation
Tahlequah June 20th 1889

There being no evidence in support of the above named case the Commission decide that Daniel E Brown age 22 years is not a Cherokee by blood. Post Office address Ark.

Will.P. Ross

Chairman

Attest

DS Williams

Asst Clk Com

R. Bunch   Com

John E. Gunter   Com

BARKER

Docket #798

CENSUS ROLLS

APPLICANT FOR CHEROKEE CITIZENSHIP

POST OFFICE:		ATTORNEY: L B Bell	
NO	NAMES	AGE	SEX
1	Elihu Barker		Female

ANCESTOR: Sarah Morgan

Rejected June 20th 1889

Office Commission on Citizenship

Cherokee Nation

Tahlequah June 20th 1889

There being no evidence in the above case and no reference to roll on which the name of alleged ancestor can be found the Commission decide that Mrs Elihu Barker is not of Cherokee blood and not entitled to Citizenship in the Cherokee Nation. Post office address

Will. P. Ross

Chairman

Attest

D.S. Williams

Asst Clk Com

R. Bunch   Com

John E. Gunter   Com

BARTON

Docket #799

CENSUS ROLLS 1835 to 52

APPLICANT FOR CHEROKEE CITIZENSHIP

POST OFFICE: North View Mo		ATTORNEY: Boudinot & R[sic]	
NO	NAMES	AGE	SEX
1	Tommi Gert Barton	24	Female
2	Myrtle Bell Barton	7	

58

3	James T Barton	4	
4	Hattie Lee Barton	1	

ANCESTOR: Bashaba Goodrich

Rejected June 20th 1889

Office Commission on Citizenship
Cherokee Nation
Tahlequah June 20th 1889

There being no evidence in support of the above named case the Commission decide that Tommie Gertrude Barton age 24 years, Myrtle Bell Barton age 7 years, James T. male age 4 years and Hattie Lee Barton Female age 1 year are not of Cherokee blood. Post Office North View Mo.

Will.P. Ross
Attest   Chairman
    DS Williams   R. Bunch   Com
    Asst. Clk Com   John E. Gunter   Com

BONDS

Docket #800

CENSUS ROLLS 1835/52

APPLICANT FOR CHEROKEE CITIZENSHIP

POST OFFICE: Russellville Ark		ATTORNEY: Boudinot R	
NO	NAMES	AGE	SEX
1	Ella Etta Bonds	22	Female
2	Emma D Bonds	19	"
3	Robt C Bonds	17	Male
4	Sarah L Bonds	14	Female
5	Joseph C Bonds	12	Male

ANCESTOR: Bashaba Goorich[sic]

Rejected June 20th 1889

Office Commission on Citizenship
Cherokee Nation
Tahlequah June 20th 1889

There being no evidence in support of the above named case the Commission decide that Ella Etta Bonds age 22 years and the following named children Emma D. 19 years, Robert C male 17 years, Sarah L Female 14 years, and

Joseph C. Bonds male age 12 years are not Cherokees by blood. Post Office Russellville Ark.

		Will.P. Ross	
Attest		Chairman	
	DS Williams	R. Bunch	Com
	Asst Clk Com	John E. Gunter	Com

BEAN

Docket #801
CENSUS ROLLS

APPLICANT FOR CHEROKEE CITIZENSHIP

POST OFFICE: Sheep Ranch Cal		ATTORNEY: Wm Jackson	
NO	NAMES	AGE	SEX
1	Nancy A Bean	57	Female
2	William A Henry	37	Male
3	Edmond E Bean	31	Male
4	Emily J Raggio	27	Female
5	James R Bean	25	Male
6	Robt L Bean	23	"
7	Bell B Bean	19	female
8	Mark R Bean	19	Male
9	Geo S Bean	14	"
10	Bertram Raggio	4	"
11	Ralston Raggio	1	"
12	W S Smith	13	"
13	Ella Smith	10	female

ANCESTOR: Nancy A Fuller

Now on this the 9th day of Nov. 1887 comes the above case for a final hearing. And the parties having made application pursuant to the provisions of an Act of the National Council approved Dec. 8th 1886. And all the evidence being duly examined and found to be sufficient and satisfactory to the Commission and the name of the Ancestor Nancy A Fuller appearing on the rolls of 1835. It is adjudged and determined to the Commission that Nancy A Bean, William A. Henry, Edmond E Bean, Emily J Bean, James R Bean, Robert L Bean, Bell B Bean, Mark R Bean, Geo S Bean, Bertram Raggio, Ralston Raggio, W S Smith, Ellen Smith are Cherokees by blood and are hereby re-admitted to all the rights privileges and immunities of Cherokees by blood. And a certificate of said decision of the Commission and readmission are made & furnished to said parties accordingly.

J T Adair   Chairman Commission
John E Gunter   Commissioner

C.C. Lipe
Clerk Commission

BARNES

Docket #802
CENSUS ROLLS 1835

APPLICANT FOR CHEROKEE CITIZENSHIP

POST OFFICE: Sheep Ranch Cal		ATTORNEY:	
NO	**NAMES**	**AGE**	**SEX**
1	Nancy A Barnes	55	Female
2	Laura F Bowley	26	"
3	Mary H Stephens	24	"
4	Edna V Bowley	8	"
5	Annie L Bowley	6	"
6	James R Stephens	1	Male

ANCESTOR: John R Blythe

Now on this the 1st day of June 1888 comes the above case up for final hearing and the Commission say: "We the Commission on Citizenship after examining the evidence and the census rolls of 1835, find the above applicants are Cherokees by blood and the said Nancy A Barns and her two daughters and three grandchildren viz: Laura F Bowley, Mary H Stephens (daughters), Edna V. and Annie L Bowley and James R Stephens (gr. children) are hereby readmitted to all the rights and privileges of Cherokee citizens by blood.

J.T. Adair   Chairman Commission
John E Gunter   Commissioner
D.W. Lipe   Commissioner

BURCHFIELD

Docket #803

CENSUS ROLLS 1835/52

APPLICANT FOR CHEROKEE CITIZENSHIP

POST OFFICE: Spavin Ark		ATTORNEY: Boudinot & R[sic]	
NO	**NAMES**	**AGE**	**SEX**
1	Elizabeth Burchfield	45	Female
2	William B Hodge	19	Male
3	Louis F Hodge	17	"
4	Mollie F Hodge	16	Female

ANCESTOR: Nancy Reeves

Rejected June 20th 1889

Office Commission on Citizenship
Cherokee Nation
Tahlequah June 20th 1889

There being no evidence in support of the above named case the Commission decide that Elizabeth Burchfield age 45 years, William B Hodge male age 19 years, Louis F Hodge Female[sic] 16[sic] years Post Office Spavin Ark. are not Cherokees by blood.

Will.P. Ross

Attest   Chairman

D.S. Williams   R. Bunch   Com
Asst. Clk Com   John E Gunter   Com

BETHEL

Docket #804

CENSUS ROLLS 1835/52

APPLICANT FOR CHEROKEE CITIZENSHIP

POST OFFICE: Farmer Ark		ATTORNEY: Boudinot & R[sic]	
NO	**NAMES**	**AGE**	**SEX**
1	Amanda Bethel	32	Female

ANCESTOR: Leah Reeves

Rejected

Office Commission on Citizenship
Cherokee Nation Ind. Ter.
Tahlequah June 13th 1889

Cherokee Citizenship Commission Docket Books
(1880-84, 1887-89) Volume III
Tahlequah, Cherokee Nation

There being no evidence in support of the above named case the Commission decide that Amanda Bethel age 32 years is <u>not</u> of Cherokee by blood. Post Office address Farmer Ark

E.G. Ross
    Clerk Commission

Will.P. Ross
        Chairman
J.E. Gunter Com

BROOKS

Docket #805

CENSUS ROLLS 1835/52

APPLICANT FOR CHEROKEE CITIZENSHIP

POST OFFICE: Siloam Springs		ATTORNEY: L S Sanders	
NO	NAMES	AGE	SEX
1	William F Brooks	57	

ANCESTOR: Thomas F Brooks

Rejected

Commission on Citizenship
Cherokee Nation I T
Tahlequah June 20th 1889

There being no evidence filed in support of the application in the above case the Commission decide that William F Brooks aged fifty seven years of Siloam Springs Arkansas, is not of Cherokee blood and <u>not</u> entitled to Citizenship in the Cherokee Nation.

Attest
    E.G. Ross
        Clerk Commission

Will.P. Ross   Chairman
R. Bunch   Com

BRYANT

Docket #806

CENSUS ROLLS 1835/52

APPLICANT FOR CHEROKEE CITIZENSHIP

POST OFFICE: Mulberry Ark		ATTORNEY: A E Ivey	
NO	NAMES	AGE	SEX
1	Lucy M Bryant	27	Fem
2	Alonzo Bryant	3	Male

63

3	Elizabeth Bryant	1	Fem

ANCESTOR: Andrew Moton

Office Commission on Citizenship
Cherokee Nation June 25, 1889

There being no evidence in support of the above named case the Commission decide that Lucy M Bryant age 27 years and her children Alonzo Female[sic] aged 3 years, Elizabeth Female aged 1 year are <u>not</u> Cherokees by blood.

Will.P.Ross
Chairman
J E Gunter   Com

Attest

E.G. Ross
Clk. Com

BRASHER

Docket #807
CENSUS ROLLS 1835/52

APPLICANT FOR CHEROKEE CITIZENSHIP

POST OFFICE: Whitesboro Tex		ATTORNEY: Boudinot & R[sic]	
NO	**NAMES**	**AGE**	**SEX**
1	Susan Brasher	26	Fem

ANCESTOR: Moton

Office Commission on Citizenship
Cherokee Nation June 25, 1889

There being no evidence in support of the above named case the Commission decide that Susan Bradshaw[sic] aged twenty six years is <u>not</u> a Cherokee by blood. Post Office Whitesboro Texas.

Attest   Will.P.Ross
     E.G. Ross   Chairman
          Clerk Commission   R. Bunch   Com
                               JE Gunter   Com

BROWN

Docket #808

CENSUS ROLLS

APPLICANT FOR CHEROKEE CITIZENSHIP

POST OFFICE: Plainfield Ind		ATTORNEY: C H Taylor	
NO	NAMES	AGE	SEX
1	Nancy J Brown	39	Fem

ANCESTOR: Annie Wickey

Rejected April 3rd 1889

The application of Nancy J. Brown aged 39 who applies for Citizenship for herself, and unnamed children having been submitted by the Attorney J.M. Taylor representing C.H. Taylor for applicant and the Attorney for the Nation for decision on this the 3rd day of April 1889. Commission find that Nacy[sic] J. Brown alleges herself to be of Cherokee blood by descent from her great grand mother Annie Wickey, the allegation is supported by no evidence as there has been none presented in the case nor does the applicant ever allege that the name of Annie Wickey may be found on either of the rolls named in the 7th Sec. of the Act of December 8th 1886, or any rolls whatever. The Commission therefore decide that applicant is not of Cherokee blood and is not entitled to Citizenship in the Cherokee Nation. This decission[sic] embraces the applications of Martha A. Brown aged 35 years, John T. Brown aged 33 years, Zana Brown aged 29 years, Brazelton T. Brown aged 31 years, Joseph O. Brown aged 26 years, Jemima E. Brown aged 24 years, who claim descent from the same ancestor Annie Wickey and whose cases are presented in the same manner as that of Nancy J. Brown. The applications of said parties was[sic] filed before the Commission Oct. 4, 1889. Their Post Office address is Plainfield Indiana.

	Will.P. Ross	Chairman
This April 3rd 1889	John E. Gunter	Commissioner

Attest
    D.S. Williams
    Clk Com.

BROWN

Docket #809

CENSUS ROLLS

APPLICANT FOR CHEROKEE CITIZENSHIP

POST OFFICE: Plainfield Ind   **ATTORNEY:** C H Taylor

NO	NAMES	AGE	SEX
1	Martha A Brown	35	Fem

ANCESTOR: Annie Wickey

Rejected April 3rd 1889

Adverse

Embraced in decission[sic] on page 524
Book B. in the Nancy J. Brown case.
rendered April 3rd 1889
Will.P. Ross
Chairman
John E. Gunter   Commissioner

Office Com on Citizenship
Tahlequah I.T.
April 3rd 1889
Attest
D.S. Williams
Clk. Com.

BROWN

Docket #810

CENSUS ROLLS

APPLICANT FOR CHEROKEE CITIZENSHIP

POST OFFICE: Plainfield Ind   **ATTORNEY:** C.H. Taylor

NO	NAMES	AGE	SEX
1	John T Brown	33	Male

ANCESTOR: Annie Wickey

Rejected April 3rd 1889

Adverse

Embraced in decission[sic] on page 524
Book B. in the Nancy J. Brown case.
rendered April 3rd 1889
Will.P. Ross   Chairman
John E. Gunter   Commissioner

Office Com on Citizenship
Tahlequah I.T.

April 3rd 1889
Attest
D.S. Williams
Clk. Com.

BROWN

Docket #811
CENSUS ROLLS

APPLICANT FOR CHEROKEE CITIZENSHIP

POST OFFICE: Plainfield Ind   **ATTORNEY:** C.H. Taylor

NO	NAMES	AGE	SEX
1	Brazelton T Brown	31	Fem[sic]

ANCESTOR: Annie Wickey

Rejected April 3rd 1889

Adverse
Embraced in decission[sic] on page 524
Book B. in the Nancy J. Brown case.
rendered April 3rd 1889
Will.P. Ross   Chairman
John E. Gunter   Commissioner

Office Com on Citizenship
Tahlequah I.T.
April 3rd 1889
Attest
D.S. Williams
Clk. Com.

BROWN

Docket #812
CENSUS ROLLS

APPLICANT FOR CHEROKEE CITIZENSHIP

POST OFFICE: Plainfield Ind   **ATTORNEY:** C H Taylor

NO	NAMES	AGE	SEX
1	Jemima E Brown	24	Fem

ANCESTOR: Annie Wickey

Rejected April 3rd 1889

Adverse

Embraced in decission[sic] on page 524

Book B. in the Nancy J. Brown case.

rendered April 3rd 1889

Will.P. Ross   Chairman

John E. Gunter   Commissioner

Office Com on Citizenship

Tahlequah I.T.

April 3rd 1889

Attest

D.S. Williams

Clk. Com.

BROWN

Docket #813

CENSUS ROLLS

APPLICANT FOR CHEROKEE CITIZENSHIP

POST OFFICE: Plainfield Ind.   **ATTORNEY:** CH Taylor

NO	NAMES	AGE	SEX
1	Zana Brown	29	Male

ANCESTOR: Annie Wickey

Rejected April 3rd 1889

Adverse

Embraced in decission[sic] on page 524

Book B. in the Nancy J. Brown case.

rendered April 3rd 1889

Will.P. Ross   Chairman

John E. Gunter   Commissioner

Office Com on Citizenship

Tahlequah I.T.

April 3rd 1889

Attest

D.S. Williams

Clk. Com.

BROWN

Docket #814

CENSUS ROLLS

APPLICANT FOR CHEROKEE CITIZENSHIP

POST OFFICE: Plainfield Ind. **ATTORNEY:** CH Taylor

NO	NAMES	AGE	SEX
1	Joseph O. Brown	26	Male

ANCESTOR: Annie Wickey

Rejected April 3rd 1889

Adverse

Embraced in decission[sic] on page 524
Book B. in the Nancy J. Brown case.
Rendered April 3rd 1889

Will.P. Ross   Chairman
John E. Gunter   Commissioner

Office Com on Citizenship
Tahlequah I.T.
April 3rd 1889
Attest

D.S. Williams
Clk. Com.

BROWN

Docket #815

CENSUS ROLLS 1835

APPLICANT FOR CHEROKEE CITIZENSHIP

POST OFFICE: Alma Ark **ATTORNEY:** AE Ivey

NO	NAMES	AGE	SEX
1	Mary E Brown	57	Fem

ANCESTOR: John Chambers

Rejected

Office Commission on Citizenship
Cherokee Nation June 26 1889

There being no evidence in support of the above named case the Commission decide that Mary E Brown aged 57 years is not a Cherokee by blood. Post Office Alma Ark

	Will.P. Ross	Chairman
Attest	J E Gunter	Com
EG Ross		
Clerk Commission		

BROWN

Docket #816

CENSUS ROLLS 1835

APPLICANT FOR CHEROKEE CITIZENSHIP

POST OFFICE: Alma Ark   **ATTORNEY:** A E Ivey

NO	NAMES	AGE	SEX
1	Benjamin F Brown	40	Male
2	Rosa Isabella Brown	17	Fem
3	Geo Robt Brown	14	Male
4	Newton A Brown	9	"
5	Hulda J Brown	7	Fem

ANCESTOR: Isom Brown

Rejected

Office Commission on Citizenship
Cherokee Nation June 26th 1889

There being no evidence in support of the above named case the Commission decide that Benjamin F Brown aged 40 years and the following named children Rosa Isabella aged 17 years, Robert aged 14 years, Newton A, Hulda J Brown aged 7 years are not Cherokees by blood. Post Office Alma Ark.

Attest	Will.P. Ross	Chairman
E.G. Ross	J E Gunter	Com
Clerk Commission		

BURK

Docket #817

CENSUS ROLLS 1835/52

APPLICANT FOR CHEROKEE CITIZENSHIP

POST OFFICE: Pine Hill Tex   **ATTORNEY:** A E Ivey

NO	NAMES	AGE	SEX
1	J J Burk	36	Male
2	Lydia F Burk	14	Fem

3	Georgia A Burk	12	"
4	William C Burk	10	Male
5	Thomas E Burk	8	"
6	Martin E Burk	6	"
7	Wyatt H Burk	4	"
8	Lexrie[sic] J Burk	1	Fem

ANCESTOR: Danson

Rejected

Office Commission on Citizenship
Cherokee Nation June 26, 1889

There being **no** evidence in support of the application in the above named case the Commission decide that J.J. Burk age 36 years and his children, Lydia F Burk Female aged 14 years, Georgia R Burk Female aged 12 years, William C Burk Male aged 10 years, Thomas E Burk Male aged 8 years, Martin E Burk male aged 6 years, Wyatt H. Burk male aged 4 years, Lexrie J. Burk Female aged 1 year.

Attest
E.G. Ross

Will.P. Ross Chairman
J E Gunter Com
Clerk Commission.

BURCH

Docket #818
CENSUS ROLLS

APPLICANT FOR CHEROKEE CITIZENSHIP
POST OFFICE: Hot Springs Ark **ATTORNEY:** A E Ivey

NO	NAMES	AGE	SEX
1	Benj. F Burch	42	Male

ANCESTOR: William Burch

Office Commission on Citizenship
Cherokee Nation June 26, 1889

There being no evidence in support of the above named case the Commission decide that Benj. F. Burch aged 42 years is **not** a Cherokee by blood. Post Office Hot Springs Ark.

Attest
E.G. Ross
Clerk Commission

Will.P. Ross Chairman
John E. Gunter Com

71

BURCH

Docket #819

CENSUS ROLLS 1835/52

APPLICANT FOR CHEROKEE CITIZENSHIP

POST OFFICE: Hot Springs   **ATTORNEY:** A E Ivey

NO	NAMES	AGE	SEX
1	David Burch	44	Male
2	Loretta Francis Burch	20	Fem
3	Mary Rosella Burch	18	"
4	Mina Catharine Burch	16	"
5	Wm Geo W Burch	13	Male
6	Elizabeth Burch	9	Fem
7	Manuel Ogle Burch	7	Male
8	Carnie Burch	5	Fem

ANCESTOR: Wm Burch

Rejected June 26, 1889

Office Commission on Citizenship
Cherokee Nation June 26, 1889

There being no evidence in support of the above named case the Commission decide that David Burch and the following children Loretta Francis Female age 20 years, Mary Rosella Female aged 18 years, Mina Catharine aged 16 years, Wm Geo W. Male age 13 years, Elizabeth Female aged 10 years, Manuel Ogle Male aged 7 years, and Carnie Burch Female aged 5 years, and[sic] are not Cherokees by blood.

Attest   Will.P. Ross   Chairman

   E.G. Ross

     Clerk Commission   John E. Gunter   Com

PURSON

Docket #820

CENSUS ROLLS

APPLICANT FOR CHEROKEE CITIZENSHIP

POST OFFICE: Plainfield Ind   **ATTORNEY:** C H Taylor

NO	NAMES	AGE	SEX
1	Mary E Purson	41	Fem

ANCESTOR: Annie Wickey

Office Commission on Citizenship
Cherokee Nation Ind. Ter
Tahlequah June 25, 1889

There being no evidence in support of the above named case the Commission decide that Mary E Purson, aged 41 years is not a Cherokee by blood and is not a Cherokee by blood and is **not** entitled to Citizenship in the Cherokee Nation. Post Office Plainfield Ind.

Attest

E.G. Ross
Clerk Commission

Will.P. Ross   Chairman
R. Bunch   Com

BROWN

Docket #821

CENSUS ROLLS 1835

APPLICANT FOR CHEROKEE CITIZENSHIP

POST OFFICE: Ark   **ATTORNEY:**

NO	NAMES	AGE	SEX
1	William M Brown	25	Male

ANCESTOR: Isaiah Brown

Rejected June 26, 1889

Office Commission on Citizenship
Cherokee Nation June 26, 1889

There being no evidence in support of the above named case the Commission decide that William M Brown aged 25 years is **not** a Cherokee by blood.

Will.P. Ross   Chairman

Attest

E.G. Ross
Clerk Commission

J E Gunter   Com

73

CLARK

Docket #822
CENSUS ROLLS

APPLICANT FOR CHEROKEE CITIZENSHIP

POST OFFICE: Arlington Ind   **ATTORNEY:** L B Bell

NO	NAMES	AGE	SEX
1	John Martin Clark	24	Male

ANCESTOR: Martha Elmore

The Commission decide <u>against</u> claimant. See decision in case Lible J Bogue, Docket 2183, Book E, Page 29.

Will.P. Ross   Chairman

Attest

D.S. Williams   J.E. Gunter   Com
Asst Clk Com

CLARK

Docket #823
CENSUS ROLLS

APPLICANT FOR CHEROKEE CITIZENSHIP

POST OFFICE: Arlington Ind   **ATTORNEY:** L B Bell

NO	NAMES	AGE	SEX
1	Geo. T. Clark	25	Male

ANCESTOR: Martha Elmore

The Commission decide <u>against</u> claimant, see decision in case Lible J. Bogue Docket 2183, Book E, Page 29.

Will.P. Ross   Chairman

Attest

D.S. Williams   J.E. Gunter   Com
Asst Clk Com

74

NORRIS

Docket #824
CENSUS ROLLS

APPLICANT FOR CHEROKEE CITIZENSHIP

POST OFFICE: Arlington Ind   **ATTORNEY:** L B Bell

NO	NAMES	AGE	SEX
1	Laura J C Harris	27	Fem

ANCESTOR: Martha Elmore

The Commission decide <u>against</u> claimant. See decision in case Lible J Bogue, Docket 2183, Book E, Page 29.

Will.P. Ross   Chairman

Attest

D.S. Williams   J.E. Gunter   Com
Asst Clk Com

CLARK

Docket #825
CENSUS ROLLS

APPLICANT FOR CHEROKEE CITIZENSHIP

POST OFFICE: Arlington Ind   **ATTORNEY:** L B Bell

NO	NAMES	AGE	SEX
1	John W Clark	55	Male

ANCESTOR: Martha Elmore

The Commission decide <u>against</u> claimant. See decision in case Lible J Bogue, Docket 2183, Book E, Page 29.

Will.P. Ross   Chairman

Attest

D.S. Williams   J.E. Gunter   Com
Asst Clk Com

CANNON

Docket #826

CENSUS ROLLS 1835

APPLICANT FOR CHEROKEE CITIZENSHIP

POST OFFICE: Atwood Tenn   **ATTORNEY:** C H Taylor

NO	NAMES	AGE	SEX
1	Hannah Cannon	21	Fem

ANCESTOR: John Bryant

Rejected March 18, 1889

Adverse

Embraced in decission[sic] on page 431
Book B. in the Aaron Bellew case.
rendered March 18 – 1889.

Will P. Ross
Chairman Com.
John E. Gunter   Com

Office Commission
on Citizenship
Tahlequah I.T.
March 18th 1889

D.S. Williams
Clk Com

CONDREY

Docket #827

CENSUS ROLLS 1835

APPLICANT FOR CHEROKEE CITIZENSHIP

POST OFFICE: Camp Creek IT   **ATTORNEY:** L S Sanders

NO	NAMES	AGE	SEX
1	Sterling H Condrey	52	Male
2	William R Condrey	23	"
3	James E Condrey	19	"
4	John R Condrey	17	"
5	B M Condrey	14	"
6	Sarah Bell Condrey	13	Fem
7	Montezuma Condrey	11	Male
8	Noah N Condrey	10	"
9	Sterlen W Condrey	8	"

10	Jerome F Condrey	5	"
11	Joseph T Condrey	3	"
12	Allie Condrey	1	Fem

ANCESTOR: John Beamer

In the matter of the claim of Sterling R[sic] Condry and family to Cherokee Citizenship before the Commission on the 3rd day of Oct 1888 and who having filed his application pursuant to an Act of the National Council approved December 8th 1886, and claiming as his ancestor one John Beamer - - We the Commission after a careful examination of all the evidence in the case, and all the Rolls mentioned in the law creating this Commission, declare Sterling R. Condry and his family, to wit: William R. Condry – James E Condry – John R. Condry – B. M. Condry – Sarah Bell Condry – Montezuma Condry – Noah N. Condry – Sterling W Condry – Jerome F Condry – Joseph T Condry – and Ally Condry – not to be Cherokees by blood and are not entitled to any rights privileges of citizens of this Nation, and declare them to be intruders on the public Domain of the Cherokee Nation.

J.T. Adair   Chairman Commission

H.C. Barnes   Commissioner

Attest

C.C. Lipe

Clerk Com

CLINE

Docket #828

CENSUS ROLLS 1835

APPLICANT FOR CHEROKEE CITIZENSHIP

POST OFFICE: Fayetteville Ark   **ATTORNEY:**

NO	NAMES	AGE	SEX
1	Linn Cline	24	Male

ANCESTOR: Geo Cline

Rejected June 25th 1889

Office Commission on Citizenship
Cherokee Nation June 25th 1889

There being <u>no evidence</u> in support of the above named case the Commission decide that Linn Cline aged 26 years is not of Cherokee blood. Post Office Fayetteville Ark.

	Will.P. Ross	Chairman
Attest	R. Bunch	Com
E.G. Ross	J E Gunter	Com
Clerk Commission		

CRITTENDEN

Docket #829

CENSUS ROLLS 1835

APPLICANT FOR CHEROKEE CITIZENSHIP

POST OFFICE: Van Buren Ark   **ATTORNEY:** L S Sanders

NO	NAMES	AGE	SEX
1	Harvy[sic] Crittenden	35	Male
2	John K. Crittenden	20	"

ANCESTOR: Thomas Crittenden

Office Commission on Citizenship
Cherokee Nation Ind. Ter.
Tahlequah August 17th 1889

There being no evidence in support of this case the Commission decide that Harvy Crittenden aged thirty five and John K Crittenden are <u>not</u> Cherokees by blood.

	Will. P. Ross	Chairman
Attest	R. Bunch	Com
E.G. Ross	J E Gunter	Com
Clerk Commission		

Cherokee Citizenship Commission Docket Books
(1880-84, 1887-89) Volume III
Tahlequah, Cherokee Nation

CLINE

Docket #830

CENSUS ROLLS 1835

APPLICANT FOR CHEROKEE CITIZENSHIP

POST OFFICE: Fayetteville Ark   **ATTORNEY:** L S Sanders

NO	NAMES	AGE	SEX
1	Thomas A Cline	65	Male
2	John Cline	30	
3	Geo Cline	34	

ANCESTOR: Geo Cline

Rejected Augt. 21st 1889

Office Commission on Citizenship
Cherokee Nation Ind. Ter.
Tahlequah Aug. 21st 1889

The application in this case was filed on the 4th day of Oct. 1887 and there being no evidence in support of said case the Commission decide that applicant Thomas A. Cline age 65 yrs and children, John Cline age 30 yrs and George Cline age 34 yrs are not Cherokees by blood and <u>not</u> entitled to Citizenship in the Cherokee Nation. P.O. Fayetteville Ark.

Attest   Will P. Ross   Chairman
    D.S. Williams   J.E. Gunter   Com
    Asst. Clk. Com.

COMBS

Docket #831

CENSUS ROLLS 1835

APPLICANT FOR CHEROKEE CITIZENSHIP

POST OFFICE: Fayetteville, Ark   **ATTORNEY:** L S Sanders

NO	NAMES	AGE	SEX
1	Elizabeth Combs	60	Fem
2	S G Combs	34	Male

ANCESTOR: Elizabeth Combs

Rejected July 2nd 1889

Office Commission on Citizenship
Cherokee Nation Ind. Ter.
Tahlequah July 2nd 1889

There being no evidence in support of the above named case the Commission decide that Elizabeth Combs age 60 years and her son S.G. Combs 34 yrs are not Cherokees by blood. Post Office Fayetteville Ark.

Attest   Will.P. Ross
    D.S. Williams   Chairman
Asst. Clerk Commission   John E. Gunter
                                                  Com

CLINE

Docket #832
CENSUS ROLLS

APPLICANT FOR CHEROKEE CITIZENSHIP
POST OFFICE: Fayetteville Ark   **ATTORNEY:** L S Sanders

NO	NAMES	AGE	SEX
1	Jane Cline	70	Fem

ANCESTOR: Geo Cline

Rejected Aug. 21st 1889

Office Commission on Citizenship
Cherokee Nation Ind. Ter.
Tahlequah Aug 21st 1889

The application in this case was filed on the 4th day of Oct. 1889, and there being no evidence in support of application the Commission decide that applicant Jane Cline age 70 yrs. is not a Cherokee by blood & not entitled to Citizenship in the Cherokee Nation – Post Office Fayetteville, Ark.

Attest   Will. P. Ross   Chairman
    D.S Williams   J.E. Gunter   Com
    Asst. Clerk Com

CARTER

Docket #833
CENSUS ROLLS 1835

APPLICANT FOR CHEROKEE CITIZENSHIP

POST OFFICE: Atwood Tenn   **ATTORNEY:** C H Taylor

NO	NAMES	AGE	SEX
1	Tennessee Carter	30	Fem
2	Sallie Carter	6	"
3	*(Illegible)* Carter	4	

ANCESTOR: John Bryant

Rejected March 18, 1889

Adverse

Embraced in decision[sic] on page 431
Book B. in the Aaron Bellew case.
rendered March 18 – 1889.

Will P. Ross
Chairman Com.
John E. Gunter   Com

Office Commission
on Citizenship
Tahlequah I.T.
March 18th 1889
D.S. Williams
Clk Com

CANDAY

Docket #834
CENSUS ROLLS

APPLICANT FOR CHEROKEE CITIZENSHIP

POST OFFICE: Afton I.T.   **ATTORNEY:** L.B. Bell

NO	NAMES	AGE	SEX
1	Rhoda Canday	19	Fem

ANCESTOR: Anna Crews

The Commission decide against claimants. See decission[sic] in case of Andrew Meredith Docket 2180 Book E, Page 26 and John Henly Docket 1250, Book C Page 376.

Will. P. Ross
Chairman
J.E. Gunter   Com

Attest
D.S. Williams
Asst. Clk Com

CARLOCK

Docket #835
CENSUS ROLLS 1835

APPLICANT FOR CHEROKEE CITIZENSHIP

POST OFFICE: Huntsville Ark   **ATTORNEY:** C H Taylor

NO	NAMES	AGE	SEX
1	Cassa A Carlock	31	Fem
2	John N Carlock	15	Male
3	Mary A Carlock	14	Fem
4	William J Carlock	12	Male
5	Rachael Carlock	9	Fem
6	Geo W Carlock	7	Male
7	Mose F Carlock	5	"
8	Daniel W Carlock	2	"

ANCESTOR: Nancy Woodall

Rejected June 26 1889

Office Commission on Citizenship
Cherokee Nation June 26, 1889

There being no evidence in support of the above named case the Commission decide that Cassa A Carlock aged 31 years and the following children John N. Male aged 15 years, Mary A Female aged 14 years, William J male aged 12 years, Rachel Female aged 9 years, George W, male aged 7 years and Daniel W. Carlock aged 2 years are not Cherokees by blood.

Attest   Will.P. Ross   Chairman
    E.G. Ross   R. Bunch   Com
        Clerk Commission   J.E. Gunter   Com

COFFIN

Docket #836
CENSUS ROLLS

APPLICANT FOR CHEROKEE CITIZENSHIP

POST OFFICE: Chicago Ill   **ATTORNEY:** L B Bell

NO	NAMES	AGE	SEX
1	Frank Coffin		Male

ANCESTOR: Anna Crews

The Commission decide against claimants. See Decission[sic] in case of Andrew Meredith Docket 2180 Book E, Page 26 and John Healy Docket 1250, Book C, Page 326.

Will.P.Ross   Chairman
R. Bunch   Com
John E Gunter   Com

Attest

D.S. Williams
Asst Clk Com

COFFIN

Docket #837
CENSUS ROLLS

APPLICANT FOR CHEROKEE CITIZENSHIP

POST OFFICE: Russellville Ind   **ATTORNEY:** L.B. Bell

NO	NAMES	AGE	SEX
1	Leanna Coffin		Fem

ANCESTOR: Anna Crews

The Commission decide against claimants. See Decission[sic] in case of Andrew Meredith Docket 2180 Book E, Page 26 and John Healy Docket 1250, Book C, Page 326.

Will.P.Ross   Chairman
R. Bunch   Com
John E Gunter   Com

Attest

D.S. Williams
Asst Clk Com

COFFIN

Docket #838
CENSUS ROLLS

APPLICANT FOR CHEROKEE CITIZENSHIP

POST OFFICE:

ATTORNEY: L B Bell

NO	NAMES	AGE	SEX
1	Charles W. Coffin		Male

ANCESTOR: Anna Crews

The Commission decide <u>against</u> claimants. See Decission[sic] in case of Andrew Meredith Docket 2180 Book E, Page 26 and John Healy Docket 1250, Book C, Page 326.

Will.P.Ross   Chairman
R. Bunch   Com
John E Gunter   Com

Attest

D.S. Williams
Asst Clk Com

CLARK

Docket #839
CENSUS ROLLS

APPLICANT FOR CHEROKEE CITIZENSHIP

POST OFFICE: *(Illegible)*

ATTORNEY: L B Bell

NO	NAMES	AGE	SEX
1	John G Clark		Male

ANCESTOR: *(Name Illegible)*

The Commission decide <u>against</u> claimant. See decission[sic] in case Lible J Bogue Docket 2183, Book E, Page 29.

Will.P.Ross   Chairman
R. Bunch   Com
J.E. Gunter   Com

Attest

D.S. Williams
Asst Clk Com

84

CAIN

Docket #840

CENSUS ROLLS 1835

APPLICANT FOR CHEROKEE CITIZENSHIP

POST OFFICE: Plymouth Org   **ATTORNEY:** L S Sanders

NO	NAMES	AGE	SEX
1	Mary Ellen Cain	31	Fem
2	Jessie Ambrosa Cain	12	Male
3	Lillie Bell Cain	11	Fem
4	Ben Lee Cain	7	Male
5	Geo Cain	6	"

ANCESTOR: Emaline Boatright

Rejected Aug 21st 1889

Office Commission on Citizenship
Cherokee Nation Ind. Ter.
Tahlequah Aug. 21st 1889

The application in this case was filed on the 3rd day of Oct, 1887, and there being no evidence in support of said case the Commission decide that Applicant Mary Ellen Cain 31 yrs, and children Jesse Ambrosa Cain age 12 yrs, Lillie Bell Cain age 11 yrs, Bennie Lee Cain age 7 yrs and George Cain age 6 yrs are <u>not</u> Cherokees by blood. P.O. Plymouth Org.

Attest

D.S. Williams

Asst. Clk. Com

Will. P. Ross   Chairman
R. Bunch   Com
J.E. Gunter   Com

CLARK

Docket #841

CENSUS ROLLS

APPLICANT FOR CHEROKEE CITIZENSHIP

POST OFFICE: Casthrope Ind   **ATTORNEY:** L B Bell

NO	NAMES	AGE	SEX
1	Hezakiah Clark		Fem

ANCESTOR: Martha Elmore

The Commission decide <u>against</u> claimant. See decission[sic] in case Lible J Bogue Docket 2183, Book E, Page 29.

Cherokee Citizenship Commission Docket Books
(1880-84, 1887-89) Volume III
Tahlequah, Cherokee Nation

Will.P.Ross   Chairman
R. Bunch   Com
J.E. Gunter   Com

Attest
      D.S. Williams
Asst Clk Com

CLARK

Docket #842
CENSUS ROLLS

APPLICANT FOR CHEROKEE CITIZENSHIP

POST OFFICE: Arlington Ind   **ATTORNEY:** L B Bell

NO	NAMES	AGE	SEX
1	William S Clark	31	Male

ANCESTOR: Martha Elmore

The Commission decide **against** claimant. See decission[sic] in case Lible J Bogue Docket 2183, Book E, Page 29.

Will.P.Ross   Chairman
R. Bunch   Com
J.E. Gunter   Com

Attest
      D.S. Williams
Asst Clk Com

CANDY

Docket #843
CENSUS ROLLS

APPLICANT FOR CHEROKEE CITIZENSHIP

POST OFFICE: Afton Ind Terry   **ATTORNEY:** L B Bell

NO	NAMES	AGE	SEX
1	William Penn Candy	17	Male

ANCESTOR: Anna Crews

The Commission decide **against** claimant. See decission[sic] in case of Andrew Meredith Docket 2180 Book E, Page 26 and John Henly Docket 1250, Book C, Page 376.

Cherokee Citizenship Commission Docket Books
(1880-84, 1887-89) Volume III
Tahlequah, Cherokee Nation

Will.P.Ross   Chairman
R. Bunch   Com
J.E. Gunter   Com

Attest
    D.S. Williams
Asst Clk Com

COOK

Docket #844
CENSUS ROLLS

APPLICANT FOR CHEROKEE CITIZENSHIP

POST OFFICE: Afton IT   **ATTORNEY:** L B Bell

NO	NAMES	AGE	SEX
1	Emma J Cook	35	Fem

ANCESTOR: Anna Crews

The Commission decide <u>against</u> claimant. See decission[sic] in case of Andrew Meredith Docket 2180 Book E, Page 26 and John Henly Docket 1250, Book C, Page 376.

Will.P.Ross   Chairman
R. Bunch   Com
J.E. Gunter   Com

Attest
    D.S. Williams
Asst Clk Com

CLARK

Docket #845
CENSUS ROLLS

APPLICANT FOR CHEROKEE CITIZENSHIP

POST OFFICE: Clarksville Ohio   **ATTORNEY:** L B Bell

NO	NAMES	AGE	SEX
1	John W Clark		Male
2	W S Clark		"
3	Isabella Clark		Fem
4	Laura Clark		"
5	Geo T Clark		Male

6	Morton Clark		"

ANCESTOR: Martha Elmore

The Commission decide <u>against</u> claimant. See decission[sic] in case Lible J Bogue Docket 2183, Book E, Page 29.

Will.P.Ross   Chairman
R. Bunch   Com
J.E. Gunter   Com

Attest
D.S. Williams
Asst Clk Com

CANDY

Docket #846
CENSUS ROLLS

APPLICANT FOR CHEROKEE CITIZENSHIP

POST OFFICE: Afton   **ATTORNEY:** L B Bell

NO	NAMES	AGE	SEX
1	Chas H Candy	30	Male

ANCESTOR: Anna Crews

The Commission decide <u>against</u> claimant. See decission[sic] in case of Andrew Meredith Docket 2180 Book E, Page 26 and John Henly Docket 1250, Book C, Page 376.

Will.P.Ross   Chairman
R. Bunch   Com
J.E. Gunter   Com

Attest
D.S. Williams
Asst Clk Com

CHANEY

Docket #847
CENSUS ROLLS

APPLICANT FOR CHEROKEE CITIZENSHIP

POST OFFICE: Decalin[sic] Texas   **ATTORNEY:** C H Taylor

NO	NAMES	AGE	SEX
1	Mary P Chaney	28	Fem

ANCESTOR: Mary Ray

Rejected June 26, 1889

Office Commission on Citizenship
Cherokee Nation June 26, 1889

There being no evidence in support of the above named case the Commission decide that Mary P Chauncy[sic] aged 28 years is <u>not</u> a Cherokee by blood. Post Office Decatur Texas.

Attest   Will.P. Ross   Chairman
     E.G. Ross   R. Bunch   Com
         Clerk Commission   JE Gunter   Com

CLARK

Docket #848
CENSUS ROLLS

APPLICANT FOR CHEROKEE CITIZENSHIP

POST OFFICE: Clarksville Ind   **ATTORNEY:** L B Bell

NO	NAMES	AGE	SEX
1	Hezakeah S Clark		Male
2	Geo C Clark		"

ANCESTOR: Martha Elmore

The Commission decide <u>against</u> claimant. See decission[sic] in case Lible J Bogue Docket 2183, Book E, Page 29.

                 Will.P.Ross   Chairman
                 R. Bunch   Com
                   J.E. Gunter   Com
Attest
     D.S. Williams
Asst Clk Com

COX

Docket #849

CENSUS ROLLS

APPLICANT FOR CHEROKEE CITIZENSHIP

POST OFFICE: Valley Mill Ind   **ATTORNEY:** L B Bell

NO	NAMES	AGE	SEX
1	Liddia Cox		Fem

ANCESTOR: Sarah Morgan

Rejected July 2nd 1889

Office Commission on Citizenship
Cherokee Nation Ind Ter
Tahlequah July 2nd 1889

There being no evidence in support of this case the Commission decide that Liddia Cox age is not known is <u>not</u> a Cherokee by blood.
Post Office Valley Mills Ind.

Will.P. Ross

Attest   Chairman

    D.S. Williams   John E. Gunter   Com

Asst. Clerk Commission

CHAMBERS

Docket #850

CENSUS ROLLS

APPLICANT FOR CHEROKEE CITIZENSHIP

POST OFFICE: Emporia Kansas   **ATTORNEY:** L B Bell

NO	NAMES	AGE	SEX
1	Ai[sic] Chambers		Male

ANCESTOR: Sarah Morgan

Rejected July 2nd 1889

Office Commission on Citizenship
Cherokee Nation Ind. Ter.
Tahlequah July 2nd 1889

There being no evidence in support of the above named case the Commission decide that Ai Chambers age is not given, is <u>not</u> a Cherokee by blood. Post Office Emporia Kansas.

	Will.P. Ross	
Attest	Chairman	
D.S. Williams		
Asst Clerk Commission	John E. Gunter	Com

CRAWFORD

Docket # *(Omitted on microfilm)*
CENSUS ROLLS 1835

APPLICANT FOR CHEROKEE CITIZENSHIP

POST OFFICE: Chouteu[sic] I.T.   **ATTORNEY:** A E Ivey

NO	NAMES	AGE	SEX
1	Rebecca Crawford	70	Fem

ANCESTOR: Ward

Rejected July 5th 1889

Office Commission on Citizenship Cher. Nat
July 5th 1889

There being no evidence in support of the above named case the Commission decide that Rebecca Chambers age 70 yrs. is <u>not</u> a Cherokee by blood.

Post Office Choteau I.T.

D.S. Williams	Will P. Ross
Clerk Commission	Chairman
	John E. Gunter
	Com

COUCH

Docket #852
CENSUS ROLLS 1835

APPLICANT FOR CHEROKEE CITIZENSHIP

POST OFFICE: Lancaster Ark   **ATTORNEY:** A E Ivey

NO	NAMES	AGE	SEX
1	Andrew Couch	45	Male
2	A.L. Couch	20	"
3	Maggie Couch	17	Fem
4	Manny Couch	19	"
5	William H Couch	17	Male
6	Joseph Couch	13	"

7	James Couch	7	"
8	Sarah Couch	7	Fem
9	Lavada Couch	2	"
10	Lizzie Couch	1	Fem

ANCESTOR: Mima Edwards

Now on this the 9th day of January 1888, comes the above case for a final hearing and the parties having made application pursuant to the provisions of an Act of the National Council approved December 8th 1886. And all the evidence being duly examined and found <u>not</u> to be sufficient and satisfactory to the Commission and the name of the ancestor not appearing on the Rolls as claimed in application.

It is adjudged and determined by the Commission, that Andrew Couch, A.L. Couch, Maggie Couch, Manny Couch, William Couch, Joseph Couch, James Couch, Sarah Couch, Lavada Couch and Lizzie Couch are <u>not</u> Cherokees by blood and are hereby rejected and declared intruders.

J.T. Adair   Chairman Commission
John E. Gunter   Commissioner
L.W. Lipe   Commissioner

Attest

C.C. Lipe
     Clerk Commission

CATE

Docket #853
CENSUS ROLLS 1835/52

APPLICANT FOR CHEROKEE CITIZENSHIP

POST OFFICE: Alma Ark   **ATTORNEY:** AE Ivey

NO	NAMES	AGE	SEX
1	Julia A Cate	22	Fem

ANCESTOR: Samuel Ramsy

Rejected June 28th 1889

Office Commission on Citizenship
Cher. Nat.
June 28th 1889

Cherokee Citizenship Commission Docket Books
(1880-84, 1887-89) Volume III
Tahlequah, Cherokee Nation

There being no evidence in support of the above named case the Commission decide that Julia A Cate, age 22 yrs is not a Cherokee by blood.
Post Office Alma Ark.

	Will.P. Ross	
D.S. Williams		Chairman
Clerk of Commission	John E. Gunter	Com

COUCH

Docket #854
CENSUS ROLLS 1835

APPLICANT FOR CHEROKEE CITIZENSHIP

POST OFFICE: Rayne La   **ATTORNEY:** AE Ivey

NO	NAMES	AGE	SEX
1	Henry M Couch	49	Male

ANCESTOR: Mima Edwards

Now on this the 9th day of January, 1888, comes the above case for a final hearing, and the parties having made application pursuant to the provisions of an Act of the National Council approved December 8th 1886. And all the evidence being duly examined and found not to be sufficient and satisfactory to the Commission, and the name of the ancestor not appearing on the Rolls as claimed in the application.

It is adjudged and determined by the Commission that Henry M Couch is not a Cherokee by blood and is hereby rejected and declared to be an intruder.

	J.T. Adair	Chairman Commission
	John E. Gunter	Commissioner
	L.W. Lipe	Commissioner
Attest		
C.C. Lipe		
Clerk Commission		

CHAMBERS

Docket #855
CENSUS ROLLS 1851

APPLICANT FOR CHEROKEE CITIZENSHIP

POST OFFICE: **ATTORNEY:** AE Ivey

NO	NAMES	AGE	SEX
1	Lee Chambers	26	Male
2	Joseph C Chambers	1	"

ANCESTOR: Asa Chambers

Rejected Sept. 10th 1889

Office Commission on Citizenship
Cherokee Nation Ind Ter.
Tahlequah Sept. 10th 1889

The above case was called three times and no response from applicant or Attorney and there being no evidence in support of claim the Commission decide that Lee Chambers age 26 years, and Joseph C. Chambers age 1 year, are not Cherokees by blood.

Will.P. Ross   Chairman

Attest   JE Gunter   Com

EG Ross
    Clerk Commission

COUCH

Docket #856
CENSUS ROLLS

APPLICANT FOR CHEROKEE CITIZENSHIP

POST OFFICE: Texas   **ATTORNEY:** AE Ivey

NO	NAMES	AGE	SEX
1	William Couch	28	Male

ANCESTOR: Henry M Couch

Now on this the 9th day of January, 1888, comes the above case up for a final hearing, the applicant having made application pursuant to the provisions of an Act of the National Council approved Dec. 8th 1886, and all the evidence being fully considered in the Mary A. Couch case, which was by agreement of Attys. made a list one, to govern all cases claiming a direct ancestry from the same ancestor, Mima Edwards; it [sic] adjudged and determined by the

Commission that William Couch is not a Cherokee by blood and in consequence **not** entitled to the rights of such.

The decision in the Mary A Couch case, found on page 100 Docket "A" governs this case.

J.T. Adair   Chairman Commission

D.W. Lipe   Commissioner

Commissioner

Attest

       C.C. Lipe

           Clerk Com.

CRAIN

Docket #857

CENSUS ROLLS 1835

APPLICANT FOR CHEROKEE CITIZENSHIP

POST OFFICE: Viola Mo   **ATTORNEY:** AE Ivey

NO	NAMES	AGE	SEX
1	William H Crain	46	Male
2	Minnie E Crain	14	Fem
3	Emma J Crain	12	"
4	Chas O Crain	10	Male

ANCESTOR: Robt Daugherty

Rejected June 28th 1889

Office Commission on Citizenship

Cher. Nat.

June 28th 1889

There being no evidence in support of the above named case the Commission decide that William H. Crain age 46, and the following children, Minnie E. Crain, age 14 female, Emma J Crain Female age 12, Chas O Crain male age 10 yrs, are **not** Cherokees by blood. Post Office Viola Mo.

Will.P. Ross

D.S. Williams   Chairman

Clerk Commission   John E. Gunter   Com

CHRISTOPHER

Docket #858

CENSUS ROLLS 1835

APPLICANT FOR CHEROKEE CITIZENSHIP

POST OFFICE:

ATTORNEY: AE Ivey

NO	NAMES	AGE	SEX
1	Millie E Christopher	20	Fem
2	Gertrude Christopher	2	"

ANCESTOR: Annie Barnes

See decision in this case in that of George W. Parker in Book "A" page 119 – <u>Adverse</u> to claimant.

Cornell Rogers –
Clk Com. on Citizenship

Office Com on Citizenship
Tahlequah I.T. Sept. 25th 1888

CARNES

Docket #859

CENSUS ROLLS 1835

APPLICANT FOR CHEROKEE CITIZENSHIP

POST OFFICE: Ball Ground Ga.

ATTORNEY: AE Ivey

NO	NAMES	AGE	SEX
1	J D Carnes	25	Male
2	~~Jefferson D Crain~~		
2	Henry A Carnes	3	"
3	John J Carnes	1	"

ANCESTOR: Daniel Carnes

Now on this the 20th day of May 1888 comes the above case up for final hearing and the Commission say, "We the Commission on Citizenship after "examining the evidence and the census & pay rolls of 1851 & 52, find the "above applicants to be Cherokees by blood, and the said J.A. Carnes and his "two children, Henry A and John J. Carnes are hereby re-admitted to all the "rights and privileges of Cherokee citizens by blood.

J.T. Adair   Chairman Commission
John E. Gunter   Commissioner
D.W. Lipe   Commissioner

CASTLE

Docket #860

CENSUS ROLLS 1835

APPLICANT FOR CHEROKEE CITIZENSHIP

POST OFFICE: Rock Hall Station Ky   **ATTORNEY:** AE Ivey

NO	NAMES	AGE	SEX
1	Louisa Castke	45	Fem

ANCESTOR: Weaver

Rejected June 28, 89

Office Commission on Citizenship

Cher. Nat.

June 28th 1889

There being no evidence in support of the above named case, the Commission decide that Louisa Castle age 45 yrs is <u>not</u> a Cherokee by blood. Post Office Rock Hill Station Ky.

Will.P. Ross

Chairman

D.S. Williams   John E. Gunter   Com

Clerk Commission

CARROLL

Docket #861

CENSUS ROLLS 1835

APPLICANT FOR CHEROKEE CITIZENSHIP

POST OFFICE: Mayesville[sic] Ark   **ATTORNEY:** C H Taylor

NO	NAMES	AGE	SEX
1	Rachel E Carroll	31	Fem
2	Eiffie[sic] G. Carroll	8	"
3	Joseph C Carroll	6	Male
4	James P. Carroll	4	"
5	Margarett[sic] O Carroll	2	Fem

ANCESTOR: John Daniel

Rejected June 28th 1889

Office Commission on Citizenship

Cher Nat June 28th 1889

There being no evidence in support of the above named case, the Commission decide that Rachel E Carroll age 31 yrs and the following named children, Effie G. Female age 8, Joseph C. male age 6 yrs, James P. male age 4 yrs and Margaret O. Carroll age 2 female, are not Cherokees by blood. Post Office Mays Ville Ark.

Will.P. Ross
Chairman

D.S. Williams
Clerk Commission

John E. Gunter Com

COLTON

Docket #862

CENSUS ROLLS 1835

APPLICANT FOR CHEROKEE CITIZENSHIP

POST OFFICE: Evansville Ark   **ATTORNEY:**

NO	NAMES	AGE	SEX
1	Clorena Colton	4	Fem

ANCESTOR: William Lee

Rejected June 28th 1889

Office Commission on Citizenship
Cher. Nat. June 28th 1889

There being no evidence in support of the above named case the Commission decide that Clorena Colton aged 4 yrs is not a Cherokee by blood. Post Office Evansville Ark.

Will.P. Ross
Chairman

D.S. Williams
Clerk Commission

John E. Gunter Com

CLEMMONS

Docket #863

CENSUS ROLLS 1835

APPLICANT FOR CHEROKEE CITIZENSHIP

POST OFFICE: Kingston Tex   **ATTORNEY:** C H Taylor

NO	NAMES	AGE	SEX
1	J.R. Clemmons	37	Male
2	Jas E Clemmons	10	"

ANCESTOR: Agnes Childers

Rejected June 28th 1889

Office Commission on Citizenship

Cher. Nat

June 28th 1889

There being no evidence in support of the above named case, the Commission decide that J.R. Clemmons age 37 yrs and his son Joseph E Clemmons age 10 yrs are not Cherokees by blood.

Post Office Kingston Texas.

Will.P. Ross

D.S. Williams   Chairman

Clerk Commission   John E. Gunter   Com

CLEMMONS

Docket #864

CENSUS ROLLS 1835

APPLICANT FOR CHEROKEE CITIZENSHIP

POST OFFICE: Kingston Tex   **ATTORNEY:** C H Taylor

NO	NAMES	AGE	SEX
1	Geo B Clemmons		Male
2	Oscar Clemmons	2	

ANCESTOR: Agnes Childers

Rejected June 28th 1889

Office Commission on Citizenship

Cher. Nat. June 28th 1889

There being no evidence in support of the above named case the Commission decide that George B. Clemmons age – and his son Oscar Clemmons age 2 yrs are not Cherokees by blood. P.O. Kingston Texas.

Will.P. Ross

D.S. Williams   Chairman

Clerk Commission   John E. Gunter   Com

99

Cherokee Citizenship Commission Docket Books
(1880-84, 1887-89) Volume III
Tahlequah, Cherokee Nation

CLEMMONS

Docket #865

CENSUS ROLLS 1835

APPLICANT FOR CHEROKEE CITIZENSHIP

POST OFFICE: Kingston   **ATTORNEY:** C.H. Taylor

NO	NAMES	AGE	SEX
1	E C Clemmons	26	Male

ANCESTOR: Agnes Childers

Rejected June 28th 1889

Office Commission on Citizenship

Cher. Nat.

June 28th 1889

There being no evidence in support of the above named case the Commission decide that E C Clemmons age 26 yrs is not a Cherokee by blood.

Post Office Kingston Texas.

Will.P. Ross

D.S. Williams   Chairman

Clerk Commission   John E. Gunter   Com

CHANCELLOR

Docket #866

CENSUS ROLLS 1835

APPLICANT FOR CHEROKEE CITIZENSHIP

POST OFFICE: Osage Mill Ark   **ATTORNEY:** C H Taylor

NO	NAMES	AGE	SEX
1	Laura Chancellor	35	Fem
2	Robert F Chancellor	8	Male
3	Johney Chancellor	6	"
4	Henry P. Chancellor	5	"

ANCESTOR: Mose Guest

Rejected June 28th 1889

Office Commission on Citizenship

Cher. Nat.

June 28th 1889

There being no evidence in support of the above named case the Commission decide that Laura Chancellor age 35 yrs, and the following children, Robert F.

100

Chancellor age 8 male, Johney Chancellor male age 6, Henry P Chancellor male age 5 are not Cherokees by blood.

Post Office Osage Mills Ark.

Will.P. Ross

D.S. Williams   Chairman

Clerk Commission   John E. Gunter   Com

CRAIG

Docket #867

CENSUS ROLLS 1835/52

APPLICANT FOR CHEROKEE CITIZENSHIP

POST OFFICE: Cincinnati Ohio   **ATTORNEY:** L S Sanders

NO	NAMES	AGE	SEX
1	Rosel D Craig	34	Male
2	Amanda E Craig	14	Fem
3	Sarah B Craig	12	"
4	Ephriam F Craig	9	Male
5	Minnie M Craig	7	Fem
6	Rosa Lee Craig	4	"
7	Osa James Craig	2	Male

ANCESTOR: Bryant

Rejected Augt. 21st 1889

Office Commission on Citizenship
Cherokee Nation Ind. Ter.
Tahlequah Augt. 21st 1889

The application in this case was filed on the 3rd day of Oct. 1887, and there being no evidence in support of said case the Commission decide that applicant Rosel D. Craig age 34 yrs & children Amanda E Craig age 14 yrs, Sarah B Craig age 12 yrs, Ephriam F Craig age 9 yrs, Minnie M Craig age 7 yrs, Rose Lee Craig age 4 yrs, Osa James Craig age 2 yrs, are not Cherokees by blood.

Post Office Cincinnatti[sic] Ark[sic]

Will P. Ross   Chairman

Attest   J.E. Gunter   Com

D.S. Williams

Asst Clk. Com.

101

CLAYBROOK

Docket #868

CENSUS ROLLS 1835/52

APPLICANT FOR CHEREKEE CITIZENSHIP

POST OFFICE: Whitesboro Tex   **ATTORNEY:**

NO	NAMES	AGE	SEX
1	J.T. Claybrook		Male

ANCESTOR: Mina Hix

Rejected June 28, 1889

Office Commission on Citizenship
Cher. Nat.

June 28th 1889

There being no evidence in support of the above named case the Commission decide that J.T. Claybrook age (-) is not a Cherokee by blood. Post Office Whitesboro Tex.

Will. P. Ross
Chairman

D.S. Williams   John E. Gunter   Com
Clk Commission

CARNES

Docket #869

CENSUS ROLLS 1835

APPLICANT FOR CHEREKEE CITIZENSHIP

POST OFFICE: Ophis[sic] Ga   **ATTORNEY:** A E Ivey

NO	NAMES	AGE	SEX
1	Andrew J Carnes	29	Male
2	Joseph E Carnes	4	"
3	Bessie J Carnes	1	

ANCESTOR: Dinah Carnes

Now on this the 30th day of May 1888, comes the above case for final hearing and the Commission say, "We the Commission on Citizenship after "examining the testimony and the census ~~rolls of~~ & pay rolls of 1851 & 52, find "the above applicants to be Cherokees ~~citizens~~ by blood, and the said A.J. "Carnes and his two children, Joseph E and Bessie J. Carnes are hereby re- "admitted to all the rights and privileges of Cherokee citizens by blood.

Cherokee Citizenship Commission Docket Books
(1880-84, 1887-89) Volume III
Tahlequah, Cherokee Nation

J.T. Adair	Chairman Commission
John E. Gunter	Commissioner
D.W. Lipe	Commissioner

CLAUNTS

Docket #870

CENSUS ROLLS 1835

APPLICANT FOR CHEROKEE CITIZENSHIP

POST OFFICE: Burnsville[sic] Ark   **ATTORNEY:** A E Ivey

NO	NAMES	AGE	SEX
1	Emma Claunts	21	Fem
2	Allie Claunts	1	

ANCESTOR: Mama ~~Franklin~~ Edwards

Now on this the 9th day of January, 1888, comes the above case for a final hearing. The parties having made application pursuant to the provisions of an Act of the National Council approved December 8th 1886. And all the evidence being duly considered and found to be insufficient and unsatisfactory, it is adjudged and declared by the Commission that

Emma Claunts and Allie Claunts, are **not** Cherokees, and are not entitled to any rights privileges and immunities of Cherokee Citizens by blood.

J.T. Adair	Chairman Commission
John E. Gunter	Commissioner
D.W. Lipe	Commissioner

Attest

C.C. Lipe

Clk Com

The decision I the Mary A Couch case found on Book A, page 100 and Testimony on Journal page 276 to 278, governs this case.

WARD

Docket #871

CENSUS ROLLS 1835

APPLICANT FOR CHEROKEE CITIZENSHIP

POST OFFICE: Chouteau IT   **ATTORNEY:** A E Ivey

NO	NAMES	AGE	SEX
1	Jasper Ward	41	Male

ANCESTOR: Ward

(No further information given)

CARLISLE

Docket #872

CENSUS ROLLS 1835/52

APPLICANT FOR CHEROKEE CITIZENSHIP

POST OFFICE: Van Buren Ark   **ATTORNEY:**

NO	NAMES	AGE	SEX
1	John C Carlisle	23	Male

ANCESTOR: Colen Carlisle

Rejected June 28, 1889

Office Commission on Citizenship
Cher. Nat. June 28th 1889

There being no evidence in support of the above named case the Commission decide that John C. Carlisle age 23 yrs is _not_ a Cherokee by blood.
Post Office Van Buren Ark.

Will.P. Ross

D.S. Williams   Chairman
Clerk Commission   John E. Gunter   Com

CARLISLE

Docket #873

CENSUS ROLLS 1835

APPLICANT FOR CHEROKEE CITIZENSHIP

POST OFFICE: Van Buren Ark   **ATTORNEY:**

NO	NAMES	AGE	SEX
1	James T Carlisle	26	Male

ANCESTOR: Colen Carlisle

Rejected June 28th 1889

Office Commission on Citizenship
Cher. Nat. June 28th 1889

There being no evidence in support of the above named case the Commission decide that James T. Carlisle age 26 yrs is <u>not</u> a Cherokee by blood. P.O. Van Buren Ark.

Will.P. Ross

D.S. Williams
Chairman

Clerk Commission
John E. Gunter   Com

CAVENDER

Docket #874

CENSUS ROLLS 1835/52

APPLICANT FOR CHEROKEE CITIZENSHIP

POST OFFICE: Van Buren Ark   **ATTORNEY:**

NO	NAMES	AGE	SEX
1	Mary M Cavender	22	Fem
2	John E Cavender	4	Male

ANCESTOR: Colen Carlisle

Rejected June 28th 1889

Office Commission on Citizenship
Cher. Nat. June 28th 1889

There being no evidence in support of the above named case the Commission decide that Mary M. Cavender age 22 yrs and his[sic] son John E. Cavender age 4 years are <u>not</u> Cherokees by blood. Post Office Van Buren Ark.

Will.P. Ross

D.S. Williams
Chairman

Clerk Commission
John E. Gunter   Com

Cherokee Citizenship Commission Docket Books
(1880-84, 1887-89) Volume III
Tahlequah, Cherokee Nation

PALMOUR

DOCKET #875

CENSUS ROLLS 1851 & 1852

APPLICANT FOR CHEROKEE CITIZENSHIP

POST OFFICE: Palmour Ga   ATTORNEY: A.E. Ivey

No	NAMES	AGE	SEX
1	David P Palmour	33	Male
2	Emma L Palmour	11	female
3	Roni M Palmour	8	"
4	Fannie B R Palmour	6	"
5	Emily L Palmour	5	"
6	John R Palmour	1	Male

ANCESTOR: John D Palmour

Now on this the 25 day of August, 1887, comes the above case for a final hearing and the parties having made application pursuant to provisions of an Act of the National Council approved Dec 8 1886. And all the evidence being duly examined and found to be sufficient and satisfactory to the Commission and the name of the ancestor John D. Palmour appearing on the rolls of 1851 & 1852. It is adjudged and determined by the Commission that David P Palmour, Emma L Palmour, Roni M Palmour, Fannie ? ? Palmour, Emily L Palmour John R Palmour are Cherokees by blood and are hereby re-admitted to all the rights privileges and immunities of Cherokee by blood. And a certificate of said decission[sic] of the Commission and re-admission was made and furnished said parties accordingly.

	J.T. Adair	Chairman Commission
Attest	D.W. Lipe	Commissioner

C.C. Lipe
Clk Com

WHITAKER

DOCKET #876

CENSUS ROLLS 1851 & 1852

APPLICANT FOR CHEROKEE CITIZENSHIP

POST OFFICE: *(Illegible)* N C   ATTORNEY: C H Taylor

No	NAMES	AGE	SEX
1	Elizabeth Whitaker	67	female
2	David Whitaker	??	male
3	J. Mc. Whitaker	39	"

4	Martha A Whitaker	37	female
5	Sarah A Whitaker	36	"

ANCESTOR: Polly Taylor

Now on this the 13 day of Oct 1887 comes the above case for a final hearing and the parties having made application pursuant to the provisions of an Act of the National Council approved Dec 8th 1886. And all the evidence being duly examined and found to be sufficient and satisfactory to the Commission and the name of the ancestor, Polly Taylor, appearing on the rolls of 1851 & 52. It is adjudged and determined by the Commission that Elizabeth Whitaker, David Whitaker, J. Mc. Whitaker, Martha A Whitaker, Sarah A Whitaker are Cherokees by blood and are hereby re-admitted to all the rights privileges of Cherokees by blood. And a certificate of said decission[sic] of the Commission and re-admission was made and furnished to said parties accordingly.

	J.T. Adair	Chairman Commission
Attest	D.W. Lipe	Commissioner

C.C. Lipe
Clk Com

HOWELL

DOCKET #877
CENSUS ROLLS 1835, 51 & 52

APPLICANT FOR CHEROKEE CITIZENSHIP

POST OFFICE: Marietta Ga.   ATTORNEY: Henry C. Rogers

No	NAMES	AGE	SEX
1	Stephen E Howell	36	Male

ANCESTOR: George M Waters

Now on this the 3 day of Oct. 1887, comes the above case for a final hearing and the parties having made application pursuant to the provisions of an Act of the National Council approved Dec 8th 1886. And all the evidence being duly examined and found to be sufficient & satisfactory to the Commission and the name of the Ancestor George M Waters appearing on the rolls of 1835, 51 & 52. It is adjudged and determined by the Commission that Stephen E Howell is a Cherokee by blood and are[sic] hereby re-admitted to all the rights privileges and immunities of Cherokees by blood. And a certificate of said decission[sic] was made and furnished to said parties accordingly.

D.W. Lipe	Actg Chairman Com.
John E. Gunter	Commissioner

Attest

C.C. Lipe
Clk. Com.

HOWELL

DOCKET #878

CENSUS ROLLS 1835, 51 & 52

APPLICANT FOR CHEROKEE CITIZENSHIP

POST OFFICE: Marietta Ga   ATTORNEY: Henry C. Rogers

No	NAMES	AGE	SEX
1	William L Howell	22	Male

ANCESTOR: George M Waters

Now on this the 13 day of Oct. 1887, comes the above case for a final hearing. And the parties having made application pursuant to the provisions of an Act of the National Council approved Dec 8 1886, and all the evidence being duly examined and found to be sufficient and satisfactory to the Commission and the name of the Ancestor, George M Waters appearing on the rolls of 1835, 51 & 52. It is adjudged and determined by the Commission that William L Howell is a Cherokee by blood and are[sic] hereby re-admitted to all the rights privileges and immunities of Cherokees by blood. And a certificate of said decission[sic] of the Commission & re-admission was made & furnished to said parties accordingly.

D.W. Lipe	Chairman Com
John E. Gunter	Commissioner

Attest

C.C. Lipe
Clerk Com

HOWELL

DOCKET #879

CENSUS ROLLS 1835, 51 & 52

APPLICANT FOR CHEROKEE CITIZENSHIP

POST OFFICE: Marietta Ga   ATTORNEY: Henry C Rogers

No	NAMES	AGE	SEX
1	Lillie P Howell	?6	female

ANCESTOR: George M Waters

Now on this the 12 day of Oct. 1887, comes the above case for a final hearing. And the parties having made application pursuant to the provisions of an Act of the National Council approved Dec 8 1886. And all the evidence being duly examined and found to be sufficient and satisfactory to the Commission and the name of the Ancestor, George Waters appearing on the rolls of 1835, 51 & 52. It is adjudged and determined by the Commission that Lillie P Howell is a Cherokee by blood and are[sic] hereby re-admitted to all the rights privileges and immunities of Cherokees by blood. And a certificate of said decission[sic] of the Commission & re-admission was made & furnished to said parties accordingly.

D.W. Lipe   Actg Chairman
of the Com.
John E. Gunter   Commissioner

Attest

C.C. Lipe
Clerk Com

DOCKET #880   *(Entire entry illegible)*

HOWELL

DOCKET #881

CENSUS ROLLS 1835, 51 & 52

APPLICANT FOR CHEROKEE CITIZENSHIP

POST OFFICE: Marietta Ga   ATTORNEY: Henry C Rogers

No	NAMES	AGE	SEX
1	Emily C Howell	33	female

ANCESTOR: George M Waters

Now on this the 12 day of Oct. 1887, comes the above case for a final hearing. And the parties having made application pursuant to the provisions of an Act of the National Council approved Dec 8 1886. And all the evidence being duly examined and found to be sufficient and satisfactory to the Commission and the name of the Ancestor, George M. Waters appearing on the rolls of 1835, 51 & 52. It is adjudged and determined by the Commission that Emily C Howell is a Cherokee by blood and are[sic] hereby re-admitted to all the rights privileges and immunities of Cherokees by blood. And a certificate of said decission[sic] of the Commission & re-admission was made & furnished to said parties accordingly.

D.W. Lipe   Actg Chairman
of the Com.

John E. Gunter   Commissioner

Attest

     C.C. Lipe
       Clerk Com

HOWELL

DOCKET #882

CENSUS ROLLS 1835, 51 & 52

APPLICANT FOR CHEROKEE CITIZENSHIP

POST OFFICE: Marietta Ga   ATTORNEY: Henry C Rogers

No	NAMES	AGE	SEX
1	James C Howell		Male

ANCESTOR: George M Waters

Now on this the 12 day of Oct. 1887, comes the above case for a final hearing. And the parties having made application pursuant to the provisions of an Act of the National Council approved Dec 8 1886. And all the evidence being duly examined and found to be sufficient and satisfactory to the Commission and the name of the Ancestor, George Waters appearing on the rolls of 1835, 51 & 52. It is adjudged and determined by the Commission that James C Howell is a Cherokee by blood and is hereby re-admitted to all the rights privileges and immunities of Cherokees by blood. And a certificate of said decission[sic] of the Commission & re-admission was made & furnished to said parties accordingly.

D.W. Lipe   Actg Chairman
of the Com.

John E. Gunter   Commissioner

Attest

    C.C. Lipe

       Clerk Com

HOWELL

DOCKET #883

CENSUS ROLLS 1835, 51 & 52

APPLICANT FOR CHEROKEE CITIZENSHIP

POST OFFICE: Marietta Ga   ATTORNEY: Henry C Rogers

No	NAMES	AGE	SEX
1	Julia B Howell	23	female

ANCESTOR: George M Waters

Now on this the 12 day of Oct. 1887, comes the above case for a final hearing. And the parties having made application pursuant to the provisions of an Act of the National Council approved Dec 8 1886. And all the evidence being duly examined and found to be sufficient and satisfactory to the Commission and the name of the Ancestor, George M Waters, appearing on the rolls of 1835, 51 & 52. It is adjudged and determined by the Commission that Julia B Howell is a Cherokee by blood and are[sic] hereby re-admitted to all the rights privileges and immunities of Cherokees by blood. And a certificate of said decission[sic] of the Commission & re-admission was made & furnished to said parties accordingly.

             D.W. Lipe   Actg Chairman Com

             John E. Gunter   Comm.

Attest

    C.C. Lipe

       Clerk Com

HOWELL

DOCKET #884

CENSUS ROLLS 1835, 52 & 52

APPLICANT FOR CHEROKEE CITIZENSHIP

POST OFFICE: Marietta Ga   ATTORNEY: Henry C Rogers

No	NAMES	AGE	SEX
1	Ellen E Howell	??	female

ANCESTOR: George M Waters

Cherokee Citizenship Commission Docket Books
(1880-84, 1887-89) Volume III
Tahlequah, Cherokee Nation

Now on this the 12 day of Oct. 1887, comes the above case for a final hearing. And the parties having made application pursuant to the provisions of an Act of the National Council approved Dec 8 1886. And all the evidence being duly examined and found to be sufficient and satisfactory to the Commission and the name of the Ancestor, George M Waters appearing on the rolls of 1835, 51 & 52. It is adjudged and determined by the Commission that Ellen E Howell is a Cherokee by blood and are[sic] hereby re-admitted to all the rights privileges and immunities of Cherokees by blood. And a certificate of said decission[sic] of the Commission & re-admission was made & furnished to said parties accordingly.

D.W. Lipe   Actg Chairman
of the Com.

John E. Gunter   Commissioner

Attest

     C.C. Lipe
       Clerk Com

HENRY

DOCKET #885

CENSUS ROLLS 1835, 51 & 52

APPLICANT FOR CHEROKEE CITIZENSHIP

POST OFFICE: Guntersville Ala   ATTORNEY: Boudinot & Rasmus

No	NAMES	AGE	SEX
1	Hugh B Henry	30	Male
2	Herbert Henry	5	"

ANCESTOR: Annie Henry

Now on this the 30 day of Sept. 1887, comes the above case for a final hearing. And the parties having made application pursuant to the provisions of an Act of the National Council approved Dec 8 1886. And all the evidence being duly examined and found to be sufficient and satisfactory to the Commission and the name of the Ancestor, Annie Henry appearing on the rolls of 1835, 51 & 52. It is adjudged and determined by the Commission that Hugh B. Henry, Herbert Henry are Cherokees by blood and are hereby re-admitted to all the rights privileges and immunities of Cherokees by blood. And a certificate of said decission[sic] of the Commission & re-admission was made & furnished to said parties accordingly.

J T Adair   Chairman Com
John E. Gunter   Commissioner

Cherokee Citizenship Commission Docket Books
(1880-84, 1887-89) Volume III
Tahlequah, Cherokee Nation

Attest

    C.C. Lipe

      Clerk Com

CABIN

DOCKET #886

CENSUS ROLLS 1835

APPLICANT FOR CHEROKEE CITIZENSHIP

POST OFFICE: Polk County Tenn   ATTORNEY: J M Bell

No	NAMES	AGE	SEX
1	Rebecca Cabin		Female

ANCESTOR: Elizabeth & *(Name Illegible)*

Office Commission on Citizenship
Cherokee Nation
July 3rd 1889

There being no evidence in support of the above named case the Commission decide that Rebecca Carbin[sic] whose age is not known is not a Cherokee by blood. Post Office Colk[sic] County Tenn.

                Will. P. Ross   Chairman

Attest

    D.S. Williams   R. Bunch   Com

    Asst. Clk Com   J.E. Gunter   Com

COLLINS

DOCKET #887

CENSUS ROLLS 1851 & 52

APPLICANT FOR CHEROKEE CITIZENSHIP

POST OFFICE: *(Illegible)*   ATTORNEY: *(Illegible)*

No	NAMES	AGE	SEX
1	Joseph Boudinot Collins	40	Male
2	~~*(Illegible)* Parker Collins~~	26	"
3	~~Martha Hall Collins~~	38	Female
4	~~Mary Malissa Collins~~	27	"

ANCESTOR: *(Name Illegible)*

Now on this the 20th day of May, 1887, comes the above case up for a final hearing. And the Commission say, "We the Commission on Citizenship after examining the testimony and also the pay rolls of 1851 taken East of Mississippi River in the above case find that the applicant Joseph Boudinot Collins is a Cherokee by blood and is hereby re-admitted to all the rights and privileges of a Cherokee Citizen by blood.

J.T. Adair   Chairman Commission

D.W. Lipe   Commissioner

CHANCELLOR

DOCKET #889[sic]

CENSUS ROLLS 1835 to 52

APPLICANT FOR CHEROKEE CITIZENSHIP

POST OFFICE: Bowie Texas   ATTORNEY: Boudinot & R[sic]

No	NAMES	AGE	SEX
1	Lucy Chancellor	18	Female

ANCESTOR: Moton

Office Commission on Citizenship

Cherokee Nation Ind. Ter.

Tahlequah Aug 19th 1889

There being no evidence in support of this case the Commission decide that Lucy Chancellor age 18 years is not a Cherokee by blood. Post Office Bowie Texas.

Will.P. Ross   Chairman

Attest

E.G. Ross   J.E. Gunter   Com

Clerk Commission

114

COLTON

DOCKET #890

CENSUS ROLLS 1835 to 1852

APPLICANT FOR CHEROKEE CITIZENSHIP

POST OFFICE: Evansville Ark   ATTORNEY:

No	NAMES	AGE	SEX
1	Charles S Colton	7	Male

ANCESTOR: William Lee

Office Commission on Citizenship
Cherokee Nation
July 3rd 1889

There being no evidence in support of the above named case the Commission decide that Charles S Colton age 7 yrs is not a Cherokee by blood.
Post Office Evansville Ark.

Attest

D.S. Williams
Asst Clk Com

Will.P. Ross   Chairman

J.E. Gunter   Com

COLEY

DOCKET #*(Illegible)*

CENSUS ROLLS 1835

APPLICANT FOR CHEROKEE CITIZENSHIP

POST OFFICE: Melvin Texas   ATTORNEY: C H Taylor

No	NAMES	AGE	SEX
1		36	Female
2	*(All names are illegible)*	14	"
3		12	Male
4		10	Female

ANCESTOR: John Bryant

Adverse
Embraced in decission[sic] on page 431
Book B. in the Aaron Bellew case
Rendered March 18 – 1889.

Cherokee Citizenship Commission Docket Books (1880-84, 1887-89) Volume III Tahlequah, Cherokee Nation

Will.P. Ross
Chairman Com
John E. Gunter   Commissioner

Office Commission on Citizenship
Tahlequah I.T.   March 18 – 1889.

D.S. Williams
Clk Com

CANDY

DOCKET #892

CENSUS ROLLS 1835 to 52

APPLICANT FOR CHEROKEE CITIZENSHIP

POST OFFICE: McKinney Texas   ATTORNEY: W.A. Thompson

NO	NAMES	AGE	SEX
1	Samuel Candy	46	Male

ANCESTOR: Thomas Candy

Office Commission on Citizenship
Cherokee Nation
July 5th 1889

The application in the above case was filed on the 4th day of Oct, 1887, and comes up this day for final hearing. Now the Commission upon examining the evidence submitted with the Census Roll taken and made in the year 1852 known as the Old Settler Pay Roll in which the name of Thomas Candy the alleged ancestor should appear, the Commission decide that Sam Candy is a Cherokee by blood and entitled to all the rights and privileges to Citizenship in the Cherokee [sic] under an Act of the National Council approved Dec. 5th 1888.

Will.P. Ross   Chairman

Attest

D.S. Williams
Asst Clk Com   J.E. Gunter   Com

Cherokee Citizenship Commission Docket Books
(1880-84, 1887-89) Volume III
Tahlequah, Cherokee Nation

CANDY

DOCKET #893

CENSUS ROLLS 1835 to 52

APPLICANT FOR CHEROKEE CITIZENSHIP

POST OFFICE: Vinita IT   ATTORNEY: L.S. Sanders

No	NAMES	AGE	SEX
1	John H Candy	3?	Male

ANCESTOR: John Beamer

Office Commission on Citizenship
Cherokee Nation
July 5th 1889

There being no evidence in support of the above named case the Commission decide that John H Candy age 35 yrs is not a Cherokee by blood. Post Office Vinita IT

Will.P.Ross   Chairman

Attest

D.S. Williams   R. Bunch   Com

Asst Clk Com   J.E. Gunter   Com

COLE

DOCKET #894

CENSUS ROLLS 1835

APPLICANT FOR CHEROKEE CITIZENSHIP

POST OFFICE: Gibson Station   ATTORNEY: C H Taylor

No	NAMES	AGE	SEX
1	George Cole	26	Male

ANCESTOR: Mary Cole

Now on this the 20th day of March, 1889, comes the above case to wit: George Cole for a final hearing he having made application pursuant to the provisions of an Act of the National Council approved December 8th 1886, for re-admission to Citizenship in the Cherokee Nation alleging his descent from Mary Cole who he claims was of Cherokee blood. The testimony of John Taylor shows that the claimant relied upon the decision of the Commission in the case of Elizabeth Phipps his relative and the census roll of 1835 for the establishment of his claim. The decission[sic] in the case of Phipps was adverse to the applicant and the roll of neither 1835 nor of 1851 and 1852 shows the

117

name of Mary Cole. It is therefore adjudged by the Commission that George Cole is not of Cherokee blood and is not entitled to the rights privileges of Native Cherokees in the Cherokee Nation and so decree.

See decision in case of G.W. Cole et.al.

Will.P. Ross

Page 20th   Chairman Com

Attest   E.G. Ross   John E. Gunter

Clerk Commission

COLE

DOCKET #895

CENSUS ROLLS 1835

APPLICANT FOR CHEREOKEE CITIZENSHIP

POST OFFICE: Gibson Station I.T.   ATTORNEY: C.H. Taylor

No	NAMES	AGE	SEX
1	G W Cole	51	Male
2	Henry Cole	15	"
3	Cora Cole	17	Female
4	*(Name Illegible)*	7	Male
5	William Cole	8	Male
6	Stephen Cole	31	"
7	William Cole	28	"
8	Frank Cole	20	"
9	Peter Cole	19	"
10	Kate Cole	22	Female

ANCESTOR: Mary Cole

Now on this the 20th day of March 1887 comes the above case to wit: G.W. Cole for himself and family, viz: Henry Cole, Cora Cole, Stephen Cole, William Cole, Frank Cole, Peter Cole, Kate Cole children Sidna Redric and William Redric Granchildren[sic] for a final hearing, he having made application pursuant to the provisions of an Act of the National Council approved Dec 8th 1886, for re-admission to Citizenship in the Cherokee Nation alleging his descent from Mary Cole who he claims was of Cherokee blood. The testimony of John Taylor shows that the claimant relied upon the decision of the Commission in the case of Elizabeth Phipps, his relative and the census roll of 1835 for the establishment of his claim. The decision in the case of Phipps, was adverse to the applicant and the roll of neither 1835 nor of 1851 and 1852 shows the name of Mary Cole. It is therefore adjudged by the Commission

Cherokee Citizenship Commission Docket Books
(1880-84, 1887-89) Volume III
Tahlequah, Cherokee Nation

that Geo. W. Cole et al, are not of Cherokee blood and are <u>not</u> entitled to the rights and privileges of Native Cherokees in the Cherokee Nation and so decree.

E.G. Ross
    Clerk Commission

Will.P. Ross   Chairman
John E. Gunter   Com

CLEVENGER

DOCKET #896
CENSUS ROLLS 1835

APPLICANT FOR CHEROKEE CITIZENSHIP

POST OFFICE: Hollowell Kansas   ATTORNEY: C H Taylor

No	NAMES	AGE	SEX
1	George Clevenger	25	Male
2	Maud Clevenger	1	Female

ANCESTOR: John Monteath

Office Commission on Citizenship
Cherokee Nation
July 3rd 1889

There being no evidence in support of the above named case the Commission decide that George Clevenger age 25 yrs and his daughter Maud Clevenger age 1 yr are not Cherokees by blood and are not entitled to Citizenship in the Cherokee Nation. Post Office Hollowell Kans.

Attest
    D.S. Williams
    Asst. Clk Com

Will. P. Ross   Chairman

J E Gunter   Com

CLEVENGER

DOCKET #897
CENSUS ROLLS 1835

APPLICANT FOR CHEROKEE CITIZENSHIP

POST OFFICE: Hollowell Kansas   ATTORNEY: C H Taylor

No	NAMES	AGE	SEX
1	Amanda Clevenger	53	Female
2	John Clevenger	19	Male
3	Evaline Clevenger	16	Female

4	Mary Clevenger	14	"

ANCESTOR: John Monteath

Office Commission on Citizenship
Cherokee Nation
July 3rd 1889

There being no evidence in support of the above named case the Commission decide that Amanda Clevenger age 53 yrs and the following children Jon male age 19 yrs, Evaline Female age 16 yrs and Mary Clevenger Female age 14 yrs are not Cherokees by blood. Post Office Hollowell Kans.

Attest

D.S. Williams
Asst. Clk Com

Will. P. Ross   Chairman

J E Gunter   Com

CLEVENGER

DOCKET #898

CENSUS ROLLS 1835

APPLICANT FOR CHEROKEE CITIZENSHIP

POST OFFICE: Baxter Springs Kans   **ATTORNEY:** C H Taylor

No	NAMES	AGE	SEX
1	William Clevenger	27	Male
2	Charlie Clevenger	2	"
3	Darcus Clevenger	1	"

ANCESTOR: John Monteath

Office Commission on Citizenship
Cherokee Nation
July 3rd 1889

There being no evidence in support of the above named case the Commission decide that William Clevenger age 27 yrs and the following children, Charlie Clevenger male age 2 yrs and Darcus Clevenger Female 1 yr, are not Cherokees by blood. Post Office Colk[sic] County Tenn.

Attest

D.S. Williams
Asst. Clk Com

Will. P. Ross   Chairman

J E Gunter   Com

CLEVENGER

DOCKET #899

CENSUS ROLLS 1835

APPLICANT FOR CHEROKEE CITIZENSHIP

POST OFFICE: Hollowell Kans   ATTORNEY: C H Taylor

No	NAMES	AGE	SEX
1	Laura Clevenger	33	Female
2	Erna Clevenger	9	"
3	Anderson Clevenger	6	Male
4	Redman Clevenger	1	"

ANCESTOR: John Monteath

Office Commission on Citizenship
Cherokee Nation
July 3rd 1889

There being no evidence in support of the above named case the Commission decide that Laura Clevenger age 33 yrs and her children Erna Clevenger, Female age 9 yrs, Anderson male age 6 yrs and Redman Clevenger age 1 yr, are not Cherokees by blood. Post Office Hollowell Kans.

Attest

D.S. Williams
Asst. Clk Com

Will. P. Ross   Chairman

J E Gunter   Com

CROCKET

DOCKET #900

CENSUS ROLLS

APPLICANT FOR CHEROKEE CITIZENSHIP

POST OFFICE: Prairie City I.T.   ATTORNEY: C.H. Taylor

No	NAMES	AGE	SEX
1	Elizabeth J Crockett	26	Female
2	Ethel Crocket	1	"

ANCESTOR: Agnes Bain

Cherokee Citizenship Commission Docket Books
(1880-84, 1887-89) Volume III
Tahlequah, Cherokee Nation

Office Commission on Citizenship
Cherokee Nation
July 3rd 1889

There being no evidence in support of the above case the Commission decide that Elizabeth J Crocket age 26 yrs and her daughter Ethel Crocket Female age 1 yr. are not Cherokees by blood.

Post Office Prairie City I.T.

Attest
    D.S. Williams
    Asst Clk Com

Will.P.Ross   Chairman

J.E. Gunter   Com

COSAND

DOCKET #901
CENSUS ROLLS

APPLICANT FOR CHEROKEE CITIZENSHIP

POST OFFICE: New London Ind   ATTORNEY: L.B. Bell

No	NAMES	AGE	SEX
1	Pricilla Cosand	52	Female
2	Addie Cosand		"
3	Albert Cosand		Male
4	Mary Cosand		Female
5	Violetta Cosand		"
6	*(Illegible)* Cosand		Male

ANCESTOR: Alonzo *(Illegible)*

The Commission decide against claimant. See decision in case of *(remainder illegible)*

E.G. Ross
    Clerk Com

Will.P. Ross   Chairman

John E Gunter   Commissioner

CAMBELL

DOCKET #902

CENSUS ROLLS

APPLICANT FOR CHEROKEE CITIZENSHIP

POST OFFICE: Indianapolis Ind   ATTORNEY: L.B. Bell

No	NAMES	AGE	SEX
1	Willie L Cambell	33	Female
2	Henard Cambell	7	Male

ANCESTOR: Anna Crews

The Commission decide against claimant. See decision in the case of Andrew Meredith Docket 2180, Book E, Page 26 and John Henly Docket 1250, Book E, Page 376.

Will.P.Ross   Chairman

E.G. Ross
    Clerk Commission

John E. Gunter   Com

CROMWELL

DOCKET #903

CENSUS ROLLS 1851

APPLICANT FOR CHEROKEE CITIZENSHIP

POST OFFICE: Valley Town NC   ATTORNEY: C H Taylor

No	NAMES	AGE	SEX
1	Margaret Cromwell	36	Female
2	Campbell T Cromwell	6	Male

ANCESTOR: Elizabeth Whitaker

Now on this the 10th day of February 1888, comes the above case for a final hearing, and the parties having made application pursuant to the provisions of an Act of the National Council approved December 8th 1886, and all the evidence being duly examined and found to be sufficient and satisfactory to the Commission, it [sic] adjudged and determined by the Commission that Margaret Cromwell and Campbell T. Cromwell are Cherokees by blood and they are hereby re-admitted to all the rights privileges and immunities of Cherokee Citizens by blood.

And a certificate of said decision[sic] of the Commission and of re-admission was made a furnished to said parties accordingly.

J.T. Adair,	Chairman Commission
John E. Gunter	Commissioner
	Commissioner

Attest

C.C. Lipe

Clerk Commission

CAGLE

DOCKET #904

CENSUS ROLLS 1835

APPLICANT FOR CHEROKEE CITIZENSHIP

POST OFFICE: Leadhill Ark.   ATTORNEY: C H Taylor

No	NAMES	AGE	SEX
1	Nancy Cagle	38	Female
2	Mary E Cagle	18	"

ANCESTOR: Seba Brown

Office Commission on Citizenship
Cherokee Nation Ind. Ter.
Tahlequah July 2nd 1889

There being no evidence in support of the above named case the Commission decide that Nancy Cagle age 38 yrs and her daughter Mary E Cagle female age 18 yrs are not Cherokees by blood. P.O. Leadhill Ark.

Attest   Will.P. Ross   Chairman

D.S. Williams

Asst Clerk Commission   J.E. Gunter   Com

CLARK

DOCKET #905

CENSUS ROLLS 1835

APPLICANT FOR CHEROKEE CITIZENSHIP

POST OFFICE: Chetopa Kansas   ATTORNEY: A E Ivey

No	NAMES	AGE	SEX
1	Laura Clark	19	Female
2	Ida M Clark	2	"

3	Baby Clark	6 mo	Male

ANCESTOR: James Smith

Office Commission on Citizenship
Cherokee Nation Ind. Ter.
Tahlequah May 19th 1889

There being no evidence in support of the above named case the Commission decide that Laura Clark age 19 years and the following children, Ida M Clark age 2 years and Baby Clark age 6 months are not Cherokees by blood. Post Office Chetopa Kansas.

Attest   Will.P. Ross   Chairman
    E.G. Ross
        Clerk Commission   J.E. Gunter   Com

COSAND

DOCKET #906
CENSUS ROLLS

APPLICANT FOR CHEROKEE CITIZENSHIP

POST OFFICE: New London Ind   **ATTORNEY:** L.B. Bell

No	NAMES	AGE	SEX
1	Mary Cosand	21	Female

ANCESTOR: Anna Crews

The ~~abov~~ Commission decide against claimant. See decision in case Andrew Merideth Docket 2180 Book E Page 26 and case John Hanly[sic] Docket 1260 Book C Page 376.

Will.P. Ross   Chairman
    J E Gunter   Com

Cherokee Citizenship Commission Docket Books
(1880-84, 1887-89) Volume III
Tahlequah, Cherokee Nation

COUCH

DOCKET #907

CENSUS ROLLS 1835 to 1852

APPLICANT FOR CHEROKEE CITIZENSHIP

POST OFFICE: Texas　　　　ATTORNEY: A E Ivey

No	NAMES	AGE	SEX
1	John Ann Couch	26	Female

ANCESTOR: Mima Edwards

Now on this the 9th day of January 1888 comes the above case for a final hearing. And the parties having made application pursuant to the provisions of an Act of the National Council approved December 8th 1886. And all the evidence having been duly examined and found not to be sufficient and satisfactory to the Commission, and the name of the ancestor not appearing on the Rolls as claimed in the application.

It is adjudged and determined by the Commission that John Ann Couch, is not a Cherokee by blood and is hereby rejected and declared to be an intruder.

J.T. Adair	Chairman Commission
John E Gunter	Commissioner
D.W. Lipe	Commissioner

Attest

C.C. Lipe

Clerk Commission

CANTWELL

DOCKET #908

CENSUS ROLLS 1835 to 52

APPLICANT FOR CHEROKEE CITIZENSHIP

POST OFFICE: Veneton[sic] Ark　　　　ATTORNEY: A E Ivey

No	NAMES	AGE	SEX
1	Mary E Cantwell	38	Female
2	Lee Cantwell	16	
3	Jack Cantwell	14	

ANCESTOR: Sarah Thomas

126

Cherokee Citizenship Commission Docket Books
(1880-84, 1887-89) Volume III
Tahlequah, Cherokee Nation

Office Commission on Citizenship
Cherokee Nation Ind. Ter.
Tahlequah July 9th 1889

There being no evidence in support of the above named case the Commission decide that Mary E Cantwell age 38 yrs and the following children, Lee male age 16 yrs and Jack Cantwell Female[sic] age 14 yrs are not Cherokees by blood. Post Office Veneton Ark.

Will. P. Ross   Chairman

Attest

D.S. Williams
Asst Clk Com

J.E. Gunter   Com

CHASTIAN

DOCKET #909

CENSUS ROLLS 1835 to 52

APPLICANT FOR CHEROKEE CITIZENSHIP

POST OFFICE: Alene[sic] Ark   ATTORNEY: A.E. Ivey

No	NAMES	AGE	SEX
1	Joseph C Chastian	49	Male
2	William H Chastian	17	"
3	John E Chastian	15	"
4	Mary O Chastian	13	Female
5	Roda D Chastian	11	"
6	Henry W Chastian	9	Male
7	Charles Chastian	7	"
8	Walter W Chastian	6	"
9	Ulysess[sic] G Chastian	2	"

ANCESTOR: John Rogers

Now on this the 17th day of March 1888, comes the above case for a final hearing. And the parties having made application pursuant to the provisions of an Act of the National Council approved December 8th 1886, and all the evidence being duly considered and found to be insufficient and unsatisfactory, it is adjudged and determined by the Commission that

Joseph C Chastian, William H Chastian, John E Chastian, Mary O. Chastian, Roda D Chastian, Henry W Chastian, Charles Chastian, Walter W.

Chastian and Ulysess[sic] G. Chastian are not Cherokees and they are not entitled to the rights privileges and immunities of Cherokee Citizens by blood.

J.T. Adair	Chairman Commission
John E Gunter	Commissioner
D.W. Lipe	Commissioner

Attest
> C.C. Lipe
> > Clerk Com.

The decision in the James C.C. Rogers case found in Book C, page 627 and testimony on Journal page 325 to 333, governs this case.

CLINE

DOCKET #910
CENSUS ROLLS 1835 to 52

APPLICANT FOR CHEROKEE CITIZENSHIP

POST OFFICE: Fowler Texas   ATTORNEY: A.E. Ivey

No	NAMES	AGE	SEX
1	D.W. Cline	34	Male
2	Jessie Lee Cline	10	Female
3	Wm W Cline	7	Male
4	Secred H Cline	5	"
5	Geo L Cline	3	"

ANCESTOR: David Cline

Office Commission on Citizenship
Cherokee Nation Ind. Ter
Tahlequah July 9th 1889

There being no evidence in support of the above named case the Commission decide that D.W. Cline age 34 yrs and the following children Jessie Lee Female age 10 yrs, Wm W. Male age 7 yrs, Secred H. Cline male age 5 yrs and Geo. L. Cline male age 3 yrs are not Cherokees by blood. Post Office Fowler Texas.

Will.P. Ross   Chairman
Attest   J.E. Gunter   Com
> D.S. Williams
> Asst Clk Com

CLINKINBEARD

DOCKET #911

CENSUS ROLLS 1835

APPLICANT FOR CHEROKEE CITIZENSHIP

POST OFFICE: White Right Texas   ATTORNEY:

No	NAMES	AGE	SEX
1	Jennie Clinkinbeard	38	Female
2	Lock Clinkinbeard	6	Male
3	Jellie Clinkinbeard	4	Female
4	Roscoe Clinkinbeard	2	Male

ANCESTOR: John Ross

Office Commission on Citizenship
Cherokee Nation Ind Ter
Tahlequah July 9th 1889

There being no evidence in support of the above named case the Commission decide that Jennie Clinkinbeard age 38 yrs and the following children Lock male age 6 yrs, Jellie Female age 4 yrs, Roscoe Clinkinbeard male age 2 yrs are not Cherokees by blood. Post Office White Right Texas.

Attest   Will. P. Ross   Chairman
   D S Williams
   Asst Clk Com   J.E. Gunter   Com

CLINE

DOCKET #912

CENSUS ROLLS 1835

APPLICANT FOR CHEROKEE CITIZENSHIP

POST OFFICE: Fowler Texas   ATTORNEY: A.E. Ivey

No	NAMES	AGE	SEX
1	D A Cline	32	Male
2	Claudie O Cline	2	"

ANCESTOR: David Cline

Rejected July 9th 1889

Office Commission on Citizenship
Cherokee Nation Ind Ter
Tahlequah July 9th 1889

There being no evidence in support of the above named case the Commission decide that D.A. Cline age 32 yrs and his son Claudie O Cline male age 2 yrs are not Cherokees by blood. Post Office Fowler Texas.

Attest   Will.P. Ross   Chairman
    D.S. Williams
    Asst. Clk Com.

J.E. Gunter   Com

CUMMING

DOCKET #913
CENSUS ROLLS 1835

APPLICANT FOR CHEROKEE CITIZENSHIP

POST OFFICE: *(Illegible)* Mo.   ATTORNEY: A.E. Ivey

No	NAMES	AGE	SEX
1	Flora B Cumming	19	Female
2	Maggie E Cumming	5	"

ANCESTOR: John Rogers

Now on this the 2nd day of July 1888, the above case comes up for final hearing and the Commission say, "We the Commission on Citizenship after carefully examining the evidence in the above case and also the Old Settler pay rolls of 1851, find that Flora B Cumming and her daughter, Maggie E Cumming are Cherokees by blood and are hereby re-admitted to all the rights and privileges of Cherokee citizens by blood which is in compliance with an Act of the National Council dated Dec. 8th 1886, and the amendment there to dated and approved Febry 7th 1888.

J.T. Adair   Chairman Commission
D.W. Lipe   Commissioner

Cherokee Citizenship Commission Docket Books
(1880-84, 1887-89) Volume III
Tahlequah, Cherokee Nation

OTENHOUSE

DOCKET #914

CENSUS ROLLS 1835

APPLICANT FOR CHEROKEE CITIZENSHIP

POST OFFICE: McKinney Texas   ATTORNEY: W.A. Thompson

No	NAMES	AGE	SEX
1	Hamett Otenhouse	48	Female
2	Sarah C Otenhouse	19	"
3	Henry E Otenhouse	15	Male
4	Martha A Otenhouse	12	Female
5	Ida M Otenhouse	10	"
6	Harriett J Otenhouse	7	"
7	James R Otenhouse	4	Male

ANCESTOR: George McGanoh

Office Commission on Citizenship
Cherokee Nation
Tahlequah June 26th 1889

There being no evidence in support of the above named case the Commission decide that Hamett Otenhouse age 48 years and the following children – Sarah C, Female age 19 years, Henry E Female[sic] age 15 years, Martha A Female age 12 years, Ida M. age 10 years, Female, Harriett J. Female age 7 years and James R Otenhouse male age 4 years are not Cherokees by blood and are not entitled to Citizenship in the Cherokee Nation. Post Office McKinny[sic] Texas.

Will.P.Ross   Chairman

Attest

    D.S. Williams
    Asst Clk Com

J E Gunter   Com

DOCKET #915   *(All names illegible)*

Cherokee Citizenship Commission Docket Books
(1880-84, 1887-89) Volume III
Tahlequah, Cherokee Nation

ROGERS

DOCKET #916

CENSUS ROLLS 1835 to 52

APPLICANT FOR CHEROKEE CITIZENSHIP

POST OFFICE: *(Illegible)* Ind. Ter.   ATTORNEY: Henry C Rogers

No	NAMES	AGE	SEX
1	Leona Rogers	8	Female
2	Laura Rogers	10	"
3	John Rogers	6	Male

ANCESTOR: John Rogers

Now on this the 6 day of Oct. 1887, comes the above case for final hearing and the parties having made application pursuant to the provisions of an Act of the National Council approved Dec 8 1886. And all the evidence being duly examined and found to be sufficient and satisfactory to the Commission and the name of the ancestor, John Rogers, appearing on the rolls of 1835 to 52. It is adjudged and determined by the Commission that Leona Rogers, Laura Rogers & John Rogers are Cherokees by blood and are hereby re-admitted to all the rights & privileges and immunities of Cherokees by blood.

And a certificate of said decission[sic] by the Commission and re-admission are made and furnished to said parties accordingly.

D.W. Lipe   Actg Chairman Com
John E Gunter   Commissioner

Attest

C.C. Lipe
Clerk Com

THOMAS

DOCKET #917

CENSUS ROLLS 1835 to 52

APPLICANT FOR CHEROKEE CITIZENSHIP

POST OFFICE: *(Illegible)* Ind Tery   ATTORNEY: Henry C Rogers

No	NAMES	AGE	SEX
1	Minnie Thomas	20	Female
2	Jennie I Thomas	2	"
3	Edward *(Illegible)* Thomas	?	Male

ANCESTOR: John Rogers

132

Now on this the 8 day of Oct. 1887, comes the above case for a final hearing. And the parties having made application pursuant to the provisions of an Act of the National Council approved Dec 8 1886. And all the evidence being duly examined and found to be sufficient & satisfactory to the Commission and the name of the ancestor, John Rogers, appearing on the rolls of 1835 to 52. It is adjudged and determined by the Commission that Minnie Thomas, Jennie I Thomas and Edward *(Illegible)* Thomas are Cherokees by blood and are hereby re-admitted to all the rights privileges & immunities of Cherokees by blood. And a certificate of said decission[sic] of the Commission & re-admission are made & furnished to said parties accordingly.

D.W. Lipe Actg. Chairman Com
John E Gunter   Com.

Attest
     C.C. Lipe
     Clk Com

ROGERS

DOCKET #918
CENSUS ROLLS 1835 to 52

APPLICANT FOR CHEREKEE CITIZENSHIP

POST OFFICE: *(Illegible)* Ind Tery   ATTORNEY: Henry C Rogers

No	NAMES	AGE	SEX
1	Walter S Rogers	38	Male
2	Walter Pen Rogers	6 mo	Male
3	Laura Rogers	17	Female
4	Lenora Rogers	14	"
5	John *(Illegible)* Rogers	11	Male

ANCESTOR: John Rogers

Now on this the 6 day of Oct. 1889, comes the above case for a final hearing and all the evidence for a final hearing[sic] and the parties having made application pursuant to the provisions of an Act of the National Council approved Dec 8 1886, all[sic] all the evidence being duly examined and [sic] to be sufficient and satisfactory to the Commission and the name of the ancestor appearing on the rolls of 1835 to 52. It is adjudged and determined by the Commission that Walter S Rogers & Walter Pen Rogers are Cherokees by blood and are hereby re-admitted to all the rights privileges and immunities of

Cherokees by blood, and a certificate of said decission[sic] of the Commission and re-admission was made & furnished to said parties accordingly.

D.W. Lipe Actg Chairman Com

John E Gunter   Commissioner

Attest

C.C. Lipe

Clerk Com

(Remainder illegible)

ROGERS

DOCKET #919

CENSUS ROLLS 1835 to 52

APPLICANT FOR CHEREE CITIZENSHIP

POST OFFICE: *(Illegible)* Ind Tery   ATTORNEY: Henry C Rogers

No	NAMES	AGE	SEX
1	Lorenzo Rogers		
2	George Rogers	?	Male
3	*(Illegible)* Rogers		"

ANCESTOR: Geo W Rogers

We the Commission on Citizenship after examining the above cast in it[sic] details find that Lorenzo Rogers is the son of George W Rogers a Cherokee Indian whose name appears on the rolls of Cherokees, and that Lorenzo Rogers and his two sons George and *(Illegible)* Rogers are Cherokees by blood and entitled to the privileges and rights as other Cherokees on account of their Cherokee blood and are hereby re-admitted to the same.

D.W. Lipe   Actg Chairman Commission

H.C. Barnes   Commissioner

Office Commission on Citizenship
Tahlequah, I.T. Sept. 5th 1888

CEARLEY

DOCKET #920

CENSUS ROLLS 1851 & 52

APPLICANT FOR CHEROKEE CITIZENSHIP

POST OFFICE: Ivy Log Ga   ATTORNEY:

No	NAMES	AGE	SEX
1	Sarah L Cearley	29	Female
2	*(Illegible)* A. Cearley	9	Male
3	John G Cearley	7	"

ANCESTOR: *(Illegible Name)*

Now on this the 9th day of March 1888, comes the above case for a final hearing [sic] having made application pursuant to the provisions of an Act of the National Council approved Dec 8th 1886, and all the evidence being duly examined and found to be sufficient and satisfactory to the Commission and the name of the ancestor sufficient and satisfactory to the Commission it is adjudged and determined by the Commission that Sarah L Cearley, *(Illegible)* A Cearley and John G Cearley are Cherokees by blood and are hereby re-admitted to all the rights privileges and immunities of Cherokee citizens by blood.

A certificate of said decision of the Commission and if re-admission are made and furnished to said parties accordingly.

J.T. Adair   Chairman Commission
John E. Gunter   Commissioner

Cornell Rogers
    Clerk Commission

DOCKET #921   *(All names illegible)*

CHASTIAN

DOCKET #922

CENSUS ROLLS 1835 to 52

APPLICANT FOR CHEROKEE CITIZENSHIP

POST OFFICE: *(Illegible)* Ark   ATTORNEY:

No	NAMES	AGE	SEX
1	Nancy M Chastian	70	Female

ANCESTOR: John Rogers

Cherokee Citizenship Commission Docket Books
(1880-84, 1887-89) Volume III
Tahlequah, Cherokee Nation

Now on this the 19th day of March 1888, comes the above case for a final hearing, and the parties having made application pursuant to the provisions of an Act of the National Council approved December 8th 1886. And all the evidence being duly examined and found to be sufficient and satisfactory to the Commission and the name of the ancestor insufficient and unsatisfactory, it is adjudged and declared that Nancy M Chastian is not a Cherokee, and she is not entitled to any rights privileges and immunities of a Cherokee by blood.

J.T. Adair	Chairman Commission
John E Gunter	Commissioner
D.W. Lipe	Commissioner

Attest

C C Lipe

Clk Com

The decision in the case C C Rogers are found in Book C, page 627, and testimony on Journal pages 325 to 333 governs this case.

DOCKET #923   *(All names illegible)*

CHASTIAN

DOCKET #924

CENSUS ROLLS 1835 to 52

APPLICANT FOR CHEROKEE CITIZENSHIP

POST OFFICE: *(Illegible)*   ATTORNEY: A E Ivey

No	NAMES	AGE	SEX
1	Lafayette G Chastian	30	Male
2	Benjamin L Chastian	6	"
3	Laura O L Chastian	3	Female
4	Mary E Chastian	1	"

ANCESTOR: John Rogers

Now on this the 19th day of March, 1888, comes the above case for a final hearing. And the parties having made application pursuant to the provisions of an Act of the National Council approved December 8th 1886. And all the evidence being duly examined and found to be sufficient and satisfactory to the Commission and the name of the ancestor insufficient and unsatisfactory it is adjudged and declared by the Commission, that

Cherokee Citizenship Commission Docket Books
(1880-84, 1887-89) Volume III
Tahlequah, Cherokee Nation

Lafayette G. Chastian, Benjamin L. Chastian, Laura O.L. Chastian and Mary E Chastian are not Cherokees and they are not entitled to any of the rights privileges and immunities of Cherokee citizens by blood.

J.T. Adair	Chairman Commission
John E Gunter	Commissioner
D W Lipe	Commissioner

Attest

C.C. Lipe

Clerk Com

The decision in the James C C Rogers case found in Book C, page 627, and testimony on Journal pages 325 to 333 governs this case.

CROCKET

DOCKET #925

CENSUS ROLLS 1835 to 1852

APPLICANT FOR CHEROKEE CITIZENSHIP

POST OFFICE: *(Illegible)* City Ind. Tery   ATTORNEY: A E Ivey

NO	NAMES	AGE	SEX
1	Mary Ann Crocket	50	Female

ANCESTOR: *(Illegible)* Crocket

Office Commission on Citizenship
Cherokee Nation Ind. Tery
Tahlequah July 9th 1889

There being no evidence in support of the above named case the Commission decide that Mary Ann Crocket age 50 yrs is not a Cherokee by blood. Post Office *(Illegible)* City Ind. Tery.

Attest

D.S. Williams

Asst Clk Com

Will P Ross

Char.

J E Gunter   Com

DOCKET #926   *(All names illegible)*

137

Cherokee Citizenship Commission Docket Books
(1880-84, 1887-89) Volume III
Tahlequah, Cherokee Nation

DOCKET #927   *(All names illegible)*

CARNES

DOCKET #928

CENSUS ROLLS 1851

APPLICANT FOR CHEROKEE CITIZENSHIP

POST OFFICE: Ophir Ga   ATTORNEY: A E Ivey

No	NAMES	AGE	SEX
1	G.W. Carnes	32	Male
2	Henry L Carnes	9	"
3	Geo B Carnes	7	"
4	Ida Carnes	5	Female

ANCESTOR: Deanah Carnes

Now on this the 30th day of May, 1888, comes the above case up for final hearing and the Commission say, "We the Commission on Citizenship after "examining the evidence and the census & pay rolls of 1851 & 52, find the "above applicants to be Cherokees by blood, and the said G.W. Carnes and his "three children, Henry L, George B and Ida Carnes are hereby re-admitted to all "the rights and privileges of Cherokee citizens by blood.

J.T. Adair	Chairman Commission
John E Gunter	Commissioner
D W Lipe	Commissioner

CARNES

DOCKET #929

CENSUS ROLLS 1851

APPLICANT FOR CHEROKEE CITIZENSHIP

POST OFFICE: Ophir Ga   ATTORNEY: A E Ivey

No	NAMES	AGE	SEX
1	Deannah Carnes	57	Female
2	Elizabeth ? Carnes		"
3	John W Carnes	21	Male
4	Sarah A Carnes		Female

5	Annie ? Carnes	14	"

ANCESTOR: George Welch

Now on this the 30th day of May, 1888, comes the above case up for a final hearing and the Commission say, "We the Commission on Citizenship after "examining the evidence and the census & pay rolls of 1851 & 52, find the "above applicants to be Cherokees by blood, and the said Deannah Carnes and "her four above named children, Elizabeth ? – John W – Sarah A – Annie T. "Carnes are hereby re-admitted to all the rights and privileges of Cherokee "citizens by blood.

J.T. Adair	Chairman Commission
John E Gunter	Commissioner
D W Lipe	Commissioner

CHARITY

DOCKET #930

CENSUS ROLLS 1835 to 52

APPLICANT FOR CHEROKEE CITIZENSHIP

POST OFFICE: Chetopa Kansas   **ATTORNEY:** A E Ivey

No	NAMES	AGE	SEX
1	J Charity	50	Male

ANCESTOR: James Smith

Office Commission on Citizenship
Cherokee Nation Ind Ter
Tahlequah July 9th 1889

There being no evidence in support of the above named case the Commission decide that J Chairty[sic] age 50 yrs is not a Cherokee by blood. Post Office Chetopa Kansas.

Will.P. Ross   Chairman

Attest

D.S. Williams
Asst Clk Com

J.E. Gunter   Com

DOCKET #931   *(All names illegible)*

CAMPBELL

DOCKET #932

CENSUS ROLLS 1835 to 52

APPLICANT FOR CHEROKEE CITIZENSHIP

POST OFFICE: Van Buren Ark   ATTORNEY: A E Ivey

NO	NAMES	AGE	SEX
1	Laura Campbell	41	Female

ANCESTOR: John Edgly

Rejected July 9th 1889

> Office Commission on Citizenship
> Cherokee Nation Ind. Ter.
> Tahlequah July 9th 1889

There being no evidence in support of the above named case the Commission decide that Laura Campbell age 41 yrs is not a Cherokee by blood. Post Office Van Buren Ark.

Will.P.Ross   Chairman

Attest

D.S.Williams   J.E. Gunter   Com
Asst. Clk Com.

COUCH

DOCKET #933

CENSUS ROLLS 1835 to 52

APPLICANT FOR CHEROKEE CITIZENSHIP

POST OFFICE: Van Buren Ark   ATTORNEY: A. E. Ivey

NO	NAMES	AGE	SEX
1	William Couch	60	Male

ANCESTOR: Mima Edwards

Now on this the 9th day of January 1888, comes the above case for a final hearing. And the parties having made application pursuant to the provisions of an Act of the National Council approved December 8th 1886. And all the evidence being duly examined and found not to [sic] sufficient and satisfactory

140

to the Commission and the name of the Ancestor not appearing on the Rolls as claimed in the application.

It is adjudged and determined by the Commission that William Couch is not a Cherokee by blood and is hereby rejected and declared an intruder.

J.T. Adair	Chairman Commission
John E Gunter	Commissioner
D.S. Lipe	Commissioner

Attest

    C.C. Lipe

        Clerk Commission

COLE

DOCKET #934

CENSUS ROLLS 1835 to 52

APPLICANT FOR CHEROKEE CITIZENSHIP

POST OFFICE: Aberline[sic] Texas   ATTORNEY: A.E. Ivey

No	NAMES	AGE	SEX
1	Anna Cole	63	Female
2	Henry Lemans	48	Male
3	Lark Cole	39	Male
4	Alex Cole	33	"
5	Sallie Pony	29	Female
6	Bob Cole	23	Male

ANCESTOR: *(Illegible)*

Rejected July 9th 1889

Office Commission on Citizenship

Cherokee Nation Ind. Ter

Tahlequah July 9th 1889

There being no evidence in support of the above named case the Commission decide that Anna Cole age 63 yrs and the following children Henry Lemans male age 48 yrs, Lark Cole age 39 yrs, Alex male age 33 yrs, Sallie Pony Female age 29 yrs and Bob Cole male age 23 yrs are not Cherokees by blood. Post Office Aberline[sic] Texas

Cherokee Citizenship Commission Docket Books
(1880-84, 1887-89) Volume III
Tahlequah, Cherokee Nation

Will.P. Ross   Chairman

Attest
   D.S. Williams
   Asst Clk Com   J.E. Gunter   Com

CAMPBELL

DOCKET #935
CENSUS ROLLS 1835 to 52

APPLICANT FOR CHEROKEE CITIZENSHIP

POST OFFICE: *(Illegible)* I.T.   ATTORNEY: A.E. Ivey

No	NAMES	AGE	SEX
1	S A Campbell	33	Female

ANCESTOR: Mrs. Badson

Rejected July 9th 1889

Office Commission on Citizenship
Cherokee Nation Ind Ter
Tahlequah July 9th 1889

There being no evidence in support of the above named case the Commission decide that S.A. Campbell age 33 yrs is not a Cherokee by blood. Post Office *(Illegible)* I.T.

Will.P. Ross   Chairman

Attest
   D.S. Williams
   Asst Clk Com   J.E. Gunter Com

CAMPBELL

DOCKET #936
CENSUS ROLLS 1835 to 52

APPLICANT FOR CHEROKEE CITIZENSHIP

POST OFFICE: Closeman Ind Ter   ATTORNEY: A E Ivey

No	NAMES	AGE	SEX
1	R.V. Campbell	62	Male

ANCESTOR: Mrs. Badson

Office Commission on Citizenship
Cherokee Nation Ind. Ter
Tahlequah July 9th 1889

142

Cherokee Citizenship Commission Docket Books
(1880-84, 1887-89) Volume III
Tahlequah, Cherokee Nation

There being R.V. Campbell age 62 yrs is not a Cherokee by blood. Post Office Closemon C.N.

Will.P. Ross   Chairman

Attest

    D.S. Williams   J.E. Gunter   Com
    Asst Clk Com

CORTEN

DOCKET #937
CENSUS ROLLS 1835 to 52

APPLICANT FOR CHEROKEE CITIZENSHIP

POST OFFICE: Sunset Texas   ATTORNEY: A.E. Ivey

No	NAMES	AGE	SEX
1	Joe C Corten	35	Male

ANCESTOR: A.E. Ivey

Office Commission on Citizenship
Cherokee Nation Ind Ter
Tahlequah July 9th 1889

There being no evidence in support of the above named case the Commission decide that Joe C Corten age 35 yrs is not a Cherokee by blood. Post Office Sunset Texas.

Will.P. Ross   Chairman

Attest

    D.S. Williams   J.E. Gunter   Com
    Asst Clk Com

CADDELL

DOCKET #938
CENSUS ROLLS 1835 to 52

APPLICANT FOR CHEROKEE CITIZENSHIP

POST OFFICE: Closemon I.T.   ATTORNEY: A E Ivey

No	NAMES	AGE	SEX
1	J.D. Caddell	24	Male

ANCESTOR: *(Illegible Name)*

Rejected July 9th 1889

143

Cherokee Citizenship Commission Docket Books
(1880-84, 1887-89) Volume III
Tahlequah, Cherokee Nation

Office Commission on Citizenship
Cherokee Nation Ind. Tery.
Tahlequah July 9th 1889

There being no evidence in support of the above named case the Commission decide that J.D. Caddell age 24 yrs is not a Cherokee by blood. Post Office Closemon I.T.

Will.P. Ross   Chairman

Attest

D.S. Williams   J.E. Gunter   Com
Asst Clk Com

CLAY

DOCKET #939
CENSUS ROLLS 1835 to 52

APPLICANT FOR CHEROKEE CITIZENSHIP

POST OFFICE: Closemon I.T.   ATTORNEY: A.E. Ivey

No	NAMES	AGE	SEX
1	S.F. Clay	26	Male
2	J B Clay	9	"
3	F B. Clay	5	"
4	J E Clay	2	"

ANCESTOR: Mrs. Bradson

Rejected July 9th 1889

Office Commission on Citizenship
Cherokee Nation Ind. Ter.
Tahlequah   July 9th 1889

There being no evidence in support of the above named case the Commission decide that S.F. Clay age 26 yrs, J.B. Clay male age 9 yrs, F.B. Clay male age 5 yrs, J.E. Clay male age 1 year are not Cherokees by blood. Post Office Closemon I.T.

Will.P. Ross   Chairman

Attest

D.S. Williams
Asst Clk Com   JE Gunter   Com

Cherokee Citizenship Commission Docket Books
(1880-84, 1887-89) Volume III
Tahlequah, Cherokee Nation

CANADA

DOCKET #940

CENSUS ROLLS 1835 to 52

APPLICANT FOR CHEROKEE CITIZENSHIP

POST OFFICE: Coffeyville Kansas   ATTORNEY:

No	NAMES	AGE	SEX
1	James L Canada	24	Male

ANCESTOR: *(Illegible Name)*

Rejected July 9th 1889

Office Commission on Citizenship
Cherokee Nation Ind. Ter.
Tahlequah July 9th 1889

There being no evidence in support of the above named case the Commission decide that James L Canada age 24 yrs is not a Cherokee by blood. Post Office Coffeville[sic] Kansas.

Will.P. Ross   Chairman

Attest

D.S. Williams
Asst Clk Com   J.E. Gunter   Com

COUCH

DOCKET #941

CENSUS ROLLS 1835 to 52

APPLICANT FOR CHEROKEE CITIZENSHIP

POST OFFICE: Texas   ATTORNEY: A E Ivey

No	NAMES	AGE	SEX
1	William Couch	28	Male

ANCESTOR: Mima Edwards

Now on this the 9th day of January 1888 comes the above case for a final hearing. And the parties having made application pursuant to the provisions of an Act of the National Council approved December 8th 1886. And all the evidence being duly examined and found <u>not</u> to be sufficient and satisfactory to the Commission and the name of the ancestor not appearing on the Rolls as claimed in the application.

It is adjudged and determined by the Commission that William Couch is not a Cherokee by blood and is hereby rejected and declared intruders[sic].

145

Cherokee Citizenship Commission Docket Books
(1880-84, 1887-89) Volume III
Tahlequah, Cherokee Nation

J.T. Adair	Chairman Commission
John E Gunter	Commissioner
D.W. Lipe	Commissioner

Attest

    C.C. Lipe

        Clerk Commission

CRAWFORD

DOCKET #942

CENSUS ROLLS 1835 to 52

APPLICANT FOR CHEROKEE CITIZENSHIP

POST OFFICE: Van Buren Ark   ATTORNEY: A.E. Ivey

No	NAMES	AGE	SEX
1	Rebecca Crawford	36	Female
2	Mack Crawford	13	Male
3	Elizabeth Crawford	12	Female
4	Lousa[sic] Crawford	5	"
5	Hannah Crawford	2	"

ANCESTOR: Sam & Hulda *(Illegible)*

Rejected July 9th 1889

        Office Commission on Citizenship

           Cherokee Nation Ind. Ter.

             Tahlequah July 9th 1889

    There being no evidence in support of the above named case the Commission decide that Rebecca Crawford age 36 yrs and the following children Mack, male age 13 yrs, Elizabeth Female age 12 yrs, Lousa Female age 5 yrs, and Hanah[sic] Crawford Female age 2 yrs, are not Cherokees by blood. Post Office Van Buren, Ark.

        Will.P. Ross   Chairman

Attest

    D.S. Williams   J.E. Gunter   Com

    Asst Clk Com

COTTON

DOCKET #942[sic]
CENSUS ROLLS 1835 to [sic]

APPLICANT FOR CHEROKEE CITIZENSHIP

POST OFFICE: Morehead[sic] I.T.   ATTORNEY: A.E. Ivey

No	NAMES	AGE	SEX
1	Alice Cotton	30	Female

ANCESTOR: Calliew

Rejected July 9th 1889

Office Commission on Citizenship
Cherokee Nation Ind. Ter.
Tahlequah July 9th 1889

There being no evidence in support of the above named case the Commission decide that Alice Cotton age 30 yrs is not a Cherokee by blood. Post Office Morehead I.T.

Attest

    D.S. Williams

    Asst Clk Com

Will.P. Ross   Chairman

        JE Gunter   Com

CHASTIAN

DOCKET #943
CENSUS ROLLS 1835 to 52

APPLICANT FOR CHEROKEE CITIZENSHIP

POST OFFICE: Dyers Ark   ATTORNEY: A.E. Ivey

No	NAMES	AGE	SEX
1	B T Chastian	39	Male
2	T.E. Chastian	16	Female
3	N.M. Chastian	14	"
4	M.J. Chastian	12	"
5	G.M. Chastian	9	Male
6	E M Chastian	7	"
7	M.C. Chastian	5	Female
8	R.T. Chastian	2	Male

ANCESTOR: John Rogers

Cherokee Citizenship Commission Docket Books
(1880-84, 1887-89) Volume III
Tahlequah, Cherokee Nation

Now on this the 7th day of March 1888 comes the above case for a final hearing. And the parties having made application pursuant to the provisions of an Act of the National Council approved December 8th 1886. And all the evidence being duly considered and found to be insufficient and unsatisfactory it is adjudged and declared by the Commission that

B.T. Chastian, T.E. Chastian, N.M. Chastian, M.J. Chastian, G.M. Chastian, E.M. Chastian, M.C. Chastian and R.T. Chastian are not Cherokees and are not entitled to the rights privileges and immunities of Cherokee citizens by blood.

J.T. Adair	Chairman Commission
John E Gunter	Commissioner
D.W. Lipe	Commissioner

Attest
    C.C. Lipe
        Clerk Com

The decision in the James C.C. Rogers case found in Book C, page 627 and testimony on Journal page 325 to 333, governs this case.

CREEKMORE

DOCKET #944
CENSUS ROLLS 1835 to 52

APPLICANT FOR CHEROKEE CITIZENSHIP

POST OFFICE: Van Buren Ark   ATTORNEY: A.E. Ivey

No	NAMES	AGE	SEX
1	M.E. Creekmore	37	Female
2	E.M. Creekmore	16	Male
3	M.T. Creekmore	18	"
4	M.A. Creekmore	13	Female
5	W.N. Creekmore	7	Male
6	J.C. Creekmore	1	"

ANCESTOR: John Rogers

Now on this the 17th day of March 1888, comes the above case for a final hearing. And the parties having made application pursuant to the provisions of an Act of the National Council approved December 8th 1886. And all the evidence being duly examined and found to be insufficient and unsatisfactory to the Commission it is adjudged and declared that

148

Cherokee Citizenship Commission Docket Books
(1880-84, 1887-89) Volume III
Tahlequah, Cherokee Nation

M.E. Creekmore, E.M. Creekmore, M.T. Creekmore, M.A. Creekmore, W.N. Creekmore and J.C. Creekmore are not Cherokees and are not entitled to the rights privileges & immunities of Cherokee citizens by blood.

J.T. Adair	Chairman Commission
John E Gunter	Commissioner
D.W. Lipe	Commissioner

Attest

C.C. Lipe

Clerk Com

The decision in the James C.C. Rogers case found in Book C, page 627 and testimony on Journal page 325 to 333, governs this case.

COTTON

DOCKET #945

CENSUS ROLLS 1835

APPLICANT FOR CHEROKEE CITIZENSHIP

POST OFFICE: Morehead I.T.   ATTORNEY: A.E. Ivey

No	NAMES	AGE	SEX
1	John Cotton, Sr	29	Male
2	John Cotton, Jr	5	"
3	Allice[sic] Cotton	3	Female
4	Cora D Cotton	8 mo	"

ANCESTOR: John Griffin

Rejected July 9th 1889

Office Commission on Citizenship
Cherokee Nation Ind. Ter.
Tahlequah July 9th 1889

There being no evidence in support of the above named case the Commission decide that John Cotton age 29 yrs & the following children John male age 5 yrs, Alice Female age 3 yrs and Cora D Cotton Female age 8 months are not Cherokees by blood. Post Office Morehead I.T.

Attest   Will.P. Ross   Chairman

D.S. Williams

Asst Clk Com

J.E. Gunter   Com

COKE

DOCKET #946

CENSUS ROLLS 1835

APPLICANT FOR CHEROKEE CITIZENSHIP

POST OFFICE: Vana[sic] Grove Ark   ATTORNEY: C H Taylor

No	NAMES	AGE	SEX
1	Alice Coke	16	Female

ANCESTOR: River Jourdan

Office Commission on Citizenship
Cherokee Nation Ind. Ter.
Tahlequah July 9th 1889

There being no evidence in support of the above named case the Commission decide that Alice Coke age 16 yrs is not a Cherokee by blood. Post Office Vana Grove Ark.

Will.P. Ross   Chairman

Attest

D.S. Williams   JE Gunter   Com
Asst Clk Com

CAGLE

DOCKET #947

CENSUS ROLLS 1835

APPLICANT FOR CHEROKEE CITIZENSHIP

POST OFFICE: Lead Hill   ATTORNEY: C H Taylor

No	NAMES	AGE	SEX
1	W.E. Cagle		Male

ANCESTOR: Seba Brown

Office Commission on Citizenship
Cherokee Nation July 2, 1889

There being no evidence in support of the above named case the Commission on Citizenship decide that W.E. Cagle is not a Cherokee by blood.

Post Office Lead Hill Ark

D.S. Williams
Asst Clerk Commission

Will.P. Ross — Chairman

J E Gunter — Com

CAGLE

DOCKET #948
CENSUS ROLLS 1835

APPLICANT FOR CHEROKEE CITIZENSHIP

POST OFFICE: Lead Hill Ark

ATTORNEY: C H Taylor

No	NAMES	AGE	SEX
1	A.J. Cagle		Male

ANCESTOR: Seba Brown

Office Commission on Citizenship
July 2nd 1889

There being no evidence in support of the above named case the Commission decide that A.J. Cagle *(illegible)* years is not a Cherokee by blood.

Post Office Lead Hill Ark.

D.S. Williams — Clerk Commission

Will.P. Ross — Chairman

J.E. Gunter — Com

COLVERT

DOCKET #949
CENSUS ROLLS 1835 to 1852

APPLICANT FOR CHEROKEE CITIZENSHIP

POST OFFICE: Mayesville[sic] Ark

ATTORNEY: C H Taylor

No	NAMES		AGE	SEX
1	Louisa Colvert		28	Female
2	Gudger	"	7	Male
3	Murtte	"	6	Female
4	Odess	"	4	"
5	Annie	"	1	"

ANCESTOR: Elizabeth Whitaker

151

Cherokee Citizenship Commission Docket Books
(1880-84, 1887-89) Volume III
Tahlequah, Cherokee Nation

Now on this the 16th day of December 1887, comes the above case for a final hearing. And the parties having made application pursuant to the provisions of an Act of the National Council approved December 8th 1886. And all the evidence being duly considered and found to be sufficient and satisfactory to the Commission it is adjudged and determined by the Commission that Louiza[sic] Colvert, Gudger Colvert, Murtte[sic] Colvert, Odess Colvert and Annie Colvert are Cherokees by blood and they are hereby re-admitted to all the rights privileges and immunities of Cherokee citizens by blood.

And a certificate of said decission[sic] of the Commission and of re-admission was made and furnished said parties accordingly.

R.T. Hauks   J.T. Adair   Chairman Commission
Asst Clerk of Commission   John E. Gunter   Commissioner
on Citizenship

CONNER

DOCKET #950
CENSUS ROLLS 1835

APPLICANT FOR CHEROKEE CITIZENSHIP

POST OFFICE: Whitman   ATTORNEY: C H Taylor

No	NAMES	AGE	SEX
1	Virginia M Conner	23	Female
2	Morman W Conner	5	Male

ANCESTOR: *(Illegible)* Vaughn

Rejected July 10th 1889

Office Commission on Citizenship
Cherokee Nation Ind. Ter.
Tahlequah July 10th 1889

The above case was called 3 several times not less than one hour apart and no response from Applicant or by Atty and there being no evidence in support of the above named case the Commission decide that Virginia M Conner age 23 yrs and her son Morman male 5 yrs are not Cherokees by blood. Post Office Whitman.

Attest   Will.P. Ross   Chairman
            J.E. Gunter   Com
   D.S. Williams
   Clerk Commission

Cherokee Citizenship Commission Docket Books
(1880-84, 1887-89) Volume III
Tahlequah, Cherokee Nation

CAGLE

DOCKET #951

CENSUS ROLLS 1835

APPLICANT FOR CHEROKEE CITIZENSHIP

POST OFFICE: Lead Hill Ark   ATTORNEY: C H Taylor

No	NAMES	AGE	SEX
1	Mary A Cagle	47	Female
2	Elizabeth Cagle	18	"
3	William Cagle	14	Male
4	C E Cagle	11	"
5	Mary B.S. Cagle	9	Female
6	Tennessee Cagle	3	"
7	Newton C Cagle	1	Male

ANCESTOR: Seba Brown

Rejected July 7th 1889

Office Commission on Citizenship
Cher Nat July 7th 1889

There being no evidence in support of the above named case the Commission decide that Mary A Cagle age 47 yrs and the following named children Elizabeth female age 18 yrs, William male age 14 yrs, C E Cagle male age 11 yrs, Mary B.S. female age 9 yrs, Tennessee female age 3 yrs, Newton Cagle age 1 yr. are not Cherokees by blood. Post Office Lead Hill Ark.

D.S. Williams   Will. P. Ross   Chairman
Clk Commission   J.E. Gunter   Com

CAGLE

DOCKET #952

CENSUS ROLLS 1835

APPLICANT FOR CHEROKEE CITIZENSHIP

POST OFFICE: Lead Hill Ark   ATTORNEY: C H Taylor

No	NAMES	AGE	SEX
1	Polly A Cagle	49	Female
2	*(Illegible)* Cagle	2?	"
3	Martha Cagle	21	"
4	Lissa Cagle	19	"

5	William Cagle	14	Male
6	C L Cagle	10	"
7	Mary B K Cagle	7	Female
8	Tennessee Cagle	4	"

ANCESTOR: Seba Brown

Rejected July 2nd 1889

Office Commission on Citizenship
Cher Nat July 2nd 1889

There being no evidence in support of the above named case the Commission decide that Polly Ann Cagle age 49 yrs and the following children, *(Illegible Name)* female age 2? yrs, Martha female age 21 yrs, Lessa female age 19 yrs, William male age 14 yrs, C.L Cagle male 10 yrs, Mary B. female age 7, Tennessee age 4 female are not Cherokees by blood.
Post Office Lead Hill Ark.

Will.P. Ross   Chairman

D.S. Williams
Clk Commission

JE Gunter   Com

CISCO

DOCKET #953

CENSUS ROLLS

APPLICANT FOR CHEROKEE CITIZENSHIP

POST OFFICE: Huntsville Ark   **ATTORNEY:** C H Taylor

NO	NAMES	AGE	SEX
1	Hugh Cisco	54	Male

ANCESTOR: John Cisco

Rejected July 18th 1889

Office Commission on Citizenship
Cherokee Nation Ind. Ter.
Tahlequah July 18th 1889

The above case was called 3 several times not less than one hour at intervals and no response from Attorney or applicant and there being no evidence in support of Application the Commission decide that Hugh Cisco age 54 yrs is not a Cherokee by blood. Post Office Huntsville Ark.

Attest   Will.P. Ross   Chairman
D.S. Williams
Clk Commission   J.E. Gunter   Com

COUCH

DOCKET #954
CENSUS ROLLS 1835

APPLICANT FOR CHEROKEE CITIZENSHIP
POST OFFICE: Vinita IT   ATTORNEY: Boudinot & R[sic]

No	NAMES	AGE	SEX
1	Thomas ? Couch	55	Male
2	O.R. Couch		
3	L C Couch		
4	N M Couch		
5	Wallis Couch		

ANCESTOR: John Watts

Commission on Citizenship.

CHEROKEE NATION, IND. TER.

Tahlequah, July 31st 1888

T. F. Couch
     vs
Cherokee Nation

       This case was before a former Commission on Citizenship, and was rejected. Applicant claims a descent from John Watts. It now comes before this Commission under a regular application *(illegible)* as a notification issued on the 26th day of May 1888, *(illegible)* to be and appears before the Commission on Citizenship in the town of Tahlequah Cherokee Nation on the 20th day of July 1888 then and there to establish his citizenship in the Cherokee Nation, where Mesr. Boudinot and Rasmus answered for Mr. Couch, the plaintiff and the case was held in abeyance awaiting further testimony.

– Summary –

On the 31st day of July of the above written year Mr Rasmus submits the case with the testimony already in. The statement of *(Illegible)* Stephen Farmer now dead, made before Hon Allen Ross, Clerk of Tahlequah Dist. Cherokee Nation in the year 1879, goes to show that he knew a John Watts in East Tennessee, and that under the time of the treaty of 1817 and 1819 the Cherokees who resided on the North side of the Hiawassee River moved to the South side and that it was after this removal that he became acquainted with John Watts, and that as well as he can, recalled John Watts was about one half blood Cherokee and that he spoke only the Cherokee language and that he had these 3 sons that lived on *(Illegible)* Creek and that the youngest of these boys Phillip *(illegible...)* and to a Missionary School with him. Mr. Farmer fails to give the names of the other two sons of John Watts and that he did not *(illegible)* whether or not John Watts had any daughters though he may have had *(remainder illegible).*

The testimony of John L McCoy taken before this Commission on March 9th 1888, shows that he too knew a John Watts, who lived 5 or 6 miles south of the Old Cherokee Agency in the state of Tennessee and that he was a recognized Cherokee by blood and that he knew him previous to the treaty of 1835, but did not know his family and that he was at that time about 60 or 65 years old and that he spoke the Cherokee language *(remainder illegible).*

The testimony of Lawrence Glaze taken before a Justice of the Peace in Barton County, state of Missouri, shows that he was acquainted with one James Couch of the County of Bedford, state of Tenn. and that his wife was Abigail Couch daughter of John Watts formerly of the state of Georgia and that Abigail Couch was recognized as a Cherokee Indian and that Thomas F. Couch is the son of James & Abigail Couch. He further says to the best of his recollection they (the Couches) were recognized as Cherokees in Ray County, Missouri, and in Bedford County, Tennessee.

Now it will be remembered that the evidence of Mr. Glaze was of an exparte nature in favor of Applicant and that it was of a hyearsay character and *(illegible...)* under the rules and *(illegible...)* submitted to the same degree of proof as evidence that has undergone a thorough and regular cross-examination by the opposite party *(illegible...)* and further it will be *(illegible)* that the testimony of Mr. Glaze was taken before an officer of the state of Missouri without a *(illegible)* which excludes it as admissible evidence under the Rules adopted by the Commission. *(Remaining illegible)*

We fail to find the name of John Watts or the name of applicant in this case, therefore decide that Thomas F Couch, O.R. Couch, L.C. Couch, N.M. Couch and Wallis Couch to be intruders upon the public domain of the

Cherokee Nation and not entitled to the rights and privileges of such by virtue of their blood.

J.T. Adair   Chairman Commission
H.C. Barnes Commissioner

CRITTENDEN

DOCKET #955
CENSUS ROLLS 1835

APPLICANT FOR CHEROKEE CITIZENSHIP

POST OFFICE: Tahlequah I.T.   ATTORNEY: Rich M Wolf

No	NAMES	AGE	SEX
1	Jane Crittenden	5?	Female
2	L E Smith	26	

ANCESTOR: Elizabeth Henson

(No other information given.)

CHAPMAN

DOCKET #956
CENSUS ROLLS 1848

APPLICANT FOR CHEROKEE CITIZENSHIP

POST OFFICE: Tahlequah I.T.   ATTORNEY: C.H. Taylor

No	NAMES	AGE	SEX
1	Victoria Chapman	16	Female

ANCESTOR: *(Illegible Name)*

Office Commission on Citizenship
Cherokee Nation Ind. Ter.
Tahlequah July 18th 1889

The above case was called three times and not less than one hour apart no response by applicant or an Atty. There being no evidence in support of the above named case, the Commission decide that Victoria Chapman age 16 yrs is not a Cherokee by blood. Post Office Tahlequah I.T.

Attest   Will.P. Ross   Chairman
    D.S. Williams
    Clerk Commission   ~~J.E. Gunter~~ Com

157

Cherokee Citizenship Commission Docket Books (1880-84, 1887-89) Volume III
Tahlequah, Cherokee Nation

ARMSTRONG

DOCKET #957

CENSUS ROLLS 1835 to 52

APPLICANT FOR CHEROKEE CITIZENSHIP

POST OFFICE: Blue Jacket IT   ATTORNEY: Boudinot & Rasmus

No	NAMES	AGE	SEX
1	Fanny Armstrong	55	Female
2	Augustus *(Illegible)* Armstrong	16	Male

ANCESTOR: Charlott Vaughn

We the Commission on Citizenship after examining the testimony in the above case, find it of a *(illegible)* nature, the law governing this Commission passed December 8th 1886 clearly states that any *(illegible...)* and in this case we fail to find the name of Charlott Vaughn the alleged ancestor of the applicant and find the testimony taken on part of the applicant *(illegible...)* they are not of Cherokee blood, therefore we do not hesitate in declaring Fanny and Augustus Armstrong intruders upon the public domain of the Cherokee Nation, nor entitled to any rights or privileges whatever in the C.N.

J.T. Adair   Chairman Commission
              Commissioner
H.C. Barnes   Commissioner

Office Com on Citizenship
Tahlequah IT *(Illegible)* 1888

DOCKET #958   *(All names illegible)*

ADAMS

DOCKET #959

CENSUS ROLLS

APPLICANT FOR CHEROKEE CITIZENSHIP

POST OFFICE: Lawrence Ill   ATTORNEY: A E Ivey

No	NAMES	AGE	SEX
1	John C Adams	33	Male

ANCESTOR: John S Denham

Rejected June 7th 1889

158

Cherokee Citizenship Commission Docket Books
(1880-84, 1887-89) Volume III
Tahlequah, Cherokee Nation

Office Commission on Citizenship
Cherokee Nation Ind. Ter.
Tahlequah June 7th 1889

The case of John C Adams was filed on the 20th day of Sept 1887 and was submitted for final action June 7th 1889 without evidence in support of application. Therefore we the Commission are of the opinion and do decide that John C Adams age 33 years is not of Cherokee blood and is not entitled to citizenship in the Cherokee nation. Post Office address Lawrence Ill.

Attest   Will.P. Ross   Chairman
    D S Williams
    Asst Clk Com
                        J.E. Gunter   Com

ASBELL

DOCKET #960
CENSUS ROLLS 1835

APPLICANT FOR CHEROKEE CITIZENSHIP

POST OFFICE: Van Buren Ark   ATTORNEY: A E Ivey

No	NAMES	AGE	SEX
1	James Ross Asbell	29	Male
2	Rachel Asbell	23	Female
3	*(Illegible Name)*	1	Male

ANCESTOR: John Asbell

Now on this the 9th day of August 1889 comes the above case for a final hearing. And submitted by agreement between the attorney for Plaintiff and the Atty on part of the Nation *(illegible...)* and submitted in the case of James Ross Asbell, Rachel Asbell, *(Illegible)* Ross Asbell, we the Commission on Citizenship after a careful and impartial *(illegible)* of the *(illegible)* & having also examined the Census Rolls of 1835 and failed to find the name of the Ancestor John Ashbell[sic]. And the evidence on behalf of applicant not being sufficient, the Commission therefore decide that the above named parties are <u>not</u> Cherokees by blood and not entitled to any of the rights or privileges of Cherokees.

                 J.T. Adair   Chairman Com
                 John E Gunter   Com
C.C. Lipe
Clk Com

ASBELL

DOCKET #961

CENSUS ROLLS 1835

APPLICANT FOR CHEROKEE CITIZENSHIP

POST OFFICE: Van Buren Ark   ATTORNEY: A E Ivey

No	NAMES	AGE	SEX
1	William G Asbell	35	Male
2	Louisanna Asbell	13	Female
3	Nancy J Asbell	11	"
4	Thomas J Asbell	7	Male

ANCESTOR: Thomas J Asbell

Rejected July 2nd 1889

Office Commission on Citizenship
Cherokee Nation Ind Ter
Tahlequah July 2nd 1889

This applicant alleges that he is the son of one Thomas J Asbell and grandson of John Asbell who was the son of John Asbell Sr and his wife Elizabeth Ross who was of Cherokee blood. The application is not sustained by evidence nor are the names of the alleged ancestors found on the census rolls of Cherokees by blood made in the year 1835 – 46 by the United States. The Commission therefore decide that the applicant Wm J. Asbell 35 yrs of age at the filing of his application, Sept. 20th 1887, is not of Cherokee descent and is not entitled to Citizenship in the Cherokee Nation. This decission[sic] includes the daughter of said applicant, to wit: Louisanna Asbell aged 13 years and Nancy Jane Asbell aged 11 years and son Thomas J Asbell aged 7 years. P.O. address Van Buren Ark.

Will.P. Ross   Chairman

Attest

DS Williams
Asst Clerk Commission   J.E. Gunter   Com

ASBELL

DOCKET #962

CENSUS ROLLS 1835

APPLICANT FOR CHEROKEE CITIZENSHIP

POST OFFICE: Van Buren Ark   ATTORNEY: A E Ivey

No	NAMES	AGE	SEX
1	J H Asbell	48	Male
2	W B Asbell	24	"
3	G W Asbell	20	"
4	Ella Asbell	18	Female
5	Manta Asbell	16	"
6	Robt Asbell	14	Male
7	James M Asbell	12	"
8	Joseph Asbell	10	"

ANCESTOR: John Azbell[sic]

Rejected July 2nd 1889

Office Commission on Citizenship
Cherokee Nation Ind Ter
Tahlequah July 2nd 1889

There being no evidence in support of the above named case the Commission decide that J.H. Asbell age 48 yrs and the following children, W.B. male age 24 yrs, G.W. male age 20 yrs, Ella female 18 yrs, Manta female age 16 yrs, Robert male age 14 yrs, James M. age 12 yrs and Joseph Asbell male age 10 yrs are not Cherokees by blood. Post Office Van Buren Ark.

Attest   Will.P. Ross   Chairman
    D.S. Williams
Asst Clerk Commission   J.E. Gunter   Com

BRAGG

DOCKET #963

CENSUS ROLLS 1835 to 52

APPLICANT FOR CHEROKEE CITIZENSHIP

POST OFFICE: Union Town Ark   ATTORNEY: A.E. Ivey

No	NAMES	AGE	SEX
1	Nancy E Bragg	25	Female
2	Virgie Bragg	2	"

ANCESTOR: John Azbell

Cherokee Citizenship Commission Docket Books (1880-84, 1887-89) Volume III
Tahlequah, Cherokee Nation

Rejected July 10th 1889

Office Commission on Citizenship
Cherokee Nation Ind Ter
Tahlequah July 10th 1889

There being no evidence in support of the above named case the Commission decide that Nancy E Bragg age 25 yrs and his[sic] daughter Virgie Bragg, Female age 2 are not Cherokees by blood. Post Office Union Town Ark.

Attest   Will.P. Ross   Chairman
     DS Williams
     Clerk Commission   J.E. Gunter   Com

BLACKWELL

DOCKET #964
CENSUS ROLLS 1835 to 52

APPLICANT FOR CHEROKEE CITIZENSHIP

POST OFFICE: Baxter Springs Kan   **ATTORNEY:** Boudinot & R[sic]

NO	NAMES	AGE	SEX
1	Martha Blackwell	42	Female
2	Roger Blackwell	15	Male
3	Julia Blackwell	14	Female
4	Lewis Blackwell	13	Male
5	Susie Blackwell	12	Female
6	Henrietta Blackwell	11	"
7	Jacob Blackwell	7	Male
8	Garfield Blackwell	5	"
9	Charley Blackwell	3	"
10	George Blackwell	6 mo	"

ANCESTOR: Marshal & Robt Lewis

Office Commission on Citizenship
Cherokee Nation Ind. Ter.
Tahlequah August 14th 1889

The applicant in the above case alleges that she is the daughter of one Marshall Lewis and grand daughter of Robt Lewis who is said to have been a full blood Cherokee. The statement of Marshall Lewis who represented that he was about seventy five years of age in 1887 shows that he once belonged to W C

Simms of Kentucky and there is no certificate of credibility attached by Clerk of the County before whom his affidavit was taken nor to that of one *(Illegible)* Harrington who swears that the father of Marshall Lewis was an Indian of the Cherokee tribe and that Martha Blackwell is a native of an Indian tribe without stating the source of his information. The person named at no time resided in the Cherokee Nation nor or[sic] their names found on the rolls of Cherokees by blood referred to in the declaration of applicant. The Commission therefore decide that Martha Blackwell aged 42 yrs and her sons Roger aged 15 yrs, Lewis 13 yrs, Jacob 7 yrs, Garfield 5 yrs, Charley 3 yrs, George 6 months, and daughters Julia 14 yrs, Susie 12 yrs and Henrietta 11 yrs are not of Cherokee blood and not entitled to citizenship in the Cherokee Nation.

Attest   Will.P.Ross   Chairman

     E G Ross

         Clerk Com   J.E. Gunter   Com

BROWN

DOCKET #965

CENSUS ROLLS 1835

APPLICANT FOR CHEROKEE CITIZENSHIP

POST OFFICE: McKinney Texas   ATTORNEY: Wm A Thompson

No	NAMES	AGE	SEX
1	John F Brown		Male
2	Harry Brown	8	"
3	Lucy Brown	5	Female
4	Thomas Brown	3	Male
5	Richard Brown	6 mo	"

ANCESTOR: Geo McGarrah

Rejected June 26th 1889

Office Commission on Citizenship
Cherokee Nation
Tahlequah June 26th 1889

There being no evidence in support of the above named case the Commission decide that John F Brown and his children Harry male age 8 years, Lucy female age 5 years, Thomas male 3 years and Richard Brown male age 6 months are not Cherokees by blood. Post Office McKinney Texas.

Will.P. Ross   Chairman

Attest

    D.S. Williams
    Asst Clk Com   J.E. Gunter   Com

DICK

DOCKET #966

CENSUS ROLLS 1835

APPLICANT FOR CHEROKEE CITIZENSHIP

POST OFFICE: Spiceland Ind   ATTORNEY: L.B. Bell

No	NAMES	AGE	SEX
1	Nancy ? Dick	55	Female

ANCESTOR: Martha Elmore

Adversely

    The Commission decide against claimant
    See decision in case Lible J Bogue Docket
    2183 Book E. Page 29.

Attest

    D S Williams
Asst Clk. Com

DAVIS

DOCKET #967

CENSUS ROLLS

APPLICANT FOR CHEROKEE CITIZENSHIP

POST OFFICE: Decatur Texas   ATTORNEY: C H Taylor

No	NAMES	AGE	SEX
1	Sarah J Davis	65	Female

ANCESTOR: William Taylor

Rejected July 10th 1889

    Office Commission on Citizenship
    Cherokee Nation Ind Ter
    Tahlequah July 10th 1889

The above case was called three times not less that one hour apart and no response by Applicant or by Atty. and there being no evidence in support of the above named case the Commission decide that Sarah J Davis age 65 yrs is not a Cherokee by blood. Post Office Decatur Tex.

Attest   Will.P. Ross   Chairman
D S Williams
Clerk Commission   J.E. Gunter   Com

DRAKE

DOCKET #968
CENSUS ROLLS

APPLICANT FOR CHEROKEE CITIZENSHIP

POST OFFICE: Saint Louis Mo   **ATTORNEY:** L.B. Bell

No	NAMES	AGE	SEX
1	Frances C Drake		Female

ANCESTOR: Sarah Morgan

Rejected July 10th 1889

Office Commission on Citizenship
Cherokee Nation Ind Ter
Tahlequah July 10th 1889

The above named case was called three several times not less than one hour apart and no response from applicant or by Attorney. There being no evidence in support of the above named case the Commission decide that Frances C Drake is not a Cherokee by blood. Post Office St. Louis Mo

Attest
DS Williams   Will.P. Ross   Chairman
Clerk Commission   J.E. Gunter   Com

DICK

DOCKET #969
CENSUS ROLLS

APPLICANT FOR CHEROKEE CITIZENSHIP

POST OFFICE: Spiceland Ind   **ATTORNEY:** L.B. Bell

No	NAMES	AGE	SEX
1	Allen C Dick	27	Male

ANCESTOR: Martha Elmore

The Commission decide against claimant. See decision in case Lible J Bogue Docket 2183 Book E Page 29   Will.P. Ross   Chairman
           J.E. Gunter   Com

Cherokee Citizenship Commission Docket Books
(1880-84, 1887-89) Volume III
Tahlequah, Cherokee Nation

DOCKET #969   *(All names illegible)*

DOWNING

DOCKET #970

CENSUS ROLLS

APPLICANT FOR CHEROKEE CITIZENSHIP

POST OFFICE: Lane Kansas   ATTORNEY: L.B. Bell

No	NAMES	AGE	SEX
1	Sarah E Downing	25	Female

ANCESTOR: Martha Elmore

The Commission decide against claimant. See decision in
case Lible J Bogue Docket 2183 Book E Page 29.

Will.P. Ross   Chairman
J.E. Gunter   Com

DAVIS

DOCKET #971

CENSUS ROLLS 1835

APPLICANT FOR CHEROKEE CITIZENSHIP

POST OFFICE: McKinney Tex   ATTORNEY: W A Thompson

No	NAMES	AGE	SEX
1	Wm Davis	23	Male

ANCESTOR: Abigile *(Illegible)*

Rejected July 10th 1889

Office Commission on Citizenship
Cherokee Nation Ind. Ter.
Tahlequah July 10th 1889

The above case was called three several times not less than one hour apart and
no response by applicant or by Attorney. There being no evidence in support of
the above named case the Commission decide that Wm Davis age 23 yrs is not a
Cherokee by blood. Post Office McKinney Tex.

166

Cherokee Citizenship Commission Docket Books
(1880-84, 1887-89) Volume III
Tahlequah, Cherokee Nation

Will.P. Ross

Attest

Chairman

D.S. Williams

R. Bunch   Com

Clerk Commission

J.E. Gunter   Com

DOWELL

DOCKET #972

CENSUS ROLLS 1835 to 52

APPLICANT FOR CHEROKEE CITIZENSHIP

POST OFFICE: Lowell Kansas   ATTORNEY: Boudinot & Rasmus

No	NAMES	AGE	SEX
1	Geo M Dowell		

ANCESTOR: John Tomberlin

Office Commission on Citizenship
Cherokee Nation Ind Ter
Tahlequah Sept 16th 1889

The Commission decide against the claimant to citizenship in the Cherokee Nation in the above case. George Martin Dowell and his children whose names are not given for reasons set fourth in their opinion in the case of Reuben H Dowell Docket 973 Book C Page 100. PO Lowell Kansas

Attest

Will.P. Ross   Chairman

E.G. Ross

R Bunch   Com

Clerk Commission

J.E. Gunter   Com

DOWELL

DOCKET #973

CENSUS ROLLS 1835 to 52

APPLICANT FOR CHEROKEE CITIZENSHIP

POST OFFICE: Lowell Kansas   ATTORNEY: Boudinot &

No	NAMES	AGE	SEX
1	Reuben H Dowell		Male

ANCESTOR:

Cherokee Citizenship Commission Docket Books
(1880-84, 1887-89) Volume III
Tahlequah, Cherokee Nation

Office Commission on Citizenship
Cherokee Nation Ind. Ter.
Tahlequah Sept 16th 1889

The application in the above case was filed on the 4th day of October, 1887, *(illegible...)* that the applicant is the Grand son of one John Tomberlin the name he believes was enrolled on the Census rolls of Cherokees by blood taken and made in the United States in the years 1835, 48, 51, 52. In his declaration taken before J.H. Whitcraft, Clerk of the District Court Cherokee County State of Kansas on the 2nd day of February A.D. 1884, he swears that he is of Cherokee Indian descent. That he was 35 years old and was born in Madison County State of Alabama, that he is the son of one May Dowell who was born in the Cherokee Nation in 1796 and died in Muscatine County Iowa the 19th December 1856 and that she was the reported daughter of one John Tomberline born in the Cherokee Nation in 1767 and died *(illegible)* in 1849 and that he was of Cherokee Indian descent. George M Dowell age 44 years supports this *(illegible)* the same time and place by an <u>exparte</u> affidavit as does James A Dowell age 50 years before W J Benhoul Clerk District Court Scott County State of Iowa on the 24th day of March 1884. Geo M Dowell is also an applicant for admission to Citizenship in the Cherokee Nation and James A Dowell the other witness is presumably also one of the same *(illegible)*. And from this circumstance it will be sure that the mother and Grand ~~Mother~~ Father of claimant were living at the date of the taking of the census of Cherokees in 1835 the mother at the date of 1848-52 and that the applicant himself was born in the year *(illegible...)* yet neither of their names are found on the rolls of 1835-48-25. The Commission therefore decide that Reuben H Dowell is *(illegible...)* entitled to Citizenship in the Cherokee Nation by virtue of Cherokee Indian descent nor are his descendants as *(illegible...)* his declaration of Febuary[sic] 2nd 1884 to wit, *(Illegible Name)* 33 years, Sarah A Cooper 31 years, Wm H Dowell 29 years, *(Illegible)* Dowell 24 years, Stephen N Dowell 22 years, Benjamin C Dowell 20 years, Nancy B Stroud 17 years, Cora *(Illegible...)* years and Charles B Dowell ? years. P.O. Lowell Kansas.

Attest   Will P Ross
   E.G. Ross   Chairman
     Clerk Commission
               J.E. Gunter   Com

Cherokee Citizenship Commission Docket Books
(1880-84, 1887-89) Volume III
Tahlequah, Cherokee Nation

DUDLEY

DOCKET #974
CENSUS ROLLS

APPLICANT FOR CHEROKEE CITIZENSHIP

POST OFFICE: Hensville[sic] Ark.   ATTORNEY: C H Taylor

No	NAMES	Age	Sex
1	William A Dudley	27	Male
2	Hattie Dudley	4	Female
3	James B Dudley	1	Male

ANCESTOR: Nancy Woodall

Rejected July 2nd 1889

Office Commission on Citizenship
Cher Nat July 2nd 1889

There being no evidence in support of the above named case the Commission decide that William A Dudley age 27 yrs and the following named children, Hattie female age 4 yrs and James B Dudley male age 1 yrs[sic] are not Cherokees by blood. Post Office Hensville Ark.

Attest

D.S. Williams
Asst Clerk Com

J.E. Gunter   Com

DOCKET #975   *(All names illegible)*

DICKEY

DOCKET #976
CENSUS ROLLS 1835 to 52

APPLICANT FOR CHEROKEE CITIZENSHIP

POST OFFICE: Fayetteville Ark   ATTORNEY: Boudinot & Rasmus

No	NAMES	Age	Sex
1	Myra Dickey	30	Female
2	Carey Dickey	9	Male
3	Aura L Dickey	7	Female
4	Melvin Dickey	4	Male
5	Daisy *(Illegible)* Dickey	2	Female

ANCESTOR: Reuben Bradley

169

Cherokee Citizenship Commission Docket Books
(1880-84, 1887-89) Volume III
Tahlequah, Cherokee Nation

Office Commission on Citizenship
Cherokee Nation Ind Ter
Tahlequah Sept 10th 1889

The above case was called three times and no response from Applicant or by Attorney and there being no evidence on file in support of claim the Commission decide that Myra Dickey age 30 years and her children whose names are as follows Carey male age 9 years, Aura L Dickey female age 7 years, Melvin age 4 years and Daisey Dickey female age 2 years are not Cherokees by blood. Post Office Fayetteville Ark.

Attest   Will.P. Ross
     E G Ross   Chairman
         Clerk Commission   R. Bunch   Com
                            J.E. Gunter   Com

DOCKET #977   *(All names illegible)*

DANIEL

DOCKET #978
CENSUS ROLLS

APPLICANT FOR CHEROKEE CITIZENSHIP

POST OFFICE: Siloam Spgs Ark   **ATTORNEY:** C.H. Taylor

NO	NAMES	AGE	SEX
1	William H Daniel	33	Male

ANCESTOR: John Daniel

Commission on Citizenship.

CHEROKEE NATION, IND. TER.

Tahlequah,   August 21st 1889

Wm H. Daniel
     vs   Application for Cherokee Citizenship
The Cherokee Nation

            In the above case the applicant alleges that he is the son of one John Daniel but fails to state on what roll his own name or that of an ancestor ~~may be found~~ of Cherokee by blood taken and made by the United

170

States ~~of~~ if upon other in the year 1835 48 51 52 or Old Settler roll of 1851. The only evidence in the case is that of one Charles Smith taken before this Commission on July 2nd 1889. Smith swears that he is 68 years old and lives in Delaware District, Cherokee Nation, that he is acquainted with applicant and knew his father and grand Father ~~of~~ in Granger County, state of Tennessee, John Daniel *(illegible)* from Tennessee in 1846 or 1847 and *(Illegible)* in 1848 and went to Kentucky, he *(illegible)* John Daniel *(illegible...)* but understood that he died in Arkansas about 16 yrs ago. John Daniel was the son of Wm Daniel who *(illegible...)* in Tennessee when he went to Kentucky but never saw him afterwards nor did he see applicant until six or seven years ago when he got acquainted with him. He does not know whether applicant *(illegible)* Cherokee funds or enjoyed other Cherokee rights and *(illegible...)* This evidence does not *(illegible)* the Cherokee blood of applicant and where taken in connection with the fact that ~~he~~ it is not alleged that their names appear on the rolls referred to in Sec 7 of the Act of Dec 8 1886 defining the jurisdiction of this Commission and that he has not attempted to establish his connection with the *(illegible ...)* duty of the Commission to decide as they now do, that claimant is not of Cherokee blood and is not entitled to citizenship in the Cherokee Nation.

Will.P. Ross

Chairman

John E. Gunter   Com

DOCKET #979   *(All names illegible)*

DANIEL

DOCKET #980

CENSUS ROLLS

APPLICANT FOR CHEROKEE CITIZENSHIP

POST OFFICE: Maysville Ark   ATTORNEY: C.H. Taylor

No	NAMES	AGE	SEX
1	Daniel P Daniel	27	Male
2	Fielding A Daniel	2	"
3	Virgie W Daniel	10 mo	Female

ANCESTOR: John Daniel

Cherokee Citizenship Commission Docket Books (1880-84, 1887-89) Volume III
Tahlequah, Cherokee Nation

Office Commission on Citizenship
Cherokee Nation Ind. Ter.
Tahlequah Sept 10th 1889

The above named applicant was called three times and no answer and there being no evidence on file in support of the application we decide that Daniel P Daniel age 27 years. Fielding A Daniel age 2 years and Virgie Daniel age 10 months are not Cherokees by blood. Post Office Maysville Ark.

Attest   Will.P. Ross
   E G Ross   Chairman
     Clerk commission
                                          J.E. Gunter   Com

DOCKET #981   *(All names illegible)*

DOCKET #982   *(All names illegible)*

DREW

DOCKET #983
CENSUS ROLLS 1835

APPLICANT FOR CHEROKEE CITIZENSHIP

POST OFFICE: McKinney Tex   ATTORNEY: W.A. Thompson

No	NAMES	AGE	SEX
1	W.D. Drew	39	Male
2	Tilla Drew	9	"
3	Clide Drew	3	"

ANCESTOR: Jack McGarrah

Office Commission on Citizenship
Cherokee Nation
Tahlequah   June 26th 1889

There being no evidence in support of the above named case the Commission decide that W.D. Drew age 39 years and Tilla Drew age 9 years and Clide Drew male age 3 years are not Cherokees by blood. Post Office McKinney Texas.

172

Attest

D.S. Williams
Clerk Commission

Will.P. Ross
Chairman

J.E. Gunter   Com

DRAKE

DOCKET #984

CENSUS ROLLS   1835

APPLICANT FOR CHEROKEE CITIZENSHIP

POST OFFICE: Tahlequah C.N.   ATTORNEY: C.H. Taylor

No	NAMES	AGE	SEX
1	William H Drake	25	Male
2	James W Drake	6 mo	"

ANCESTOR: Mary Ray

See Decision in this case in the Sidney R. *(Illegible)* case on Book "D" page 455, Docket 1969 – adverse

Cornell Rogers
Clerk Com on Citizenship

July 28th 1888 –

DUNBAR

DOCKET #985

CENSUS ROLLS   1835

APPLICANT FOR CHEROKEE CITIZENSHIP

POST OFFICE: Dardanelle Ark   ATTORNEY: Boudinot &

No	NAMES	AGE	SEX
1	J Henrietta Dunbar	22	Female

ANCESTOR: Bashaba Goodrich

Office Commission on Citizenship
Tahlequah C.N.   June 20th 1889

There being no evidence in support of the above named case the Commission decide that J Henrietta Dunbar age 22 years is not a Cherokee by blood. Post Office Dardanelle Ark.

Attest

    E.G. Ross

        Clerk Commission   Will.P. Ross

                                             Chairman

                             J.E. Gunter   Com

DUNBAR

DOCKET #986

CENSUS ROLLS 1835

APPLICANT FOR CHEROKEE CITIZENSHIP

POST OFFICE: Dardanelle Ark   ATTORNEY: Boudinot & Rasmus

No	NAMES	AGE	SEX
1	Stella B Dunbar	27	Female

ANCESTOR: Bashaba Goodrich

Office Commission on Citizenship

Tahlequah June 20th 1889

There being no evidence in support of the above named case the Commission decide that Stella B Dunbar age 27 years is not of Cherokee blood.

Attest

    E.G. Ross

        Clerk Commission   Will.P. Ross

                                             Chairman

                             J.E. Gunter Com

DUNBAR

DOCKET #987

CENSUS ROLLS 1835

APPLICANT FOR CHEROKEE CITIZENSHIP

POST OFFICE: Dardanelle Ark   ATTORNEY: Boudinot &

No	NAMES	AGE	SEX
1	James T Dunbar	23	Male

ANCESTOR: Bashaba Goodrich

Cherokee Citizenship Commission Docket Books
(1880-84, 1887-89) Volume III
Tahlequah, Cherokee Nation

Office Commission on Citizenship
Tahlequah June 20th 1889

There being no evidence in support of the above named case the Commission decide that James T Dunbar aged 23 years is not a Cherokee by blood.

Attest

E.G. Ross
Clerk commission

Will.P. Ross
Chairman
J.E. Gunter   Com

DESHAZO

DOCKET #988

CENSUS ROLLS 1835

APPLICANT FOR CHEROKEE CITIZENSHIP

POST OFFICE: Vinita Ind Tery   ATTORNEY: B.H. Stone

No	NAMES	AGE	SEX
1	Mary A Deshazo	40	Female
2	George Deshazo		
3	Elizabeth Deshazo		
4	Thomas Deshazo		
5	Willie Deshazo		
6	Charley Deshazo		
7	Tevins *(Blank)*		

ANCESTOR: Martin Many

Office Commission on Citizenship
Cherokee Nation Ind. Ter
Tahlequah June 18th 1889

There being no evidence in support of the above named case the Commission decide that Nancy[sic] A Deshazo age 40 years and the following named children, George, Elizabeth, Thomas, Willie, Charles, Tevins Deshazo are not of Cherokee blood.

Cherokee Citizenship Commission Docket Books
(1880-84, 1887-89) Volume III
Tahlequah, Cherokee Nation

Attest

EG Ross
    Clerk Commission

Will.P. Ross
    Chairman

R. Bunch   Com

J.E. Gunter   Com

DOCKET #989   *(All names illegible)*

DOLY

DOCKET #990

CENSUS ROLLS 1835

APPLICANT FOR CHEROKEE CITIZENSHIP

POST OFFICE: Echo I.T.   ATTORNEY: C.H. Taylor

No	NAMES	AGE	SEX
1	Eliza Ann Doly	38	Female
2	Geo W Doley[sic]	15	Male
3	Ed J Doly	8	"
4	Maud Doley[sic]	10	Female

ANCESTOR: Samuel Parks

Office Commission on Citizenship
Cherokee Nation Ind. Ter.
Tahlequah Sept 16th 1889

The above case was called three times and no response from applicant or by Attorney and there being no evidence on file in support of the above Claim the Commission decide that Eliza Ann Doly age 38 years and her children whose names are as follows George W Doly age 15 years, Ed J Doly age 8 years, Maud Doly age 10 years are not Cherokees by blood. Post Office Echo I.T.

Attest

E G Ross
    Clerk Commission

Will.P. Ross
    Chairman

J.E. Gunter   Com

DOCKET #991   *(All names illegible)*

DEMORE

DOCKET #992

CENSUS ROLLS 1835

APPLICANT FOR CHEROKEE CITIZENSHIP

POST OFFICE: Bois De Ark Mo   **ATTORNEY:** A E Ivey

No	NAMES	AGE	SEX
1	Eliza Demore	24	Female

ANCESTOR: Silas Helton

Commission on Citizenship
Cherokee Nation Ind. Ter.
Tahlequah Sept 16th 1889

The above case having been called three times and there being no evidence in support of the allegation as set up by applicant, the Commission decide that Eliza Demore age 24 years is not of Cherokee blood and not entitled to Cherokee Citizenship. Post Office Bois De Ark, Mo

Attest

E.G. Ross
    Clerk Commission

Will.P. Ross
        Chairman
R. Bunch   Com
J.E. Gunter   Com

DEAN

DOCKET #993

CENSUS ROLLS 1835

APPLICANT FOR CHEROKEE CITIZENSHIP

POST OFFICE: Alma Ark   **ATTORNEY:**

No	NAMES	AGE	SEX
1	Maudda J Dean	22	Female
2	Edgar Dean	2½	Male
3	*(Illegible)* Dean	1	"

ANCESTOR: Joseph Williams

Office Commission on Citizenship
Cherokee Nation Ind. Ter.
Tahlequah Sept 10th 1889

This case having been submitted without evidence by the Attorneys the Commission decide that Maudda J Dean age twenty two years and her children Edgar Dean age 2½ years and Freo Dean age one year are not Cherokees by blood. Post Office Alma Ark.

Attest   Will.P. Ross

     E G Ross   Chairman

         Clerk Commission   R. Bunch   Com

                               J.E. Gunter   Com

DUPREE

DOCKET #994

CENSUS ROLLS 1835

APPLICANT FOR CHEROKEE CITIZENSHIP

POST OFFICE: Mineola Texas   ATTORNEY: A.E. Ivey

No	NAMES	AGE	SEX
1	Charlott Dupree	65	Female
2	Emma J Gray	33	"
3	Wm Dupree	30	
4	Lela Dupree	25	

ANCESTOR: John Bell

Office Commission on Citizenship
Cherokee Nation Ind Ter
Tahlequah Sept 10th 1889

The applicant in the above case having established the facts that she is the daughter of John Bell and his wife Charlotte Bell nee Charlotte Adair from the latter of whom she derives her Cherokee blood and that she is the Sister of James M Bell and Aunt of L.B. Bell of Delaware and that the names of John Bell and family appears on the census rolls of Cherokees by blood taken and made by the United States in the year 1835 is hereby declared to be of Cherokee blood and readmitted to the rights of Citizenship in the Cherokee Nation together with her children Emma J Gray nee Dupree 33 years old, Lela Dupree 25 years old and William Dupree 30 years old. Post Office Mineola Texas.

Will P Ross

Attest

                               Chairman

     E G Ross   J E Gunter   Com

         Clerk Com

DAY

DOCKET #995
CENSUS ROLLS 1835

APPLICANT FOR CHEROKEE CITIZENSHIP

POST OFFICE: Alma Ark **ATTORNEY:** Ivey & Welch

No	NAMES	AGE	SEX
1	Mattie Day	26	Female

ANCESTOR: *(Illegible)* Moton

Commission on Citizenship
Cherokee Nation Ind Ter
Tahlequah Sept 10th 1889

This case having been submitted by the Attorneys without evidence the Commission decide that Mattie Day age 26 years and her child name not given are not Cherokees by blood and not entitled to Cherokee Citizenship. Post Office Alma Ark.

Will P Ross

Attest
Chairman

E G Ross
J E Gunter Com

Clerk Commission

DUDLEY

DOCKET #996
CENSUS ROLLS 1835 to 52

APPLICANT FOR CHEROKEE CITIZENSHIP

POST OFFICE: Evansville Ark **ATTORNEY:** A E Ivey

No	NAMES	AGE	SEX
1	Martha Dudley	44	Female
2	Robt E Dudley	13	
3	John R Dudley	11	
4	Florence F Dudley	9	
5	Henry A Dudley	4	
6	Andrew Lenox	23	

ANCESTOR: Nathaniel Parris

179

Office Commission on Citizenship
Cherokee Nation Ind Ter
Tahlequah Sept 10th 1889

This case having been submitted by Attorney without evidence the Commission decide that Martha Dudley age 44 years and her children Robt E age 13 years, John R age 11 years, Florence F age 9 years, Henry A age 4 years. Andrew Lenox Dudley age 23 years are not Cherokees by blood and not entitled to Citizenship. PO Evansville Ark.

Attest

E G Ross   Will P Ross
    Clerk Commission   Chairman
                         J E Gunter   Com

DAY

DOCKET #997
CENSUS ROLLS 1835 to 52

APPLICANT FOR CHEROKEE CITIZENSHIP
POST OFFICE: Alma Ark   ATTORNEY: A E Ivey

NO	NAMES	AGE	SEX
1	Martha Day	30	Female
2	Alma G Day	4	"
3	Robt Day	1	Male

ANCESTOR: Andrew Morton

Office Commission on Citizenship
Cherokee Nation Ind Ter
Tahlequah Sept 10th 1889

The above applicant was called three times and no answer and there being no evidence on file in support of the application we decide that applicant Martha Day age 30 years and children Alma G Day age 4 years and Robt Day age 1 year are not Cherokees by blood. P O Alma Ark.

Attest   Will P. Ross
    E G Ross   Chairman
        Clerk Commission   J E Gunter   Com

DANGUE

DOCKET #998

CENSUS ROLLS 1835

APPLICANT FOR CHEROKEE CITIZENSHIP

POST OFFICE: Alma Ark   ATTORNEY: A E Ivey

No	NAMES	AGE	SEX
1	Jane E Dangue	27	Female
2	Mary Dangue	8	"
3	Thomas Dangue	6	Male
4	S L Dangue	4	Female

ANCESTOR: John Hall

Rejected Sept 10th 1889

Office Commission on Citizenship

Cherokee Nation Ind Ter

Tahlequah September 10th 1889

The above applicant was called 3 times & no answer. There being no evidence on file in support of the application we decide that the applicant Jane E Dangue age 27 years and children Nancy[sic] Dangue age 8 yrs, Thomas W Dangue age 6 yrs, S L Dangue age 4 yrs are not Cherokees by blood & there are hereby rejected. P O Alma Ark.

Will P Ross

Attest   Chairman

D S Williams   John E Gunter

Asst Clk Com   Commissioner

DOCKET #999   *(All names illegible)*

DRAKE

DOCKET #1000

CENSUS ROLLS 1835

APPLICANT FOR CHEROKEE CITIZENSHIP

POST OFFICE: Benjamin Tex   ATTORNEY: E A Ivey[sic]

No	NAMES	AGE	SEX
1	J T F Drake		female

ANCESTOR: Nancy Henford

Cherokee Citizenship Commission Docket Books
(1880-84, 1887-89) Volume III
Tahlequah, Cherokee Nation

Office Commission on Citizenship
Cherokee Nation Ind Ter
Tahlequah Sept 10th 1889

The above case was called three times and no response from applicant or by Attorney and there being no evidence on file in support of the above named claim the Commission decide that J T F Drake female is not a Cherokee by blood. Post Office Benjamin Tex.

Attest

E G Ross   Will P Ross
    Clerk Commission   Chairman
                                      J E Gunter   Com

DOCKET #1001   *(All names illegible)*

DOCKET #1002   *(All names illegible)*

DOCKET #1003   *(All names illegible)*

DARLEY

DOCKET #1004
CENSUS ROLLS 1835 to 52

APPLICANT FOR CHEROKEE CITIZENSHIP

POST OFFICE: Belmont Tex   ATTORNEY: A E Ivey

No	NAMES	AGE	SEX
1	J C Darley	21	Male
2	Wm J J Darley	1	"

ANCESTOR: John Rogers

Now on this the 17th day of March 1888, comes the above case for a final hearing. The parties having made application pursuant to the provisions of an Act of the National Council approved December 8th 1886. And all the evidence being duly examined and found to be insufficient and unsatisfactory it is adjudged and declared by the Commission that

Cherokee Citizenship Commission Docket Books
(1880-84, 1887-89) Volume III
Tahlequah, Cherokee Nation

J C Darley and William J.J. Darley are not Cherokees and are <u>not</u> entitled to the rights and privileges and immunities of Cherokee citizens by blood.

J.T. Adair	Chairman Commission
John E Gunter	Commissioner
D W Lipe	Commissioner

Attest

C C Lipe

Clerk Com

The decision in the James C C Rogers case found in Book C, page 627, and testimony on Journal pages 325 to 333 governs this case.

DOCKET #1005   *(All names illegible)*

DUREE

DOCKET #1006

CENSUS ROLLS 1835 to 52

APPLICANT FOR CHEROKEE CITIZENSHIP

POST OFFICE: Claremore IT   ATTORNEY: A E Ivey

No	NAMES	AGE	SEX
1	John W Duree[sic]	35	Male

ANCESTOR: Bradson

Commission on Citizenship

Cherokee Nation I T

Tahlequah Sept 10th 1889

The above applicant was called three times and no answer and there being no evidence on file in support of the application we decide that John W Duncan age 35 years is <u>not</u> a Cherokee by blood. Post Office Claremore I T

Attest

E G Ross

Clerk Commission

Will P Ross

Chairman

J E Gunter   Com

183

DOCKET #1007   *(All names illegible)*

DUREE

DOCKET #1008

CENSUS ROLLS 1835 to 52

APPLICANT FOR CHEROKEE CITIZENSHIP

POST OFFICE: Claremore I T   ATTORNEY: A E Ivey

No	NAMES	AGE	SEX
1	Lorenzo Duree	22	Male
2	Lillie Duree	1	

ANCESTOR: Mrs Badson

Office Commission on Citizenship
Cherokee Nation Ind Ter
Tahlequah Sept 10th 1889

This case having been submitted by the Attorneys without evidence the Commission decide that Lonzo[sic] Duren[sic] age 22 years and Lillie Duren age 1 year are not Cherokees by blood and <u>not</u> entitled to Cherokee Citizenship. Post Office Claremore I T.

Attest

E G Ross   Will P Ross
    Clerk Commission   Chairman
                          J E Gunter   Com

DOCKET #1009   *(All names illegible)*

Cherokee Citizenship Commission Docket Books
(1880-84, 1887-89) Volume III
Tahlequah, Cherokee Nation

DUREE

DOCKET #1010

CENSUS ROLLS 1835 to 52

APPLICANT FOR CHEROKEE CITIZENSHIP

POST OFFICE: Claremore I T   ATTORNEY: A E Ivey

No	NAMES	AGE	SEX
1	Thomas Duree	35	Male
2	Mena Duree	9	Female

ANCESTOR: Mrs Badson

Office Commission on Citizenship
Cherokee Nation Ind Ter
Tahlequah Sept 10th 1889

This case having been submitted by the Attorneys without evidence the Commission decide that Thomas Duren[sic] age 35 years and his child Mena Duren are not Cherokees by blood and not entitled to Cherokee Citizenship. Post Office Claremore I T

Attest

E G Ross
Clerk Commission

Will P. Ross
Chairman
R Bunch   Com
J E Gunter Com

DOCKET #1011   *(All names illegible)*

DUNBAR

DOCKET #1012

CENSUS ROLLS 1835

APPLICANT FOR CHEROKEE CITIZENSHIP

POST OFFICE: Montague Texas   ATTORNEY: Boudinot & Rasmus

No	NAMES	AGE	SEX
1	Thomas G Dunbar	44	Male
2	Chas H Dunbar	19	"
3	Hattie C Dunbar	16	Female
4	Edgar D Dunbar	10	Male
5	Lulu M Dunbar	6	Female
6	Salma C Dunbar	2	"

ANCESTOR: Bashaba Goodrich

185

Cherokee Citizenship Commission Docket Books
(1880-84, 1887-89) Volume III
Tahlequah, Cherokee Nation

Rejected June 20th 1889

Office Commission on Citizenship
Cherokee Nation Ind Ter
Tahlequah June 20th 1889

There being no evidence in support of the above named case the Commission decide that Thomas G Dunbar age 44 yrs and the following named children, Charley H male age 19 yrs, Hattie C Female age 16 years, Edgar D male 10 years, Lulu M Female age 6 years and Salma C Dunbar Female age 2 years are not Cherokees by blood. Post Office Montague Texas.

Will P Ross

Attest

Chairman

D S Williams
Asst Clk Com

R Bunch   Com
J E Gunter   Com

DOCKET #1013   *(All names illegible)*

DUNCAN

DOCKET #1014
CENSUS ROLLS 1835 to 52

APPLICANT FOR CHEROKEE CITIZENSHIP

POST OFFICE: Prairie City I T   ATTORNEY: L.B. Bell

No	NAMES	AGE	SEX
1	Samantha Duncan	37	Female

ANCESTOR: David Harlow

We the Commission on Citizenship after careful examination of the testimony in the above case *(illegible...)* Act of December 8th 1886, find the name of David Harlow, who is *(illegible...)* was the grandfather of Samantha Duncan *(illegible...)* the Commission declare that Samantha Duncan is a Cherokee by blood and entitled to all the rights and privileges of Cherokee citizens by blood.

J.T. Adair   Chairman Commission
H.C. Barnes Commissioner

Office Com on Citizenship
Tahlequah IT Oct 8th 1888

186

DOCKET #1015   *(All names illegible)*

DAVIS

DOCKET #1016
CENSUS ROLLS 1835 to 1852

APPLICANT FOR CHEREKEE CITIZENSHIP

POST OFFICE: Emmett IT   ATTORNEY: Boudinot & Rasmus

No	NAMES	AGE	SEX
1	Vian Davis	45	Female

ANCESTOR: Moton

Office Commission on Citizenship
Cherokee Nation Ind Ter
Tahlequah August 28th 1889

The above case was called and submitted by Attorney Rasmus without evidence. The Commission decide that Vian Davis age 45 years is <u>not</u> a Cherokee by blood and <u>not</u> entitled to citizenship in the Cherokee Nation.

Attest   Will P Ross
    E G Ross   Chairman
         Clerk Commission   JE Gunter   Com

DOCKET #1017   *(All names illegible)*

DAWSON

DOCKET #1018
CENSUS ROLLS 1835 to 1852

APPLICANT FOR CHEREKEE CITIZENSHIP

POST OFFICE: Bowie Texas   ATTORNEY: Boudinot & Rasmus

No	NAMES	AGE	SEX
1	Mary Dawson	54	Female
2	Walter Dawson	18	Male

ANCESTOR:

Cherokee Citizenship Commission Docket Books
(1880-84, 1887-89) Volume III
Tahlequah, Cherokee Nation

Office Commission on Citizenship
Cherokee Nation Ind Ter
Tahlequah Aug 28th 1889

The above case having been submitted by Wm Rasmus Attorney for claimant without evidence, the Commission decide that Mary Dawson aged 54 years and her son Walter Dawson aged 18 years are <u>not</u> of Cherokee blood. Post Office Bowie Texas.

Attest   Will P Ross

    EG Ross   Chairman

        Clerk Commission   JE Gunter   Com

DUNCAN

DOCKET #1019
CENSUS ROLLS

APPLICANT FOR CHEROKEE CITIZENSHIP

POST OFFICE: Cherokee City Ark   ATTORNEY: L S Sanders

No	NAMES	AGE	SEX
1	Rachel A Duncan	41	Female
2	William H Duncan	19	Male
3	Charles Marion Duncan	17	"
4	James Thomas Duncan	16	"
5	Jesse Albert Duncan	14	"
6	Joseph C Duncan	12	"
7	Nancy May Duncan	11	Female
8	Emma Bettie Duncan	9	"
9	Ida Lucinda Duncan	7	"
10	Liza Ermin Duncan	6	
11	Willie Benj Duncan	3	Male

ANCESTOR: Nancy Copeland

Office Commission on Citizenship
Cherokee Nation Ind Ter
Tahlequah June 6th 1889

The application in the above case is supported by the affidavits of Mary Albert aged 38 years and Eliza J Mark age 53 years of Benton Co Ark and who testify as of their own knowledge concerning the geneology[sic] of the applicant of which it does not appear they could have known anything except by

Cherokee Citizenship Commission Docket Books
(1880-84, 1887-89) Volume III
Tahlequah, Cherokee Nation

information *(illegible...)* other business. They do not attempt to show that the applicant is of Cherokee blood and as the name of Nancy Copeland is not found on the census rolls of Cherokees taken in the years 1835-1852, the Commission decide that Rachel A Duncan aged 41 years and sons Wm H age 19 years, Chas Marion aged 17 years, James Thomas aged 16 years, Jessie Albert aged 14 years, Joseph C aged 12 yrs, Willie Benjamin aged 3 years, and daughters Nancy May aged 11 years, Emma Bettie 9 years, Ida Lucinda 7 years, Liza Ermin 6 years are not of Cherokee blood.

Attest   Will P Ross

    E G Ross   Chairman
        Clerk Commission   JE Gunter   Com

DEESE

DOCKET #1020
CENSUS ROLLS 1835 to 52

APPLICANT FOR CHEROKEE CITIZENSHIP

POST OFFICE: Uniontown Ark   **ATTORNEY:** A E Ivey

No	NAMES	AGE	SEX
1	William Deese	33	Male
2	Sarah E Deese	10	Female
3	J D Deese	9	"
4	*(Illegible)* C Deese	8	"
5	T H Deese	6	"
6	Wm Edward Deese	5	Male
7	Ellen*(illegible)* Deese	2	Female
8	Hulda May Deese	5 mo	"

ANCESTOR: Nancy McCamon

William Dees, et al
Joseph Snow, et al   Applicants for
Emily Kay, et al   Cherokee Citizenship
      (vs)
Cherokee Nation

Now on this the 21st day of March, 1888, comes the above entitled cases up for final disposition, they having been submitted by applicants Attorney on the 30th inst.

Cherokee Citizenship Commission Docket Books
(1880-84, 1887-89) Volume III
Tahlequah, Cherokee Nation

The testimony of William Dees taken before a Notary Public in Crawford County State of Arkansas on the 27th day of Sept. 1887, shows that he is the son of Alexander & Eliza Dees, and grand son of Sarah Nancy McCamon[sic]. The testimony of Eliza Dees concerning the claim of her daughter Joseph Snow shows that in the year 1838 she married Alexander Dees and that they lived in Alabama at that time, and about ten years afterwards moved to Arkansas and has lived in Sebastian and Crawford Counties ever since and that she is sixty six (66) years old and that her husband, Alexander Dees was the son of Sarah Nancy McCamin (a sister of *(Illegible)* McCamin), and that she has three living children by Alexander Dees whose names are as follows to wit: Emily, who married one James Kay, William Dees, and Joseph who married one G. F. Snow.

The testimony of Mary Allison shows that she is 46 years old and that she is a Cherokee and was born and raised in Sequoyah District C.N. and that the applicant Joseph Snow is her cousin, and that she derives her Cherokee blood from her father Alexander Dees who was the son of Stevenson Dees and Nancy Dees nee McCamin, and that Stevenson Dees wife, Sarah Nancy McCamin was my grandfathers'[sic] (~~Sam McCamin~~) sister, and that her grandfather was Sam McCamin and her grand mother wife of Sam McCamin was a full blood Cherokee woman and that her grand father Sam McCamin was a half blood Cherokee and that her father and mother migrated to this country with the general emigration and that her father was one Benjamin Franklin, a white man.   The testimony of Wm P. Ross, shows that he is sixty seven (67) years old and that he used to live in Wills Valley in the old Cherokee Nation now in Alabama and that he knew Sam McCamin there, and that he also knew his wife, who was a full blood Cherokee woman, and some of their children, and that one was named Sam, and that their daughter was not married then, and that the old man Sam McCamin was a white man, and that he had seen him often at his fathers house and that he knew him well, and that one of Sam McCamin's daughters married Jackson King and another married Silas Chole.

The census and pay rolls of Cherokees taken in the Old Nation in the years 1835, 1851 and 1852 submitted as testimony *(illegible...)* these cases.

All the reliable evidence addressed goes to establish the fact that these applicants were descendants of Sarah Nancy McCamin, a sister of Sam McCamin, *(illegible)* a white man.   The testimony of Wm P. Ross is corroborated by the rolls of the year 1835 which show that Sam McCamin was a resident of Wills Valley in the Old Nation, and enrolled as the head of a

Cherokee Citizenship Commission Docket Books
(1880-84, 1887-89) Volume III
Tahlequah, Cherokee Nation

Cherokee family and that he was a white man, consequently his sister Sarah Nancy McCamin was a white woman, and the rolls fail to show her or her husband, Stevenson Dees, a Cherokee Indian, or either of them a white person, the head of a Cherokee family.

Mrs. Mary Allison whom she states that Sam McCamin, her grand father was a half blood Cherokee Indian, makes a mistake for such is not the case. – The rolls fail to show upon any of their pages the names o any persons by the name of Dees; therefore, we the Commission on Citizenship find that William Dees and his children, namely: Sarah E. – J.D. – Emily C. - L. N. – Wm. Edward – Ellinor E. – and Hula May Dees, together with Joseph Snow and her[sic] children, namely: Effie and Mamie Snow together with Emily Kay and her two children, namely: *(Illegible)* A. – and Ollie P. Kay, are not Cherokees by blood, and in consequence not entitled to the rights and privileges of such.

~~Therefore~~ They are declared to be white persons.

J.T. Adair   Chairman Commission
John E Gunter   Commissioner
D.W. Lipe   Commissioner

The testimony in this case will be found on Journal page 351 to 353.

Attest
Cornell Rogers

DOCKET #1021   *(All names illegible)*

GEORGE

DOCKET #1022
CENSUS ROLLS 1835 – 1852

APPLICANT FOR CHEROKEE CITIZENSHIP
POST OFFICE: Brightwater Ark   ATTORNEY: A E Ivey

No	NAMES	AGE	SEX
1	J.B. George	26	Male

ANCESTOR: John Hensy

191

Cherokee Citizenship Commission Docket Books
(1880-84, 1887-89) Volume III
Tahlequah, Cherokee Nation

Office Commission on Citizenship
Cherokee Nation Ind Ter
Tahlequah Sept 12th 1889

The above application being accompanied by no proof and the claimant having been called three several times at intervals of an hour without answer the Commission decide that J B George 26 yrs old is <u>not</u> of Cherokee blood.

Attest
>E G Ross
>>Clerk commission

Will P. Ross
>Chairman
J E Gunter   Com

DOCKET #1023   *(All names illegible)*

GRIFFIN

DOCKET #1024
CENSUS ROLLS 1835 – 1852

APPLICANT FOR CHEROKEE CITIZENSHIP

POST OFFICE: Galena Ark   ATTORNEY: A. E. Ivey

No	NAMES	AGE	SEX
1	Sarah Griffin	19	Female
2	Nancy Griffin	5	"
3	Joseph Griffin	2	Male

ANCESTOR: John Thompson

Office Commission on Citizenship
Cherokee Nation Ind Ter
Tahlequah Sept 12th 1889

The above applicant was called three times and no answer and there being no evidence on file in support of the application we the Commission decide that applicant Sarah Griffin age 19 years and children Nancy Griffin age 5 years and Joseph Griffin age 2 years are <u>not</u> Cherokees by blood. Post Office Galena Ark.

Attest

    EG Ross
        Clerk Commission   Will P Ross

                                        Chairman
                        J E Gunter   Com

DOCKET #1025   *(All names illegible)*

GASTON

DOCKET #1026
CENSUS ROLLS 1835 to 52

APPLICANT FOR CHEROKEE CITIZENSHIP

POST OFFICE: Galena Ark   ATTORNEY: A E Ivey

No	NAMES	AGE	SEX
1	Alice Gaston	16	Female

ANCESTOR: John Thompson

                  Office Commission on Citizenship
                      Cherokee Nation Ind Ter
                      Tahlequah Sept 12th 1889

        The application in the above case being accompanied by no proof and the applicant having been called three several times at intervals of an hour without answer the Commission decide that Alice Gaston 16 years is <u>not</u> of Cherokee blood. Post Office Galena Ark.

E G Ross
        Clerk commission   Will P. Ross

                                    Chairman
                      J E Gunter   Com

DOCKET #1027   *(All names illegible)*

Cherokee Citizenship Commission Docket Books
(1880-84, 1887-89) Volume III
Tahlequah, Cherokee Nation

GLASGOW

DOCKET #1028

CENSUS ROLLS

APPLICANT FOR CHEROKEE CITIZENSHIP

POST OFFICE: Ashton NC   ATTORNEY:

No	NAMES	AGE	SEX
1	William M Glasgow	41	Male
2	*(Illegible)* Glasgow	16	Female
3	Daniel Glasgow	14	Male
4	Ellis M Glasgow	9	"
5	Oliver M Glasgow	4	"

ANCESTOR: Isaac *(Illegible)*

Office Commission on Citizenship
Cherokee Nation Ind Ter
Tahlequah Sept 17th 1889

The above case was called three times and no response from applicant or by Attorney and there being no evidence on file in support of claim the Commission therefore decide that William M Glasgow age 41 years, *(Illegible)* Glasgow age 16 years, Daniel Glasgow male age 14 years, Ellis M Glasgow male age 9 years, Oliver M Glasgow male age 4 years are not Cherokees by blood. Post Office Ashton NC.

Attest

E G Ross   Will P Ross
        Clerk Commission   Chairman
                                 J E Gunter   Com

DOCKET #1029   *(All names illegible)*

GARNER

DOCKET #1030

CENSUS ROLLS 1835 to 52

APPLICANT FOR CHEROKEE CITIZENSHIP

POST OFFICE: ATTORNEY:

No	NAMES	AGE	SEX
1	Theodosha Garner	29	Female

194

2	Ada M Lee Garner	8	"
3	Jesse Homer Garner	5	Male
4	Tisha Adline Garner	4	Female
5	Billie Garner	1	"

ANCESTOR: Emaline Boatright

Office Commission on Citizenship
Cherokee Nation Ind Ter
Tahlequah Sept 17th 1889

The above case was called three times and no response from applicant or by Attorney and there being no evidence on file in support of claim the Commission therefore decide that Theodosha Garner age 29 years and the following children Ada M Lee Garner age 8 years, Jesse Homer Garner age 5 years, Tisha Adline Garner age 4 years and Billie Garner age 1 year are not Cherokees by blood.

Attest

E G Ross
    Clerk Commission

Will P Ross
    Chairman
    J E Gunter Com

DOCKET #1031   *(All names illegible)*

DOCKET #1032   *(All names illegible)*

DOCKET #1033   *(All names illegible)*

GLENN

DOCKET #1034
CENSUS ROLLS

APPLICANT FOR CHEROKEE CITIZENSHIP
POST OFFICE: Center NC   **ATTORNEY:**

No	NAMES	AGE	SEX
1	Mattie Glenn	32	Female
2	Leland E Glenn	15	Male

3	Robert E Glenn	13	"
4	Edwin E Glenn	11	"
5	Vernon C Glenn	9	"
6	Mariam V Glenn	5	Female
7	Dora E Glenn	2	"

ANCESTOR: Anna Crews

The Commission decide against claimant. See decision in case Andrew Meredith Docket 2180 Book E, Page 26 and case John Henly Docket 1250, Book C, Page 376.

Will.P.Ross   Chairman
J.E. Gunter   Com

DOCKET #1035   *(All names illegible)*

GRAVES

DOCKET #1036
CENSUS ROLLS 1835 to 52

APPLICANT FOR CHEROKEE CITIZENSHIP

POST OFFICE: Minneapolis[sic] Colo   ATTORNEY: Boudinot & Rasmus

No	NAMES	AGE	SEX
1	George W Graves	23	Male

ANCESTOR: Elizabeth *(Illegible)*

Office Commission on Citizenship
Cherokee Nation Ind Ter
Tahlequah Sept 12th 1889

The above applicant was called three times and no answer and there being no evidence on file in support of the application the Commission decide that applicant George W Graves age 23 years is not a Cherokee by blood. Post Office Minneapolis[sic] Colorado.
Attest
    E G Ross
        Clerk Commission

Will P Ross
        Chairman
J E Gunter   Com

196

DOCKET #1037   *(All names illegible)*

DOCKET #1038   *(All names illegible)*

DOCKET #1039   *(All names illegible)*

EASLY

DOCKET #1040

CENSUS ROLLS 1835 to 52

APPLICANT FOR CHEROKEE CITIZENSHIP

POST OFFICE: Salem Ill   ATTORNEY: W A Thompson

No	NAMES	AGE	SEX
1	G J Easly		Male

ANCESTOR: Grant

Office Commission on Citizenship Cher Nation I.T.
Tahlequah May 20th 1889

The application in the above case was filed on the 18th day of October, 1887, and is supported by no evidence. The Commission therefore decide that G.J. Easly is not of Cherokee blood and are[sic] not entitled to citizenship in the Cherokee Nation whose Post Office at the time of filing was Salem Illinois.

Attest
    D S Williams
    Asst Clk Com

                Will P Ross
                        Chairman
              J E Gunter   Com

DOCKET #1041   *(All names illegible)*

EDWARDS

DOCKET #1042

CENSUS ROLLS 1835 to 52

APPLICANT FOR CHEROKEE CITIZENSHIP

POST OFFICE: Dardanelle Ark   **ATTORNEY:** Boudinot & Rasmus

No	NAMES	AGE	SEX
1	William O Edwards	27	Male

ANCESTOR: Nathan Thomas

Office Commission on Citizenship
Cherokee Nation Ind Ter
Tahlequah Sept 11th 1889

The above applicant was called three times and no answer and there being no evidence on file in support of the application we decide that applicant William O Edwards age twenty seven years is <u>not</u> a Cherokee by blood. Post Office Dardanelle Ark.

Attest

E G Ross   Will P Ross
    Clerk Commission   Chairman
                       J E Gunter   Com

DOCKET #1043   *(All names illegible)*

ELLIS

DOCKET #1044

CENSUS ROLLS

APPLICANT FOR CHEROKEE CITIZENSHIP

POST OFFICE: Valley Mills Ind   **ATTORNEY:** L B Bell

No	NAMES	AGE	SEX
1	Malla O Ellis		Female

ANCESTOR: Sarah Morgan

Office Commission on Citizenship
Cherokee Nation Ind. Ter.
Tahlequah July 2nd 1889

Application for Cherokee Citizenship

198

The above Application was called 3 times & no answer & there being no evidence on file in support of the Application, we decide that Applicant Malla O Ellis are[sic] not of Cherokee blood. P.O. Valley Mills Ind.

Attest
    D S Williams
    Asst Clk Com

        Will P Ross
           Chairman
        J E Gunter   Com

DOCKET #1045   *(All names illegible)*

DOCKET #1046   *(All names illegible)*

DOCKET #1047   *(All names illegible)*

EASLEY

DOCKET #1048
CENSUS ROLLS 1835

APPLICANT FOR CHEROKEE CITIZENSHIP

POST OFFICE: Salem Ill   ATTORNEY: W A Thompson

No	NAMES	AGE	SEX
1	Robt M Easley		Male

ANCESTOR: Grant

Rejected May 20 – 89

Office Commission on Citizenship Cher Nat I.T.
Tahlequah May 2nd 1889

The above application was filed on the 5th day of October 1887 and is supported by no evidence. The Commission therefore decide that Robt M Esley whose Post Office at the time of filing was Salem Ill are[sic] not Cherokees[sic] by blood and are not entitled to citizenship in the Cherokee Nation.

Attest
    D S Williams
    Asst Clk Com

        Will P Ross
           Chairman
        R Bunch   Com
        J E Gunter   Com

EASLEY

DOCKET #1049

CENSUS ROLLS 1835

APPLICANT FOR CHEROKEE CITIZENSHIP

POST OFFICE: Salem Ill   ATTORNEY: W A Thompson

No	NAMES	AGE	SEX
1	John F Easley		Male

ANCESTOR: Grant

Office Commission on Citizenship Cher Nat I.T.
Tahlequah May 20th 1889

The above application was filed on the 5th day of October 1887 and is supported by no evidence. The Commission therefore decide John F Easley whose Post Office at the time of filing was Salem Ill are[sic] not Cherokee by blood and are not entitled to citizenship in the Nation.

Attest   Will P Ross

   D S Williams   Chairman

   Asst Clk Com   R Bunch   Com

                  J E Gunter   Com

EDWARDS

DOCKET #1050

CENSUS ROLLS 1835 to 52

APPLICANT FOR CHEROKEE CITIZENSHIP

POST OFFICE: Hacket[sic] City Ark   ATTORNEY:

No	NAMES	AGE	SEX
1	Benjamin F Edwards	28	Male
2	*(Illegible)* Newt Edwards	6	"
3	Mary Pearl Edwards	4	Female
4	Henry Bruce Edwards	2	Male

ANCESTOR: Mima Edwards

Now on this the 9th day of January 1888 comes the above case for a final hearing. And the parties having made application pursuant to the provisions of an Act of the National Council approved December 8th 1886. And all the evidence being duly examined and fount <u>not</u> to be sufficient & satisfactory to the Commission

It is adjudged and determined by the Commission that Benjamin F Edwards, *(Illegible)* Newt Edwards, Mary Pearl Edwards and Henry Brute[sic] Edwards are **not** Cherokees by blood and are thereby rejected and declared intruders.

J T Adair	Chairman Commission
John E Gunter	Commissioner
D W Lipe	Commissioner

Attest

    C C Lipe

        Clerk Commission

EVANS

DOCKET #1051

CENSUS ROLLS 1835 to 52

APPLICANT FOR CHEREKEE CITIZENSHIP

POST OFFICE: North View Mo   ATTORNEY: Boudinot & R[sic]

No	NAMES	AGE	SEX
1	Narcissa M Evans	51	Female
2	Nancy E Evans	14	"
3	Lona J Evans	10	"

ANCESTOR: *(Illegible Name)*

Office Commission on Citizenship

Cherokee Nation Ind Ter

June 20th 1889

There being no evidence in support of the above named case the Commission decide that Narcissa M Evans age 51 years and her children Nancy E Evans Female age 14 years and Lona J Evans Female age 10 years are not Cherokees by blood. Post Office North View Mo.

Attest

    E G Ross

        Clerk Commission

                Will P Ross

                        Chairman

                J E Gunter   Com

Cherokee Citizenship Commission Docket Books
(1880-84, 1887-89) Volume III
Tahlequah, Cherokee Nation

EDWARDS

DOCKET #1052

CENSUS ROLLS

APPLICANT FOR CHEROKEE CITIZENSHIP

POST OFFICE: Vinita IT

ATTORNEY: L B Bell

NO	NAMES	AGE	SEX
1	Stephen D C Edwards		Male
2	Alice Edwards	27	Female
3	Elie Edwards	6	Male[sic]
4	Zebna Edwards	4	"
5	Stephen Edwards	3	"
6	Benjamin Edwards	5 mo	"

ANCESTOR: Fleetwood

Office Commission on Citizenship
Cherokee Nation Ind Ter
Tahlequah Sept 11th 1889

The application in the above case refers to no census roll of Cherokees by blood on which the name of the alleged ancestor Fleetwood whose Christian name is not given and is supported by no proof.

The Commission therefore decide that claim and Stephen D C Edwards and Alice Edwards 27 yrs, Ella Edwards 6 yrs, Zebna Edwards 4 yrs, Stephens[sic] Edwards 3 yrs and Benjamin Edwards 5 months old at the filing of his application Oct. 5th 1887 are not of Cherokee blood and not entitled to citizenship in the Cherokee Nation. Post Office Vinita Ind. Ter.
Attest

E G Ross
    Clerk Commission

Will P Ross
    Chairman
J E Gunter Com

DOCKET #1053 *(All names illegible)*

ESTERLING

DOCKET #1054

CENSUS ROLLS

APPLICANT FOR CHEROKEE CITIZENSHIP

POST OFFICE: Emporia Kansas   **ATTORNEY:** L B Bell

No	NAMES	AGE	SEX
1	Amanda Esterling	30	Female

ANCESTOR: Ana Crews

The Commission decide against claimant. See decision in the case of Andrew Meredith Docket 2180 Book E, Page 26 and John Henly Docket 1250, Book C, Page 376.

Attest

E G Ross

Clerk Commission

Will P Ross

Chairman

R. Bunch   Com

J.E. Gunter   Com

DOCKET #1055   *(All names illegible)*

EDDIS

DOCKET #1056

CENSUS ROLLS 1835

APPLICANT FOR CHEROKEE CITIZENSHIP

POST OFFICE: Hindsville Ark   **ATTORNEY:** C H Taylor

No	NAMES	AGE	SEX
1	Mary E Eddis	18	Female
2	Cora M Eddis	1	"

ANCESTOR: *(Illegible)* Vaughn

Rejected July 2nd 1889

Office Commission on Citizenship

Cherokee Nation Ind. Ter.

Tahlequah July 2nd 1889

There being no evidence in support of the above named case the Commission decide that Mary E Eddis age 18 yrs and her child Cora M Eddis Female age 1 yr are not Cherokees by blood.

Post Office Hindsville Ark.

Attest   Will P Ross
     D S Williams   Chairman
Asst Clerk Commission   R Bunch   Com
                               J E Gunter   Com

DOCKET #1057   *(All names illegible)*

EVANS

DOCKET #1058
CENSUS ROLLS 1835 to 52

APPLICANT FOR CHEROKEE CITIZENSHIP

POST OFFICE: Morrisville Ark   ATTORNEY: A E Ivey

No	NAMES	Age	Sex
1	Velletta Evans	57	Female
2	Elany D Loving	26	"
3	Eliza Evans	24	"
4	William P L Evans	20	Male
5	Lydia A Evans	14	Female

ANCESTOR: Alex Brown

Office Commission on Citizenship
Cherokee Nation Ind Ter
Tahlequah Sept 11, 1889

      The above case was called three times and no response from applicant or by Attorney and there being no evidence on file in support of claim the Commission therefore decide that Valletty Eaves[sic] age fifty seven years and the following children Elney Loving age twenty six years, Elijah Eaves age twenty four years, William P L Eaves and Lydia A Eaves age fourteen years are not Cherokees by blood. Post Office Morrisville Ark.

Attest   Will P Ross
     E G Ross   Chairman
        Clerk Commission   R Bunch   Com
                              J E Gunter   Com

DOCKET #1059 *(All names illegible)*

DOCKET #1060 *(All names illegible)*

DOCKET #1061 *(All names illegible)*

EDWARDS

DOCKET #1062

CENSUS ROLLS 1835 to 52

APPLICANT FOR CHEROKEE CITIZENSHIP

POST OFFICE: Mountainburg Ark   ATTORNEY: A E Ivey

No	NAMES	AGE	SEX
1	James A Edwards	41	Male
2	Geo W Edwards	20	"
3	William B Edwards	17	"
4	Andrew J Edwards	12	"
5	Lucy Edwards	9	Female
6	James Edwards	4	Male
7	Grover C Edwards	2	"
8	Arthur L Edwards	1	"

ANCESTOR: Mima Edwards

Now on this the 9th day of January 1888 comes the above case for a final hearing. And the parties having made application pursuant to the provisions of an Act of the National Council approved December 8th 1886, and the testimony being duly examined and found not to be sufficient and satisfactory to the Commission,

It is adjudged and determined by the Commission that James A Edwards, George W Edwards, William B Edwards, Andrew J Edwards, Lucy Edwards, James Edwards, Grover C Edwards and Arthur L Edwards are not Cherokees by blood, and are hereby rejected and declared intruders.

Cherokee Citizenship Commission Docket Books
(1880-84, 1887-89) Volume III
Tahlequah, Cherokee Nation

J T. Adair	Chairman Commission
John E Gunter	Commissioner
D.W. Lipe	Commissioner

Attest

    C C Lipe

        Clerk Commission

DOCKET #1063   *(All names illegible)*

FIELDS

DOCKET #1064

CENSUS ROLLS 1835

APPLICANT FOR CHEROKEE CITIZENSHIP

POST OFFICE: Milano Texas   ATTORNEY: C H Taylor

No	NAMES	AGE	SEX
1	Sarah C Fields	57	Female

ANCESTOR: John *(Illegible)*

Office Commission on Citizenship
Tahlequah   Sept 11th 1889

    The above case was called three times and no response from applicant or by Attorney and there being no evidence on file in support of claim the Commission therefore decide that Sarah C Fields age 57 years is not a Cherokee by blood.

Attest   Will P Ross

    E G Ross   Chairman

        Clerk Commission

                J E Gunter   Com

DOCKET #1065   *(All names illegible)*

Cherokee Citizenship Commission Docket Books
(1880-84, 1887-89) Volume III
Tahlequah, Cherokee Nation

FISER

DOCKET #1066

CENSUS ROLLS 1835 to 1852

APPLICANT FOR CHEREOKEE CITIZENSHIP

POST OFFICE: Clarksville Texas   ATTORNEY: Boudinot & Rasmus

No	NAMES	AGE	SEX
1	M Kate Fiser	20	Female

ANCESTOR: Bashaba Goodrich

Rejected June 20th 1889

Office Commission on Citizenship
Cherokee Nation
Tahlequah June 20th 1889

There being no evidence in support of the above named case the Commission decide that M. Kate Fiser age 20 years is not a Cherokee by blood. Post Office Clarksville Texas.

Attest

D S Williams
Asst Clk Com

Will P Ross
Chairman
R Bunch   Com
J E Gunter   Com

DOCKET #1067   *(All names illegible)*

FOX

DOCKET #1068

CENSUS ROLLS 1835 to 52

APPLICANT FOR CHEREOKEE CITIZENSHIP

POST OFFICE: Fort Smith Ark   ATTORNEY: L S Sanders

No	NAMES	AGE	SEX
1	James M Fox	38	Male
2	Maggie L Fox	10	Female
3	Nancy L Fox	8	"
4	William L Fox	6	Male
5	Arthur L Fox	4	"
6	Pleasant M Fox	2	"

ANCESTOR: John Fox

Cherokee Citizenship Commission Docket Books
(1880-84, 1887-89) Volume III
Tahlequah, Cherokee Nation

Office Commission on Citizenship
Cherokee Nation Ind Ter
Tahlequah Sept 11th 1889

The above applicant was called three times and no answer and there being no evidence in support of the application we decide that applicant James M Fox age 38 years, Maggie L age 6[sic] years, Nancy L age 8 years, William L age 6 years, Arthur L age 4 years and Pleasant M Fox age 2 years are not Cherokees by blood. P.O. Fort Smith Ark.

Attest
    E G Ross
       Clerk Commission

Will P Ross
    Chairman
J E Gunter   Com

DOCKET #1069   *(All names illegible)*

FORD

DOCKET #1070

CENSUS ROLLS 1835 to 1852

APPLICANT FOR CHEROKEE CITIZENSHIP

POST OFFICE: Montague Texas   **ATTORNEY:** Boudinot & Rasmus

No	NAMES	AGE	SEX
1	Fannie Ford	26	Female

ANCESTOR: Moton

Office Commission on Citizenship
Cherokee Nation Ind Ter
Tahlequah Aug 28th 1889

The above named case having been submitted by Wm Rasmus Attorney for claimant without evidence the Commission decide that Fannie Ford age 26 years and family names not supplied are not of Cherokee blood. Post Office Montague Texas.

Attest
    E G Ross
       Clerk Commission

Will P Ross
    Chairman
R Bunch
    Com
J E Gunter   Com

Cherokee Citizenship Commission Docket Books
(1880-84, 1887-89) Volume III
Tahlequah, Cherokee Nation

DOCKET #1071   *(All names illegible)*

FOSTER

DOCKET #1072

CENSUS ROLLS 1835

APPLICANT FOR CHEROKEE CITIZENSHIP

POST OFFICE: Van Buren Ark   ATTORNEY: L S Sanders

No	NAMES	AGE	SEX
1	Mary S Foster	25	Female

ANCESTOR: William Alfred

Office Commission on Citizenship
Cherokee Nation Ind Ter
Tahlequah Sept 11th 1889

The above named case having been submitted without evidence and called three several times at intervals of not less than one hour without answer the Commission decide that Mary S Foster age 25 years is not of Cherokee blood and not entitled to Citizenship in the Cherokee Nation.

Attest   Will P Ross
   E G Ross   Chairman
     Clerk Commission   R Bunch   Com
                     J E Gunter   Com

DOCKET #1073   *(All names illegible)*

FULLER

DOCKET #1074

CENSUS ROLLS

APPLICANT FOR CHEROKEE CITIZENSHIP

POST OFFICE: Heidelberg Miss   ATTORNEY: L B Bell

No	NAMES	AGE	SEX
1	T M Fuller	31	Male
2	Anna Fuller	1	Female

ANCESTOR: Ana Crews

209

The Commission decide against claimant. See decision in the case of Andrew Meredith Docket 2180 Book E, Page 26 and John Henly Docket 1250, Book C, Page 376.

Will P Ross

Attest   Chairman

E G Ross   John E Gunter   Com

Clerk Commission

DOCKET #1075   *(All names illegible)*

FOREMAN

DOCKET #1076

CENSUS ROLLS 1835

APPLICANT FOR CHEREKEE CITIZENSHIP

	POST OFFICE: Ritchey Mo	ATTORNEY: L B Bell	
NO	**NAMES**	**AGE**	**SEX**
1	John Foreman		Male

ANCESTOR: David England

Office Commission on Citizenship
Cherokee Nation Ind Ter
Tahlequah Sept 11th 1889

The above case was called three times and no response from applicant or by Attorney and there being no evidence on file in support of claim the Commission therefore decide that John Foreman is not of Cherokee blood and not entitled to Citizenship in the Cherokee Nation.

Attest

E G Ross   Will P Ross

Clerk Commission   Chairman

J E Gunter   Com

DOCKET #1077   *(All names illegible)*

FULGHAM

DOCKET #1078

CENSUS ROLLS

APPLICANT FOR CHEROKEE CITIZENSHIP

POST OFFICE: Richmond Ind   ATTORNEY: L B Bell

No	NAMES	AGE	SEX
1	H Fulgham	47	Male

ANCESTOR: Mary Crews

The Commission decide against claimant. See decision in the case of Andrew Meredith Docket 2180 Book E, Page 26 and John Henly Docket 1250, Book C, Page 376.

Will P Ross
Chairman
John E Gunter   Com

DOCKET #1079   *(All names illegible)*

FISHER

DOCKET #1080

CENSUS ROLLS 1835 to 1852

APPLICANT FOR CHEROKEE CITIZENSHIP

POST OFFICE: *(Illegible)*   ATTORNEY: A E Ivey

No	NAMES	AGE	SEX
1	Lucy B Fisher		Female

ANCESTOR: Hattie Williams

(No information given)

DOCKET #1081   *(All names illegible)*

DOCKET #1082   *(All names illegible)*

DOCKET #1083   *(All names illegible)*

Cherokee Citizenship Commission Docket Books
(1880-84, 1887-89) Volume III
Tahlequah, Cherokee Nation

FOUNTAIN

DOCKET #1084

CENSUS ROLLS 1851

APPLICANT FOR CHEROKEE CITIZENSHIP

POST OFFICE: Hartwell Ga   ATTORNEY: A E Ivey

No	NAMES	AGE	SEX
1	Sarah F Fountain	13	Female

ANCESTOR: Ladskyaw Brown

We the Commission on Citizenship after examining the evidence in the case of the above applicant *(illegible...)* is the grand daughter of John Tidwell a half blood Cherokee and is therefore of Cherokee blood. Therefore we the Commission on Citizenship agree and do hereby admit Sarah F Fountain to all the rights and privileges of a Cherokee citizen by blood.

J.T. Adair   Chairman Commission
D W Lipe   Commissioner
H C Barnes   Commissioner

Office Com on Citizenship
Tahlequah Sept 21st 1888

DOCKET #1085   *(All names illegible)*

FOOTE

DOCKET #1086

CENSUS ROLLS 1835

APPLICANT FOR CHEROKEE CITIZENSHIP

POST OFFICE: McKinney Texas   ATTORNEY: W A Thompson

No	NAMES	AGE	SEX
1	L A Foote	39	Male
2	Fannie E Foote	11	Female

ANCESTOR: Jack McGarrah

Office Commission on Citizenship
Cherokee Nation June 26th 1889

There being no evidence in support of the above named case the Commission decide that L A Foote aged 39 years and child, Fannie E Foote

212

female aged 11 years are not Cherokees by blood. Post Office McKinney Texas.

Attest

E G Ross

Clerk Commission

Will P Ross

Chairman

J E Gunter   Com

FOOTE

DOCKET #1087

CENSUS ROLLS 1835

APPLICANT FOR CHEROKEE CITIZENSHIP

POST OFFICE: McKinney Tex   ATTORNEY:

No	NAMES	AGE	SEX
1	Henry S Foote	35	Male

ANCESTOR: Jack McGarrah

Office Commission on Citizenship
Cherokee Nation June 26th 1889

There being no evidence in support of the above named case the Commission decide that Henry S Foote aged thirty five years is not a Cherokee by blood. Post Office McKinney Texas.

Attest

E G Ross

Clerk Commission

Will P Ross

Chairman

R Bunch   Com

J E Gunter   Com

FOOTE

DOCKET #1088

CENSUS ROLLS 1835

APPLICANT FOR CHEROKEE CITIZENSHIP

POST OFFICE: McKinney Texas   ATTORNEY: W A Thompson

No	NAMES	AGE	SEX
1	Eliza Jane Foots	57	Female

ANCESTOR: Jack McGarrah

Rejected June 26th 1889

Office Commission on Citizenship
Cherokee Nation
Tahlequah June 26th 1889

There being no evidence in support of the above named case the Commission decide that Eliza Jane Foote age 57 years is not a Cherokee by blood. Post Office McKinney Texas.

Will P Ross
Chairman

Attest

> D.S. Williams
> Asst Clk Com

R Bunch   Com
J E Gunter   Com

DOCKET #1089   *(All names illegible)*

FAIRES

DOCKET #1090
CENSUS ROLLS Old Settlers

APPLICANT FOR CHEROKEE CITIZENSHIP

POST OFFICE: McKinney Tex   ATTORNEY: W A Thompson

No	NAMES	AGE	SEX
1	Oscar Faires	19	Male

ANCESTOR: J C McGarrah

Office Commission on Citizenship
Cherokee Nation June 26 1889

There being no evidence in support of the above named case the Commission decide that Oscar Faires aged 19 years is not a Cherokee by blood. Post Office McKinney Texas.

Will P Ross
Chairman

Attest

> E G Ross
> Clerk Commission

R Bunch Com
JE Gunter   Com

DOCKET #1091   *(All names illegible)*

Cherokee Citizenship Commission Docket Books
(1880-84, 1887-89) Volume III
Tahlequah, Cherokee Nation

FLOYD

DOCKET #1092

CENSUS ROLLS 1835 to 52

APPLICANT FOR CHEROKEE CITIZENSHIP

POST OFFICE: *(Illegible)* Texas   ATTORNEY: Boudinot & Rasmus

No	NAMES	AGE	SEX
1	Carrie Floyd	26	Female
2	Annie L Floyd	6	"
3	Amanda D Floyd	4	"
4	James D Floyd	1	Male

ANCESTOR: Jane Coody

Now on this the 29th day of June, 1888, comes the above case up for final hearing, and the Commission say, "We the Commission on Citizenship after examining the evidence in the above case and also the Old Settlers pay rolls of 1851 find that they, the applicants, are Cherokees by blood, and the above mention Carrie Floyd and her three children, Annie L. – Amanda D. – and James D. Floyd are here re-admitted to all the rights and privileges of Cherokee citizens by blood which is in compliance with an Act of the National Council dated Feby. 7th 1888."

J T Adair   Chairman Commission

D W Lipe   Commissioner

FOLSOM

DOCKET #1093

CENSUS ROLLS

APPLICANT FOR CHEROKEE CITIZENSHIP

POST OFFICE: *(Illegible)* IT   ATTORNEY: L.B. Bell

No	NAMES	AGE	SEX
1	Deborah Folsom	16	Female

ANCESTOR: Ana Crews

The Commission decide against claimant. See decision in case Andrew Meredith Docket 2180 Book E, Page 26 and case John Henly Docket 1250, Book C Page 376.

Attest   Will P Ross

E G Ross   Chairman

Clerk Com   J E Gunter   Com

215

Cherokee Citizenship Commission Docket Books
(1880-84, 1887-89) Volume III
Tahlequah, Cherokee Nation

FULLER

DOCKET #1094

CENSUS ROLLS

APPLICANT FOR CHEROKEE CITIZENSHIP

POST OFFICE: *(Illegible)*   ATTORNEY: L B Bell

No	NAMES	AGE	SEX
1	Henry Fuller	27	Male

ANCESTOR: Ana Crews

The Commission decide against claimant. See decision in case Andrew Meredith Docket 2180 Book E, Page 26 and case John Henly Docket 1250, Book C Page 376.

Attest   Will P Ross

    E G Ross   Chairman

        Clerk Com   J E Gunter   Com

FAULKNER

DOCKET #1095

CENSUS ROLLS Old Settler

APPLICANT FOR CHEROKEE CITIZENSHIP

POST OFFICE: McKinney Texas   ATTORNEY: W A Thompson

No	NAMES	AGE	SEX
1	W B Faulkner	23	Male

ANCESTOR: Jack McGarrah

Office Commission on Citizenship
Cherokee Nation June 26th 1889

There being no evidence in support of the above named case the Commission decide that W.B. Faulkner aged 23 years is not a Cherokee by blood

    Attest

        E G Ross   Will P Ross

            Clerk Commission   Chairman

                    J E Gunter   Com

FITCH

DOCKET #1096

CENSUS ROLLS 1835

APPLICANT FOR CHEROKEE CITIZENSHIP

POST OFFICE: Hindsville Ark   ATTORNEY: C H Taylor

No	NAMES	AGE	SEX
1	Andrew D Fitch	24	Male
2	Ally Fitch	1	Female

ANCESTOR: *(Illegible)* Vaughn

Rejected July 2nd 1889

Office Commission on Citizenship
Cherokee Nation Ind Ter
Tahlequah July 2nd 1889

There being no evidence in support of the above named case the Commission decide that Andrew D Fitch age 24 years and Ally Fitch Female age 1 yr are not Cherokees by blood. Post Office Hindsville Ark.

Attest

    D S Williams
Asst Clerk Commission

       Will P Ross
            Chairman
    J E Gunter   Com

FITCH

DOCKET #1097

CENSUS ROLLS 1835

APPLICANT FOR CHEROKEE CITIZENSHIP

POST OFFICE: Hindsville Ark   ATTORNEY: C H Taylor

No	NAMES	AGE	SEX
1	Thomas L Fitch	27	Male
2	Margaret Fitch	6	Female
3	Edith Fitch	4	"
4	Cothell Fitch	1	Male

ANCESTOR: *(Illegible)* Vaughn

Rejected July 9th 1889

Office Commission on Citizenship
Cherokee Nation Ind. Ter.
Tahlequah July 9th 1889

Cherokee Citizenship Commission Docket Books
(1880-84, 1887-89) Volume III
Tahlequah, Cherokee Nation

There being no evidence in support of this case the Commission decide that Thomas L Fitch age 27 yrs and the following children Margaret Female age 6 yrs, Edith Female age 4 yrs and Cothell Fitch Male age 1 yrs are not Cher. by blood. Post Office Hindsville Ark.

Attest
    D.S. Williams
Asst   Clk Com

           Will P Ross
                  Chairman
        J. E. Gunter   Com

GRAYHAM

DOCKET #1098

CENSUS ROLLS 1835

APPLICANT FOR CHEROKEE CITIZENSHIP

POST OFFICE: Natural Dam Ark   ATTORNEY: J E Welch

No	NAMES	AGE	SEX
1	Mary E Grayham	45	Female
2	Wm M Oliver *(Graham)*	21	Male
3	Alex Grayham	19	"
4	Daniel S Grayham	16	"
5	Mirtel E Estes	8	Female
6	Maud Estes		

ANCESTOR: Larkin Moton

Office Commission on Citizenship
Cherokee Nation Ind Ter
Tahlequah Sept 12th 1889

The above applicant was called three times and no answer and there being no evidence on file in support of the application the Commission decide that applicant Mary E Graham age 45 years and children Wm M Oliver Graham age 21 years, Alexander Graham age 18[sic] years Dan'l S Graham age 16 years, Myrtel E Estes age 8 years, Maud Estes age 6 years are not Cherokees by blood. P.O. Natural Dan Ark.

Attest
    E G Ross
        Clerk Commission

      Will P Ross
        Chairman
      J E Gunter Com

Docket #1099   *(Missing from archival records)*

GARRETT

DOCKET #1100

CENSUS ROLLS 1835

APPLICANT FOR CHEROKEE CITIZENSHIP

POST OFFICE: *(Illegible)* Ark   ATTORNEY:

No	NAMES	AGE	SEX
1	Elizabeth Garrett	56	Female
2	Edgar L Garrett	18	

ANCESTOR: Nancy Woodall

Office Commission on Citizenship
Cherokee Nation Ind Ter
Tahlequah   July 2nd 1889

There being no evidence in support of the above named case the Commission decide that Elizabeth Garrett age 56 yrs and her son Edgar L Garrett male age 18 yrs are not Cherokees by blood. Post Office *(Illegible)* Ark.

Attest   Will P Ross
   D S Williams   Chairman
Asst Clerk Commission   J E Gunter   Com

GARNER

DOCKET #1101

CENSUS ROLLS 1835 to 1851

APPLICANT FOR CHEROKEE CITIZENSHIP

POST OFFICE: ATTORNEY: Boudinot & Rasmus

No	NAMES	AGE	SEX
1	Lillian M Garner		

ANCESTOR: Sarah Brown

Office Commission on Citizenship
Cherokee Nation Ind Ter
Tahlequah Sept 12 1889

The above applicant was called three times and no answer and there being no evidence on file in support of the application the Commission decide that applicant Lillian M Garner is not a Cherokee by blood.

Attest
    E G Ross
        Clerk Commission

        Will P Ross
        Chairman
        J E Gunter   Com

GOSS

DOCKET #1102
CENSUS ROLLS 1851

APPLICANT FOR CHEROKEE CITIZENSHIP

POST OFFICE: Dawsonville Ga   ATTORNEY: A E Ivey

No	NAMES	AGE	SEX
1	Virginia T Goss	57	Female

ANCESTOR: Dicy Chatton

Now on this the 19th day of May 1888, comes the above case up for final hearing, and the Commission says, "We the Commission on Citizenship after examining the evidence in the case of the above applicant and also the census rolls of 1851, find that Virginia Goss is not a Cherokee by blood, and no such ancestor as Dicy Chatton appears *(illegible...)* alleges. The testimony of Robert M Julian, a resident of *(Illegible)* County Georgia who lives in the same locality where the said Virginia Goss resides, shows that she was commonly known there as Jennie Goss, and became acquainted with her 18 or so years ago and is recognized in Georgia to belong to the African race, and he was acquainted with a number of Cherokees in Georgia, and never hyears any of then recognize her as being of Cherokee blood, and further states the applicant was a slave *(illegible...)* and belongs to the *(Illegible)* family. The Commission therefore decide that Virginia T Goss is not a Cherokee by blood and not entitled to any rights and privileges of the Cherokee Nation, and is hereby rejected.

        J T Adair   Chairman Commission
        D W Lipe   Commissioner

GRAVITTE

DOCKET #1103

CENSUS ROLLS 1851

APPLICANT FOR CHEROKEE CITIZENSHIP

POST OFFICE: Crane Eater Ga.   ATTORNEY: A E Ivey

No	NAMES	AGE	SEX
1	John Gravitte	41	Male
2	Nerva J Gavitte	15	Female
3	Harris Gravitte	13	Male
4	Lester Gravitte	10	Male
5	Thomas Gravitte	7	"
6	Arlie M Gravitte	3	Female

ANCESTOR: Jane Gravitte

Office Commission on Citizenship
Cherokee Nation Ind. Ter
Tahlequah Oct 4th 1889

    The above case was submitted by A E Ivey, Attorney, for claimant on the 6th of March 1889. It has been held under advisement since then for proof of it exists, for the proper identification of applicant as the son of James Gravitt[sic] and a person of Cherokee Indian descent. This not having been done the Commission decide that John Gravitt 41 years of age and his daughters, Nerva J Gravitt 15 years, Arlie M Gravitt 3 years, and sons Harris Gravitt 13 years, Lester Gravitt 10 years, and Thomas Gravitt 7 years are not of Cherokee Indian descent. Post Office Crane Eater Ga.

Attest

    E G Ross

        Clerk Commission

Will P Ross

    Chairman

R Bunch   Com

J E Gunter   Com

DOCKET #1104   *(All names illegible)*

GRAVITTE

DOCKET #1105

CENSUS ROLLS 1851

APPLICANT FOR CHEROKEE CITIZENSHIP

POST OFFICE: Town Creek Ga   ATTORNEY: A.E. Ivey

No	NAMES	AGE	SEX
1	Catherine Gravitte	41	Female
2	John W Gravitte	5	

ANCESTOR: Annie Gravitte

Office Commission on Citizenship
Cherokee Nation Ind. Ter
Tahlequah Oct 4th 1889

The above case was submitted to the Commission for decision by A E Ivey, Attorney, for claimant on the 6th day of March 1889. It was accompanied by no evidence *(illegible...)* The Commission decide that Catherine Gravitt 41 years of age and her son John W Gravitt 5 years are not of Cherokee blood. Post Office Town Creek Ga.

Will P Ross
Chairman
Attest
E G Ross   R Bunch   Com
Clerk Commission   J E Gunter   Com

DOCKET #1106   *(All names illegible)*

GRAVITTE

DOCKET #1107

CENSUS ROLLS 1851

APPLICANT FOR CHEROKEE CITIZENSHIP

POST OFFICE: Crane Eater Ga   ATTORNEY: A E Ivey

No	NAMES	AGE	SEX
1	Thomas Gravitte	40	Male
2	Alice Gravitte	10	Female
3	Emma Gravitte	2	"
4	Bill Gravitte	6 mo	Male

ANCESTOR: Jane Gravitte

Cherokee Citizenship Commission Docket Books
(1880-84, 1887-89) Volume III
Tahlequah, Cherokee Nation

Office Commission on Citizenship
Cherokee Nation Ind. Ter
Tahlequah Oct 4th 1889

      The above case was submitted to the Commission on Citizenship on the 6th of March 1889, by A E Ivey, Attorney, without proof. It has been held under advisement until now to enable the applicant to identify himself as the son of Jane Gravitt a person of Cherokee Indian descent whose name was enrolled on the census roll of Cherokees by blood taken by the United States in the year 1851 but this not having been done the Commission decide that the said Thomas Gravitt 40 years of age and his daughters Alice Gravitt 10 years, Emma Gravitt 2 years and Bill Gravitt (son) 1½ years of age are not of Cherokee Indian blood. Post Office Crane Eater Georgia.

Attest

    E G Ross   Clerk Commission

Will P Ross Chairman
R Bunch Com
J E Gunter Com

DOCKET #1108   *(All names illegible)*

GIBBS

DOCKET #1109
CENSUS ROLLS 1851

APPLICANT FOR CHEROKEE CITIZENSHIP

POST OFFICE: Dallas Ga   ATTORNEY: A E Ivey

No	NAMES	AGE	SEX
1	Caroline Gibbs	19	Female

ANCESTOR: Pleasant Tidwell

    We the Commission on Citizenship after examining the evidence in the above case and the census rolls of 1851 *(illegible...)* –daughter of John Tidwell *(illegible...)* rights and privileges of Cherokee citizens by blood.

J T Adair   Chairman Commission
D W Lipe   Commissioner
C C Barnes Commissioner

Office Com on Citizenship
Tahlequah I.T. Sept. 21st 1888

223

Cherokee Citizenship Commission Docket Books
(1880-84, 1887-89) Volume III
Tahlequah, Cherokee Nation

DOCKET #1110   *(All names illegible)*

Docket #1111   *(Missing from archival records)*

GUNTER

DOCKET #1112
CENSUS ROLLS 1835 to 1852

APPLICANT FOR CHEROKEE CITIZENSHIP

POST OFFICE: Jacksboro Texas   ATTORNEY: A.E. Ivey

No	NAMES	AGE	SEX
1	Geo Gunter	27	Male

ANCESTOR: Zachariah Gunter

Office Commission on Citizenship
Cherokee Nation Ind Ter
Tahlequah Sept 17th 1889

The above case was called three times and no response from applicant or by Attorney and there being no evidence on file in support of claim the Commission therefore decide that George Gunter age twenty seven years is not a Cherokee by blood. Post Office Jacksboro Texas.
Attest

E G Ross   Will P Ross
    Clerk Commission   Chairman
                                 J E Gunter   Com

GRANT

DOCKET #1113
CENSUS ROLLS 1835 to 52

APPLICANT FOR CHEROKEE CITIZENSHIP

POST OFFICE: *(Illegible)* IT   ATTORNEY: A E Ivey

No	NAMES	AGE	SEX
1	John Grant	53	Male
2	R E Grant	23	"
3	J W Grant	16	"

4	James A Grant	14	"

ANCESTOR: *(Illegible)* Wofford

Office Commission on Citizenship
Cherokee Nation Ind Ter
Tahlequah Aug 30th 1889

The above case having been called three times and no answer and there being no evidence filed in support of the application we decide that claimant John Grant age 53 years and his children R E Grant age 23 years, J W Grant age 16 years and James W Grant age 14 years are not Cherokees by blood.

Attest

E G Ross
Clerk Commission

Will P Ross
Chairman
J E Gunter   Com

COBLE

DOCKET #1114

CENSUS ROLLS 1851

APPLICANT FOR CHEROKEE CITIZENSHIP

POST OFFICE: Tails Creek Ga   **ATTORNEY:** A.E. Ivey

No	NAMES	AGE	SEX
1	Benjamin M Goble	23	Male
2	James W Goble	2	Male
3	Levenia Goble	1	Female

ANCESTOR: Nancy Goble

Office Commission on Citizenship
Cherokee Nation Ind Ter
Tahlequah May 18th 1889

It having been proven to the satisfaction of the Commission that Benjamin M Goble the applicant in the above case is the son of Nancy Goble who was the daughter of Sally Langley nee Sally Parris who was of Cherokee blood and whose name is found on the census roll of Cherokees taken in the year 1851, the Commission decide that Benjamin M Goble age 23 years and his son James W Goble age 2 years and daughter Levenia Goble age 1 year are of

225

Cherokee Citizenship Commission Docket Books
(1880-84, 1887-89) Volume III
Tahlequah, Cherokee Nation

Cherokee blood and entitled to citizenship in the Cherokee Nation under the provisions of the Act dated December 5th[sic]1886 creating this Commission.

Attest   Will P Ross

     E G Ross   Chairman

         Clerk commission   J E Gunter   Com

DOCKET #1115   *(All names illegible)*

GRAYHAM

DOCKET #1116

CENSUS ROLLS 1835 to 1852

APPLICANT FOR CHEROKEE CITIZENSHIP

POST OFFICE: Rudy Ark   ATTORNEY: A E Ivey

No	NAMES	AGE	SEX
1	Amanda J Grayham	36	Female
2	Mary E Grayham	14	"
3	J W Grayham	10	Male
4	Ada Grayham	7	Female
5	Arvilla Grayham	5	"
6	Edward Grayham	12	Male
7	Levana Grayham	4	Female
8	Ora May Grayham	2	"

ANCESTOR: Caroline Bell

Office Commission on Citizenship
Cherokee Nation Ind Ter
Tahlequah Sept 17th 1889

      The applicant in the above case alleges that she is the daughter of one George Bell who is the son of one Caroline Bell whose maiden name was Caroline Harrison and claims her Cherokee blood from her mother Caroline Bell whose name she believes will be found enrolled on the census rolls of Cherokees by blood taken and made by the United states in the years 1835, 52. The evidence in support of this application is the exparte affidavit of one Sam Homes sworn to before Ben Graham Clerk of the Circuit Court of Crawford County, State of Arkansas on the 23rd day of Sept A.D. 1887. This witness believes that applicant is the identical person she presents herself to be and knows that she is recognized and known as being of Cherokee origin and has every reason to believe that she is the Grand daughter of Caroline Bell who he believes and is informed is of Cherokee descent. Aside from the insufficiency of such evidence to establish the Cherokee descent of the applicant the name of her Grand mother Caroline Bell nee Harrison is not found on the census rolls of Cherokees referred to the Commission therefore decide that claimant Amanda J Graham and children Mary E Graham age 14 years, Edward Graham age 12 years John W Graham age 10 years, Ada Graham age 7 years, Arvilla Graham age 5 years, Levans[sic] Graham age 4 years and Ora May Graham age 2 years are not of Cherokee blood. P.O. Rudy Arkansas.

Will P Ross
Chairman

Attest

E G Ross
Clerk Commission

J E Gunter   Com

GIBSON

DOCKET #1117
CENSUS ROLLS 1835 to 52

APPLICANT FOR CHEROKEE CITIZENSHIP

POST OFFICE: Mound City Ill   ATTORNEY: A E Ivey

No	NAMES	AGE	SEX
1	Jerry Gibson	51	Male

ANCESTOR: Jeff Harris

Office Commission on Citizenship
Cherokee Nation Ind Ter
Tahlequah Sept 12th 1889

The above case was called three times and no response from applicant or by Attorney.

The Commission after examining the *(illegible...)* said case fail to find any evidence in support of claim and therefore decide that Jerry Gibson age 51 years is <u>not</u> a Cherokee by blood. Post Office Mound City Ill.

Attest

E G Ross
Clerk Commission

Will P Ross
Chairman
J E Gunter   Com

227

GEORGE

DOCKET #1118

CENSUS ROLLS 1835 to 1852

APPLICANT FOR CHEROKEE CITIZENSHIP

POST OFFICE: Brightwater Ark   ATTORNEY: A.E. Ivey

No	NAMES	AGE	SEX
1	Mr. *(empty space)* George	64	Male

ANCESTOR: John Henry

Office Commission on Citizenship
Cherokee Nation Ind Ter
Tahlequah Sept 12th 1889

The above case was called three times and no response from applicant or by Attorney and there being no evidence on file in support of claim the Commission therefore decide that Mr. George age 64 years is not a Cherokee by blood.

Attest

E G Ross
Clerk Commission

Will P Ross
Chairman
R Bunch   Com

J E Gunter   Com

GOOD

DOCKET #1119

CENSUS ROLLS 1835

APPLICANT FOR CHEROKEE CITIZENSHIP

POST OFFICE: Texas[sic] Decatur Texas   ATTORNEY: C.H. Taylor

No	NAMES	AGE	SEX
1	Nancy E Good	36	Female

ANCESTOR: William Abslom Chisholm

Office Commission on Citizenship
Cherokee Nation Ind Ter
Tahlequah Sept 12th 1889

The application in this case is accompanied by no evidence and having been called three several times at intervals of one hour without answer the

Cherokee Citizenship Commission Docket Books
(1880-84, 1887-89) Volume III
Tahlequah, Cherokee Nation

Commission decide that Nancy E Good is not of Cherokee blood. In connection with this see case Docket 1688 Book B Page 174. Post Office Decatur Tex.

Attest

    E G Ross

        Clerk Commission

                            Will P Ross

                                    Chairman

                          J E Gunter   Com

GENTRY

DOCKET #1120

CENSUS ROLLS

APPLICANT FOR CHEROKEE CITIZENSHIP

POST OFFICE: Decatur Texas   ATTORNEY: C H Taylor

NO	NAMES	AGE	SEX
1	Charlotte Gentry	37	Female
2	Hattie L Gentry	18	"
3	George Gentry	16	Male
4	Nannie Gentry	14	Female
5	Lee Gentry	11	Male
6	Lauman Gentry	9	"

ANCESTOR: Mary Ray

                Office Commission on Citizenship

                    Cherokee Nation Ind Ter

                    Tahlequah Sept 12th 1889

The above application was called three times and no answer and there being no evidence on file in support of the application the Commission decide that applicant Charlotte Gentry age 37 years and children Hattie L age 18 years, George age 16 years, Nannie age 14 years, Lee age 11 years and Lauman Gentry age 9 years are not Cherokees by blood. Post Office Decatur Texas.

Attest

    E G Ross

        Clerk Commission

                            Will P Ross

                                    Chairman

                          J E Gunter   Com

GENTRY

DOCKET #1121

CENSUS ROLLS

APPLICANT FOR CHEROKEE CITIZENSHIP

POST OFFICE: Decatur Texas   ATTORNEY: C H Taylor

No	NAMES	AGE	SEX
1	Rebecca Gentry	36	Female

ANCESTOR: Mary Ray

Commission on Citizenship
Cherokee Nation Ind Ter
Tahlequah Sept 12th 1889

The above case was called and no response from applicant or by Attorney and there being no evidence on file in support of claim the Commission therefore decide that Rebecca Gentry age 36 years is not a Cherokee by blood. Post Office Decatur Texas

Attest

E G Ross
Clerk Commission

Will P Ross
Chairman
J E Gunter   Com

GRUBBS

DOCKET #1122

CENSUS ROLLS

APPLICANT FOR CHEROKEE CITIZENSHIP

POST OFFICE: Kingston Ark   ATTORNEY: L B Bell

No	NAMES	AGE	SEX
1	Katie B Grubbs		Female

ANCESTOR: Ana Crews

The Commission decide against claimant. See decision in case Andrew Meredith Docket 2180 Book E, Page 26 and case John Henly Docket 1250, Book C Page 376.

Attest

E G Ross
Clerk Commission

Will P Ross
Chairman
J E Gunter   Com

230

Cherokee Citizenship Commission Docket Books
(1880-84, 1887-89) Volume III
Tahlequah, Cherokee Nation

GUEST

DOCKET #1123

CENSUS ROLLS 1835 to 52

APPLICANT FOR CHEROKEE CITIZENSHIP

POST OFFICE: Dardanelle Ark   ATTORNEY: Boudinot & Rasmus

No	NAMES	AGE	SEX
1	J Henry Guest	22	Male
2	James ? Guest	16	Male
3	Nona Guest	14	Female
4	Eddie Guest	9	

ANCESTOR: Wm Guest

Office Commission on Citizenship
Tahlequah Sept 12th 1889

There being no evidence in support of the above named case the Commission decide that J Henry Guest age 22 years and James ? Guest age 16 years, Nona Guest age 14 years and Eddie Guest age 9 years are not Cherokees by blood. Post Office Dardanelle Ark.

Will P Ross

Attest   Chairman

E G Ross
Clerk Commission

J E Gunter   Com

GODARD

DOCKET #1124

CENSUS ROLLS 1835

APPLICANT FOR CHEROKEE CITIZENSHIP

POST OFFICE: Clifty Ark   ATTORNEY: C H Taylor

No	NAMES	AGE	SEX
1	Mary Godard	25	Female
2	B J Godard	4	Male
3	Geretta Godard	1	Female

ANCESTOR: *(Illegible)* Vaughn

Office Commission on Citizenship
Cherokee Nation Ind Ter
Tahlequah Sept 12th 1889

231

The above case was called three times and no response from applicant or by Attorney and there being no evidence on file in support of claim the Commission therefore decide that Mary Godard age 25 years, B J Godard age 4 years, Geretta Godard age 1 year are not Cherokees by blood. Post Office Clifty Ark.

Will P Ross

Chairman

Attest

    E G Ross

        Clerk Commission

J E Gunter   Com

GODARD

DOCKET #1125

CENSUS ROLLS 1835

APPLICANT FOR CHEROKEE CITIZENSHIP

POST OFFICE: Clifty Ark   ATTORNEY: C H Taylor

No	NAMES	AGE	SEX
1	Nancy A Godard	20	Female
2	Ora Godard	1	

ANCESTOR: *(Illegible)* Vaughn

Office Commission on Citizenship

Cherokee Nation Ind Ter

Tahlequah Sept 17th 1889

The above applicant was called three times and no answer and there being no evidence on file in support of the application the Commission decide that Nancy A Godard twenty years and child Ora Godard are not Cherokees by blood. Post Office Clifty Ark.

Will.P. Ross

Chairman

J E Gunter

Attest

    E G Ross

        Clerk Commission

HALE

DOCKET #1126

CENSUS ROLLS

APPLICANT FOR CHEROKEE CITIZENSHIP

POST OFFICE: *(Illegible)* NC   ATTORNEY:

No	NAMES	AGE	SEX
1	Samuel H Hale	44	Male
2	William H Hale	18	"
3	Joel E Hale	17	"
4	Edward F Hale	17	"
5	Sarah S Hale	15	Female
6	Mary A Hale	12	"
7	Adam H Hale	10	Male
8	Milton S Hale	8	"
9	*(Illegible)* A Hale	6	"
10	Nancy M Hale	5	Female

ANCESTOR: Sarah Elmore

Adverse

Adverse.

See decision of *(illegible)*
Mission in case of John R Henly, Docket 553 Book B, Page 266.

Will P Ross
Attest   Chairman
   D S Williams   J E Gunter   Com
Asst Clerk Com

HALE

DOCKET #1127

CENSUS ROLLS

APPLICANT FOR CHEROKEE CITIZENSHIP

POST OFFICE: *(Illegible)*   ATTORNEY:

No	NAMES	AGE	SEX
1	Edward H Hale	49	Male
2	*(Illegible)* A Hale	15	Female
3	Harlan B Hale	14	Male
4	Anna T Hale	12	Female
5	Alphonso C Hale	10	Male
6	*(Illegible)* E Hale	8	"

7	Luther E Hale	6	"
8	Mary J Hale	4	Female
9	William S Hale	1	Male

ANCESTOR: Sarah Elmore

Adverse. See decision of Commission
in case John R Henly, Docket 553 Book B, Page 266.

Will P Ross
Chairman
J E Gunter

Attest
   D S Williams
Asst Clk Com

HENLEY

DOCKET #1128
CENSUS ROLLS

APPLICANT FOR CHEROKEE CITIZENSHIP

POST OFFICE: Blue Jacket I.T.   ATTORNEY:

No	NAMES	AGE	SEX
1	Mary A Henley	66	Female
2	Daniel W Henley	38	Male
3	John C Henley	35	"
4	Jessie C Henley	33	"
5	Hesakiah A Henley	27	"
6	Galeathea M Henley	24	Female
7	Samuel T Henley	20	Male
8	Arthur Henley	10	"
9	Bestea Henley	8	Female
10	Nellie Henley	7	"
11	Galia Henley	5	"
12	Hezakiah Henley	2	Male
13	Geo C Henley	1	"
14	Edna G Henley	10	Female
15	Mary Lee Henley	7	"

ANCESTOR: Martha Elmore

234

The Commission decide against claimant. See decision in case Lible J Bogue, Docket 2183, Book E, Page 29.

Will.P. Ross   Chairman
J.E. Gunter   Com

Attest

D.S. Williams
Asst Clk Com

HUGHES

DOCKET #1129

CENSUS ROLLS 1835 to 52   OS

APPLICANT FOR CHEROKEE CITIZENSHIP

POST OFFICE: Oaks Tex   ATTORNEY: Boudinot & Ras[sic]

No	NAMES	AGE	SEX
1	William ? Hughes	28	Male
2	Ezekiel H Hughes	3	"

ANCESTOR: *(Illegible)* Sylver

The above case was submitted April 30th by Attorney without evidence. The Commission therefore decide that William ? Hughes aged 28 at the filing of his application the 20th day of September and his son Ezekiel H Hughes are not of Cherokee blood and **not** entitled to citizenship in the Cherokee Nation.

Will P Ross
Chairman
John E Gunter   Commissioner

Attest

E G Ross
Clerk of Commission

DOCKET #1130   *(All names illegible)*

DOCKET #1131   *(All names illegible)*

Cherokee Citizenship Commission Docket Books
(1880-84, 1887-89) Volume III
Tahlequah, Cherokee Nation

HUGHES

DOCKET #1132

CENSUS ROLLS 1835 to 1851

APPLICANT FOR CHEROKEE CITIZENSHIP

POST OFFICE: Oaks IT   ATTORNEY: Boudinot & Rasmus

No	NAMES	AGE	SEX
1	Elmira Hughes	45	Female
2	Allen Hughes	18	Male
3	Eliza Hughes	16	Female
4	Sissan Hughes	12	"
5	James H Hughes	3	Male

ANCESTOR: *(Illegible)* Syler

The above case was filed the 20th day of September 1887 and was submitted by Attorney without evidence. The Commission therefore decide that Elmira Hughes and her children Allen Hughes aged 18 years, Eliza Hughes aged 16 years, Sissan Hughes aged 12 years and James H Hughes aged 3 years are not Cherokees by blood and not entitled to admission to Citizenship in the Cherokee Nation. Post Office Oaks, Ind. Ter.

DOCKET #1133   *(All names illegible)*

DOCKET #1134   *(All names illegible)*

BONDS

DOCKET #1135

CENSUS ROLLS 1835 to 52

APPLICANT FOR CHEROKEE CITIZENSHIP

POST OFFICE: Dover Ark   ATTORNEY:

No	NAMES	AGE	SEX
1	Fruwana L Henry	21	Female
2	Rue E Bonds	19	
3	John S Bonds	17	Male
4	Robt D Bonds	15	"
5	Andrew C Bonds	15	"
6	Anna A Bonds	12	Female
7	Cora E Bonds	10	"

8	Willie D Bonds	6	Male
9	James E Bonds	4	"
10	Albert C Bonds	4	"
11	Jessie N Bonds	2	"

ANCESTOR: Bashaba Garrah

Office Commission on Citizenship
Cherokee Nation Ind Ter
June 20th 1889

There being no evidence in support of the above named case the Commission decide that Fruwana L Henry age *(illegible)* years, Rue E Bonds aged 19 years, John S male aged 17 years, Robt D male aged 15 years, Andrew C male aged 15 years, Anna A Female aged 12 years, Cora E Female aged 10 years, Willie D male 6 years, James E male aged 4 years, Albert C male aged 4 years, Jessie N Bonds male aged 2 years are not Cherokees by blood.

	Will P Ross
E G Ross	Chairman
Clerk Commission	J E Gunter Com

HERNDON

DOCKET #1136
CENSUS ROLLS Old Settler

APPLICANT FOR CHEROKEE CITIZENSHIP

POST OFFICE: McKinney Tex   **ATTORNEY:** W A Thompson

No	NAMES	AGE	SEX
1	George H Herndon	41	Male

ANCESTOR: Jack McGarrah

Office Commission on Citizenship
Cherokee Nation
Tahlequah June 26th 1889

There being no evidence in support of the above named case the Commission decide that George H Herndon age 41 yrs and his wife Lucy Herndon 31 years are not Cherokees by blood. Post Office McKinney Texas.

Cherokee Citizenship Commission Docket Books
(1880-84, 1887-89) Volume III
Tahlequah, Cherokee Nation

Will P Ross
Attest   Chairman
   D S Williams   J E Gunter Com
   Asst Clk Com.

HALE

DOCKET #1137
CENSUS ROLLS

APPLICANT FOR CHEROKEE CITIZENSHIP
POST OFFICE: *(Illegible)*   ATTORNEY: L B Bell

No	NAMES	Age	Sex
1	E N Hale		Male

ANCESTOR: Sarah Elmore

(Illegible...)   See decision of Commission case John R. Henly *(remainder illegible)*.

WillPRoss
Chairman
Attest   JE Gunter Com
   D.S. Williams
   Asst. Clk. Com

HENLY

DOCKET #1138
CENSUS ROLLS

APPLICANT FOR CHEROKEE CITIZENSHIP
POST OFFICE: Fairmont[sic] Ark   ATTORNEY: L B Bell

No	NAMES	Age	Sex
1	Alphons Henly		Male

ANCESTOR: Sarah Elmore

(Illegible...)   See decision of Commission case John R. Henly *(remainder illegible)*.

Will. P. Ross
Chairman
Attest   JE Gunter Com
   D.S. Williams
   Asst. Clk. Com

DOCKET #1139   *(All names illegible)*

DOCKET #1140   *(All names illegible)*

HUDSON

DOCKET #1141
CENSUS ROLLS 1835 to 52

APPLICANT FOR CHEROKEE CITIZENSHIP

POST OFFICE: Clarksville Ark   ATTORNEY: Boudinot & Ra[sic]

No	NAMES	AGE	SEX
1	Sarah M Hudson	45	Female
2	Edward A Hudson	13	Male
3	Viola M Hudson	7	Female
4	Harvey H Hudson	5	Male
5	Mary E Hudson	2	Female

ANCESTOR: Bashaba Goodrich

Office Commission on Citizenship
Cherokee Nation June 26th 1889

There being no evidence in support of the above named case the Commission decide that Sarah M Hudson age 45 years and the following children Edward A male aged 13 years, Viola M Female age 7 years, Harvey H Male age 5 years and Mary E Hudson Female age 2 years are not Cherokees by blood. Post Office Clarksville Ark.

Attest

E G Ross
    Clerk Commission

Will.P. Ross
        Chairman
    J E Gunter   Com

HILL

DOCKET #1142

CENSUS ROLLS 1835 to 52

APPLICANT FOR CHEROKEE CITIZENSHIP

POST OFFICE: Van Buren Ark   ATTORNEY: Boudinot & Rasmus

No	NAMES	AGE	SEX
1	N J Hill	27	Male

ANCESTOR: Nathan Adams

Office Commission on Citizenship
Cherokee Nation Ind Ter
Tahlequah Sept 18th 1889

The above appears to be a duplicate application. See decision in case of Nancy Jane *(Illegible)* Docket 1176 Book C Page 301
Attest

    E G Ross
        Clerk Commission   Will.P.Ross
                                      Chairman
                             J E Gunter   Com

HOM

DOCKET #1143

CENSUS ROLLS

APPLICANT FOR CHEROKEE CITIZENSHIP

POST OFFICE: McKinney Texas   ATTORNEY: W A Thompson

No	NAMES	AGE	SEX
1	E E Hom	27	Female
2	Hattie Hom	6	"
3	Rolle Hom	2	Male

ANCESTOR: Jack McGarrah

Office Commission on Citizenship
Cherokee Nation
Tahlequah June 26th 1889

The Attorney for Applicant having filed the above case without evidence and there being none offered in its support the Commission decide that E E Hom aged twenty seven years and her son Rolle H Hom aged two years and daughter

240

Hattie Hom aged Six years are not of Cherokee blood. Post Office McKinney Texas.

Attest

D S Williams   Will.P.Ross
Asst Clk Com   Chairman
                                 J E Gunter   Com

DOCKET #1144   *(All names illegible)*

DOCKET #1145   *(All names illegible)*

HIDE

DOCKET #1146
CENSUS ROLLS 1835 to 1852

APPLICANT FOR CHEREKEE CITIZENSHIP

POST OFFICE: Siloam Spgs Ark   ATTORNEY: L S Sanders

No	NAMES	AGE	SEX
1	William H Hide	51	Male
2	Willie R Hide	1	"

ANCESTOR: F M Millsaps

Office Commission on Citizenship
Cherokee Nation
Tahlequah May 23, 1889

In the above case the Commission this day decide that William H Hide age 51 years and his son Willie R Hide male aged one year are not of Cherokee blood and are not entitled to Citizenship in the Cherokee Nation. See the case of Nancy Ann Thompson Book D Page 94.

Attest

E G Ross
Clerk Commission   Will.P.Ross
                                     Chairman
                                J R Gunter   Com

HARLEY

DOCKET #1147

CENSUS ROLLS 1835 to 1852

APPLICANT FOR CHEROKEE CITIZENSHIP

POST OFFICE: Clarksville Ark   ATTORNEY: Boudinot & Rasmus

No	NAMES	AGE	SEX
1	Amanda E Harley	37	Female
2	Edward R Harley	18	Male
3	Mary W Harley	15	Female

ANCESTOR:

Office Commission on Citizenship
Cherokee Nation Ind Ter
Tahlequah Sept 16th 1889

The applicant in the above case claims to derive her Cherokee blood from her Great Grand Mother Susan Bowen[sic].   No proof accompanies the application but W F Rasmus Esqr, Attorney refers the Commission to the evidence in the case of Nancy V Thompson whose application for Cherokee Citizenship was rejected by the Adair Commission the 8th day of August 1888 for reason sated in their opinion. Although there is no reference to Amanda E Harley in the evidence in that case and no connection between unless it be inferred from a common ancestor, the Commission has deemeed[sic] it proper to examine fully the evidence in that case. It is contained in two affidavits exparte taken by Q B Payner Clerk of the Circuit Court of Johnson County State of Arkansas that of Margaret B Wilson age 76 on the 13th day of December 1887 and the other of *(Illegible Name)* age 47 years on the 7th day of February 1888. These witnesses derive their knowledge in regard to the Cherokee blood of Susan Brown nee Susan Smith from family *(illegible)*. One of them, Mrs. Wilson being the Great Grand Daughter of Mrs. Brown. These witnesses fail to connect the claimants or their ancestors by evidence or otherwise than stated with the Cherokee Indians. They state that they have at all times resided in Virginia or Arkansas and as they have at no previous time sought to avail themselves of any rights belonging to them as Cherokees by blood if they were such, and as the name of Susan Brown is not found on the census rolls of Cherokees by blood taken in the years 1835-48-51-51. The Commission decide that Amanda E Harley age 37 years and daughter Mary W Harley age 15 years are not entitled to Citizenship in the Cherokee Nation by virtue of Cherokee blood. Post Office Clarksville Arkansas.

Attest

    E G Ross

        Clerk commission

                Will.P.Ross

                    Chairman

                JE Gunter Com

HOWELL

DOCKET #1148

CENSUS ROLLS 1835 to 52

APPLICANT FOR CHEROKEE CITIZENSHIP

POST OFFICE: Uniontown Ark   ATTORNEY: Boudinot & Rasmus

No	NAMES	AGE	SEX
1	Mary Howell	52	Female
2	Harry Howell	21	Male
3	Amanda T Howell	17	Female
4	Geo W Howell	15	Male
5	Mila A Howell	13	Female

ANCESTOR: William Moton

        Office Commission on Citizenship

           Cherokee Nation Ind Ter

           Tahlequah Sept 18th 1889

The above case was called and submitted by Attorney without evidence.

The Commission therefore decide that Mary Howell age 52 yrs and her children whose names are as follows Harry Howell age 21 yrs, Amanda T age 17 yrs, George W age 15 yrs and Mila A Howell age 13 yrs are not Cherokees by blood. Post Office Uniontown Arkansas.

Attest

    EG Ross

        Clerk Commission

                Will.P.Ross

                    Chairman

                JE Gunter Com

HOLLMAN

DOCKET #1149

CENSUS ROLLS 1835 to 52

APPLICANT FOR CHEREE CITIZENSHIP

POST OFFICE: Tahlequah CN   ATTORNEY: B H Stone

No	NAMES	AGE	SEX
1	Amanda Hollman	34	Female
2	Lona Cantrell	14	Male
3	Cora Cantrell	9	Female
4	Ulisses Hollman	4	Male
5	*(Illegible)* Hollman	2	"

ANCESTOR: James Farris

Office Commission on Citizenship
Cherokee Nation Ind Ter
Tahlequah Sept 17th 1889

The above case was called three times and no response from applicant or by Attorney and there being no evidence on file in support of claim the Commission therefore decide that Manda Hollman age 34 years and the following children Lona *(illegible)* 14 years, Cora age 9 years, Ulisses age 4 years and *(Illegible)* Hollman age 2 years are not Cherokees by blood. Post Office Tahlequah IT.

Attest   Will.P.Ross

    E G Ross   Chairman

        Clerk Commission   J.E. Gunter   Com

HIDE

DOCKET #1150

CENSUS ROLLS 1835 to 52

APPLICANT FOR CHEREE CITIZENSHIP

POST OFFICE: Venus Mo   ATTORNEY: L S Sanders

No	NAMES	AGE	SEX
1	James W Hide	41	Male
2	Martha M Hide	15	Female
3	William B Hide	19	Male
4	James W Hide	13	"
5	Eva Bell Hide	10	Female

6	Oscar Ellis Hide	7	Male
7	Chas Eddy Hide	5	"

ANCESTOR: F M Millsaps

Office Commission on Citizenship
Tahlequah CN May 23rd 1889

In the above named case the Commission this day decide that James W Hide aged 41 years and sons William B aged 19 years, James W Hide Jr aged 13 years, Oscar Ellis Hide aged 7 years, Charles Eddy Hide aged 5 years, and daughters Martha M Hide aged 15 years, and Eva Bell Hide aged 10 years are not of Cherokee blood and not entitled to citizenship in the Cherokee Nation. See the case of Nancy Ann Thompson Docket 2008 Book D, Page 94.

Attest   Will.P. Ross
    EG Ross   Chairman
        Clerk Commission   JE Gunter Com

HODSON

DOCKET #1151
CENSUS ROLLS

APPLICANT FOR CHEROKEE CITIZENSHIP

POST OFFICE: Lowell Kansas   **ATTORNEY:** C.H. Taylor

No	NAMES	AGE	SEX
1	Sarah E Hodson	37	Female
2	Freddie Hodson	16	Male
3	Frankie Hodson	12	Female
4	Chas E Brown	19	Male

ANCESTOR: Annie Wickey

Commission on Citizenship
Cherokee Nation
Tahlequah Sept 17th 1889

The above case was called three times and no response from applicant or by Atty and there being no evidence on file in support of claim the Commission therefore decide that Sarah E Hodson age 37 yrs and the following children Freddie age 16 years, Frankie age 12 years and Charles E Brown age 19 years are not Cherokees by blood. Post Office Lowell Kansas.

Cherokee Citizenship Commission Docket Books
(1880-84, 1887-89) Volume III
Tahlequah, Cherokee Nation

Attest
E G Ross
Clerk Commission   Will.P.Ross
                                          Chairman
                                     J E Gunter Com

BALDWIN

DOCKET #1152
CENSUS ROLLS

APPLICANT FOR CHEROKEE CITIZENSHIP

POST OFFICE: Afton IT   ATTORNEY: L.B. Bell

No	NAMES	AGE	SEX
1	Martha Ellen Baldwin	35	Female

ANCESTOR: Anna Crews

The Commission decide against claimant.   See decision in case Andrew Meredith Docket 2180 Book E, Page 26 and case John Henly Docket 1250, Book C Page 376.

Will.P.Ross
Chairman
Attest   J.E. Gunter   Com
DS Williams
Asst Clk Com

HUBBARD

DOCKET #1153
CENSUS ROLLS

APPLICANT FOR CHEROKEE CITIZENSHIP

POST OFFICE: Afton IT   ATTORNEY: Anna Crews

No	NAMES	AGE	SEX
1	Thomas C Hubbard	23	Male

ANCESTOR: Ann Crews

The Commission decide against claimant.   See decision in case Andrew Meredith Docket 2180 Book E, Page 26 and case John Henly Docket 1250, Book C Page 376.

Cherokee Citizenship Commission Docket Books
(1880-84, 1887-89) Volume III
Tahlequah, Cherokee Nation

Attest

EG Ross

Clerk Commission

Will.P.Ross

Chairman

<u>John</u> E G<u>unte</u>r Com

HUBBARD

DOCKET #1154

CENSUS ROLLS

APPLICANT FOR CHEROKEE CITIZENSHIP

POST OFFICE: Afton IT

ATTORNEY: L.B. Bell

No	NAMES	AGE	SEX
1	Alfred Hubbard	22	Male

ANCESTOR: Ann Crews

The Commission decide against claimant. See decision in case Andrew Meredith Docket 2180 Book E, Page 26 and case John Henly Docket 1250, Book C Page 376.

Will.P.Ross

Chairman

John E Gunter   Com

Attest

DS. Williams

Asst Clk Com

DOCKET #1155   *(All names illegible)*

HUBBARD

DOCKET #1156

CENSUS ROLLS

APPLICANT FOR CHEROKEE CITIZENSHIP

POST OFFICE: *(Illegible)*

ATTORNEY: L.B. Bell

No	NAMES	AGE	SEX
1	Joseph W Hubbard	23	Male

ANCESTOR: Ann Crews

The Commission decide against claimant. See decision in case Andrew Meredith Docket 2180 Book E, Page 26 and case John Henly Docket 1250, Book C Page 376.

Cherokee Citizenship Commission Docket Books
(1880-84, 1887-89) Volume III
Tahlequah, Cherokee Nation

Attest

    EG Ross   Will.P.Ross

            Clerk Commission   Chairman

                                        John E Gunter Com

DOCKET #1157   *(All names illegible)*

DOCKET #1158   *(All names illegible)*

DOCKET #1159   *(All names illegible)*

DOCKET #1160   *(All names illegible)*

DOCKET #1161   *(All names illegible)*

HUBBARD

DOCKET #1162

CENSUS ROLLS

APPLICANT FOR CHEROKEE CITIZENSHIP

POST OFFICE: *(Illegible)*   ATTORNEY: *(Illegible)*

No	NAMES	AGE	SEX
1	Martin Hubbard	46	Male

ANCESTOR: *(Illegible)*

The Commission decide against claimant. See decision in case Andrew Meredith Docket 2180 Book E, Page 26 and case John Henly Docket 1250, Book C Page 376.   Will.P.Ross

                                        Chairman

                        John E Gunter Com

Attest

         DS. Williams

       Asst Clk Com

Cherokee Citizenship Commission Docket Books
(1880-84, 1887-89) Volume III
Tahlequah, Cherokee Nation

DOCKET #1163   *(All names illegible)*

DOCKET #1164   *(All names illegible)*

HENRY

DOCKET #1165
CENSUS ROLLS 1835 to 52

APPLICANT FOR CHEROKEE CITIZENSHIP

POST OFFICE: Mayesville[sic] Ark   ATTORNEY: A E Ivey

No	NAMES	AGE	SEX
1	Nancy J Henry	37	Female

ANCESTOR: Mrs. Mayfield

Office Commission on Citizenship
Cherokee Nation Ind Ter
Tahlequah Sept 16th 1889

The above applicant was called three times and no answer and there being no evidence in support of the application the Commission decide that Nancy J Henry age thirty seven years is not a Cherokee by blood. Post Office Maysville Mo[sic]

Attest

EG Ross
Clerk Commission

Will.P.Ross
Chairman
JE Gunter   Com

HUBBARD

DOCKET #1166
CENSUS ROLLS

APPLICANT FOR CHEROKEE CITIZENSHIP

POST OFFICE: Kingston Ind   ATTORNEY: L.B. Bell

No	NAMES	AGE	SEX
1	Joseph L Hubbard		Male

ANCESTOR: Ann Crews

The Commission decide against claimant. See decision in case Andrew Meredith Docket 2180 Book E, Page 26 and case John Henly Docket 1250, Book C Page 376.

Attest

EG Ross
Clk Com

Will.P.Ross
Chairman
John E Gunter Com

DOCKET #1167   *(All names illegible)*

HENDON

DOCKET #1168
CENSUS ROLLS 1835

APPLICANT FOR CHEROKEE CITIZENSHIP

POST OFFICE: Rola[sic] Ark   ATTORNEY: C H Taylor

NO	NAMES	AGE	SEX
1	Clarissa Hendon	40	Female
2	David Hendon	10	Male
3	Mikiel Hendon	8	"
4	Agnes Hendon	6	

ANCESTOR: Arch Coody

Office Commission on Citizenship
Cherokee Nation Ind Ter
Tahlequah Sept 17th 1889

The above applicant was called three times and no answer and there being no evidence on file in support of the application the Commission decide that applicant Clarissa Hendon age 40 years and children David Hendon age 10 years, Mikiel Hendon age 6 years are not Cherokees by blood. Post Office Rola[sic], Ark. *(Note: Agnes Hendon was not included in explanation.)*

Attest

E G Ross
Clerk Commission

Will.P.Ross
Chairman
J E Gunter Com

DOCKET #1169   *(All names illegible)*

HUBBARD

DOCKET #1170
CENSUS ROLLS

APPLICANT FOR CHEROKEE CITIZENSHIP

POST OFFICE: *(Illegible)*   ATTORNEY: L.B. Bell

No	NAMES	AGE	SEX
1	Ida Hubbard	22	Female

ANCESTOR: Ann Crews

The Commission decide against claimant.   See decision in case Andrew Meredith Docket 2180 Book E, Page 26 and case John Henly Docket 1250, Book C Page 376.

Will.P.Ross
Chairman
John E Gunter   Com

Attest
D.S. Williams
Asst Clk Com

DOCKET #1171   *(All names illegible)*

HASELTON

DOCKET #1172
CENSUS ROLLS

APPLICANT FOR CHEROKEE CITIZENSHIP

POST OFFICE: Indianapolis Ind   ATTORNEY: L B Bell

No	NAMES	AGE	SEX
1	Annie M Haselton	51	Female

ANCESTOR: Anna Crews

The Commission decide against claimant.   See decision in case Andrew Meredith Docket 2180 Book E, Page 26 and case John Henly Docket 1250, Book C Page 376.

Will.P.Ross
Chairman
John E Gunter   Com

Attest
>D.S. Williams
Asst Clk Com

HILL

DOCKET #1173

CENSUS ROLLS 1835 to 1852

APPLICANT FOR CHEROKEE CITIZENSHIP

POST OFFICE: *(Illegible)* Ark   ATTORNEY:

NO	NAMES	AGE	SEX
1	Elizabeth Hill		Female

ANCESTOR: Nancy Jones

Office Commission on Citizenship
Tahlequah CN May23rd 1889

The application in the above case this day *(illegible...)* against Elizabeth Hill upon the grounds set forth in the *(remainder illegible)*

E G Ross
>Clerk Commission

Will.P.Ross
>Chairman
J.E. Gunter   Com

DOCKET #1174   *(All names illegible)*

DOCKET #1175   *(All names illegible)*

DOCKET #1176   *(All names illegible)*

DOCKET #1177   *(All names illegible)*

DOCKET #1178   *(All names illegible)*

DOCKET #1179   *(All names illegible)*

DOCKET #1180   *(All names illegible)*

DOCKET #1181   *(All names illegible)*

DOCKET #1182   *(All names illegible)*

DOCKET #1183   *(All names illegible)*

HILL

DOCKET #1184
CENSUS ROLLS 1835 to 1852

APPLICANT FOR CHEROKEE CITIZENSHIP

POST OFFICE: *(Illegible)* Ark   ATTORNEY: C.H. Tayloe

NO	NAMES	AGE	SEX
1	Harriet Hill	39	Female

ANCESTOR:

Office Commission on Citizenship
Tahlequah CN May 23rd 1889

The application in the above case was this day decided against Harriet Hill upon the grounds set forth in the decision against J.J. Hill found in Book C, page 328, Docket 1203.

Will.P.Ross
Chairman

E G Ross
Clerk Commission

J.E. Gunter   Com

Cherokee Citizenship Commission Docket Books
(1880-84, 1887-89) Volume III
Tahlequah, Cherokee Nation

HILL

DOCKET #1185

CENSUS ROLLS 1835

APPLICANT FOR CHEROKEE CITIZENSHIP

POST OFFICE: Berryville Ark   ATTORNEY: C.H. Taylor

No	NAMES	AGE	SEX
1	Sally Hill	30	Female

ANCESTOR: Nancy Jones

Office Commission on Citizenship

The application in the above case was filed on the *(illegible)* day of October, 1887. Now the Commission this day decide against *(remainder illegible)*

Attest   Will.P.Ross

   E G Ross   Chairman

     Clerk Commission   J E Gunter   Com

HILL

DOCKET #1186

CENSUS ROLLS 1835

APPLICANT FOR CHEROKEE CITIZENSHIP

POST OFFICE: Berryville Ark   ATTORNEY: C.H. Taylor

No	NAMES	AGE	SEX
1	W. T. Hill	36	Female

ANCESTOR: Nancy Hill

Office Commission on Citizenship
Tahlequah CN May 23rd 1889

The application in the above case was this day decided against W.T. Hill upon the grounds set forth in the decision against J J Hill *(remainder illegible)*

E G Ross   Will.P.Ross

   Clerk Commission   Chairman

                  J E Gunter   Com

Cherokee Citizenship Commission Docket Books (1880-84, 1887-89) Volume III
Tahlequah, Cherokee Nation

HILL

DOCKET #1187
CENSUS ROLLS 1835

APPLICANT FOR CHEROKEE CITIZENSHIP

POST OFFICE: Berryville Ark   ATTORNEY: C H Taylor

No	NAMES	AGE	SEX
1	Jane Hill	33	Female

ANCESTOR: Nancy Jones

Office Commission on Citizenship
Tahlequah CN May 23rd 1889

The application in the above case was this day decided against Jane Hill upon the grounds set forth in the decision against J J Hill found in *(remainder illegible)*

E G Ross
Clerk Commission

Will.P.Ross
Chairman
J E Gunter Com

HILL

DOCKET #1188
CENSUS ROLLS 1835

APPLICANT FOR CHEROKEE CITIZENSHIP

POST OFFICE: Berryville Ark   ATTORNEY: C H Taylor

No	NAMES	AGE	SEX
1	John Hill	30	Male

ANCESTOR: Nancy Jones

Office Commission on Citizenship
Tahlequah CN May 23rd 1889

The application in the above case was this day decided against Jane Hill upon the grounds set forth in the decision against J J Hill found in Book C Page 328 Docket 1208.

E G Ross
Clerk Commission

Will.P.Ross
Chairman
J E Gunter Com

DOCKET #1189   *(All names illegible)*

HILL

DOCKET #1190

CENSUS ROLLS

APPLICANT FOR CHEROKEE CITIZENSHIP

POST OFFICE: Berryville Ark   ATTORNEY: C.H. Taylor

No	NAMES	AGE	SEX
1	Emily Hill	26	Female

ANCESTOR: Nancy Jones

Office Commission on Citizenship
Tahlequah CN May 23rd 1889

The application in the above case was this day decided against Emily Hill upon the grounds set forth in the decision against J J Hill found in Book C Page 328 Docket 1208.

E G Ross
    Clerk Commission

Will.P.Ross
    Chairman
    J E Gunter   Com

DOCKET #1191   *(All names illegible)*

DOCKET #1192   *(All names illegible)*

DOCKET #1193   *(All names illegible)*

Cherokee Citizenship Commission Docket Books
(1880-84, 1887-89) Volume III
Tahlequah, Cherokee Nation

HANNAGAN

DOCKET #1194

CENSUS ROLLS 1835

APPLICANT FOR CHEROKEE CITIZENSHIP

POST OFFICE: Van Buren Ark

ATTORNEY: A.E. Ivey

No	NAMES	AGE	SEX
1	Mary Hannagan	27	Female
2	Anna Hannagan	10	"
3	Thomas Hannagan	9	Male
4	(Illegible) Hannagan	6	"
5	Wallie Hannagan	5	"
6	Bentley Hannagan	1	"

ANCESTOR: *(Illegible Name)*

Office Commission on Citizenship
Cherokee Nation Ind Ter
Tahlequah Sept 16th 1889

The above case was called three times and no response from applicant or by Attorney and there being no evidence on file in support of claim the Commission therefore decide that Mary Hannagan aged twenty seven years and the following children Anna aged ten years, Thomas aged nine years, *(Illegible Name)* aged six years, Wallie aged five years and Bentley Hannagan aged one year are not Cherokees by blood. Post Office Van Buren Ark.
Attest

EG Ross
    Clerk Commission

Will.P.Ross
      Chairman
J.E. Gunter   Com

HILL

DOCKET #1195

CENSUS ROLLS

APPLICANT FOR CHEROKEE CITIZENSHIP

POST OFFICE: Ophir Ga

ATTORNEY: A.E. Ivey

No	NAMES	AGE	SEX
1	Daniel Hill	28	Male
2	Alice Hill	24	Female
3	Baby Hill	1	Female

ANCESTOR: *(Illegible)* Hill

257

Cherokee Citizenship Commission Docket Books (1880-84, 1887-89) Volume III
Tahlequah, Cherokee Nation

Commission on Citizenship
Cherokee Nation Ind Ter
Tahlequah Sept 15th 1889

The above applicant was called three times and no answer and there being no evidence on file in support of the application the Commission decide adversely to claimants Daniel Hill age 28 yrs, Alice Hill age 24 yrs and Baby Hill age 1 year. P.O. Ophir Ga.

Attest

    E G Ross

        Clerk Commission

Will.P.Ross
Chairman
J.E. Gunter Com

HUBBARD

DOCKET #1196

CENSUS ROLLS

APPLICANT FOR CHEROKEE CITIZENSHIP

POST OFFICE: Indianapolis Ind   ATTORNEY: L.B. Bell

No	NAMES	AGE	SEX
1	Louis E Hubbard	29	Male

ANCESTOR: Anna Crews

The Commission decide against claimant. See decision in case Andrew Meredith Docket 2180 Book E, Page 26 and case John Henly Docket 1250, Book C Page 376.

Will.P.Ross
Chairman
John E Gunter Com

Attest

    D.S. Williams

  Asst Clk Com

DOCKET #1197   *(All names illegible)*

HOWELL

DOCKET #1198

CENSUS ROLLS O.S.

APPLICANT FOR CHEROKEE CITIZENSHIP

POST OFFICE: *(Illegible)* Grove Ark   ATTORNEY: Boudinot & Rasmus

No	NAMES	AGE	SEX
1	L.E. Howell	27	Female
2	John H Ward	15	Male

ANCESTOR: Ward

Adverse
Embraced in decision in the John
Ward case Book Page 251
Attest
E G Ross
Clerk Commission

DOCKET #1199   *(All names illegible)*

HOUSE

DOCKET #1200

CENSUS ROLLS

APPLICANT FOR CHEROKEE CITIZENSHIP

POST OFFICE: Cassville Mo   ATTORNEY: C.H. Taylor

No	NAMES	AGE	SEX
1	Jerome House	33	Male

ANCESTOR: Mansfield House

Office Commission on Citizenship
Cherokee Nation Ind Ter
Tahlequah Sept 16yh 1889

The above applicant was called three times and no answer and there being no evidence on file in support of the application the Commission decide that applicant Jerome House aged thirty-three years is not a Cherokee by blood. Post Office Cassville Mo

259

Attest

    E G Ross

        Clerk Commission   Will.P.Ross

                                        Chairman

                                  J.E. Gunter Com

DOCKET #1201   *(All names illegible)*

DOCKET #1202   *(All names illegible)*

DOCKET #1203   *(All names illegible)*

HILL

DOCKET #1204

CENSUS ROLLS 1835 to 52

APPLICANT FOR CHEROKEE CITIZENSHIP

POST OFFICE: Berryville Ark   ATTORNEY: C.H. Taylor

No	NAMES	AGE	SEX
1	J.O. Hill	42	Male

ANCESTOR: Nancy Jones

Office Commission on Citizenship

Tahlequah CN May 23rd 1889

      The application in the above case was this day decided against J.O. Hill upon the grounds set forth in the decision against J J Hill found in Book C Page 328 Docket 1208.

E G Ross   Will.P.Ross

    Clerk Commission   Chairman

                                J E Gunter Com

DOCKET #1205   *(All names illegible)*

Cherokee Citizenship Commission Docket Books
(1880-84, 1887-89) Volume III
Tahlequah, Cherokee Nation

DOCKET #1206   *(All names illegible)*

DOCKET #1207   *(All names illegible)*

HUGHES
DOCKET #1208
CENSUS ROLLS 1851

APPLICANT FOR CHEROKEE CITIZENSHIP

POST OFFICE: *(Illegible)* Ark   ATTORNEY: A E Ivey

NO	NAMES	AGE	SEX
1	Tracy A Hughes	38	Female
2	William E Hughes	18	Male
3	John R Hughes	16	"
4	Larry S Hughes	14	"
5	Laura E Hughes	12	Female
6	Lizzie A Hughes	9	"
7	Lewis C Hughes	7	Male
8	Geo H. Hughes	3	"
9	Jennie L Hughes	1	Female

ANCESTOR: John Tidwell

We the Commission on Citizenship after examining the evidence in the above case and also the Siler Rolls taken East of the Mississippi River in the year 1851 find that the applicants are descendants of John Tidwell and are Cherokees by blood and the law creating this Commission *(remainder illegible...)*

J.T. Adair   Chairman Commission
D W Lipe   Commissioner
H.C. Barnes   Commissioner

Office Com on Citizenship
Tahlequah I.T. Sept. *(remainder illegible)*

Cherokee Citizenship Commission Docket Books
(1880-84, 1887-89) Volume III
Tahlequah, Cherokee Nation

HOWARD

DOCKET #1209

CENSUS ROLLS 1835 to 52

APPLICANT FOR CHEROKEE CITIZENSHIP

POST OFFICE: Lancaster Ark   ATTORNEY: A.E. Ivey

No	NAMES	AGE	SEX
1	Julia Howard	45	Female
2	Charles Howard	25	Male
3	John Howard	19	"
4	Lizzie Howard	17	Female
5	Walter Howard	15	Male
6	Mary Howard	10	Female
7	Alice Howard	8	"
8	Nettie Howard	5	"

ANCESTOR: Lawrence Slaughter

Office Commission on Citizenship
Cherokee Nation Ind Ter
Tahlequah Sept 17th 1889

The above applicant was called three times and no answer and there being no evidence on file in support of the application the Commission decide that applicant Julia Howard age 45 years and children Charles age 25 years, John age 19 years, Lizzie age 17 years, Walter age 15 years, Mary age 10 years, Alice age 8 years, Nettie Howard age 5 years are not Cherokees by blood. Post Office Lancaster Ark.

Attest

    E G Ross   Will.P.Ross
       Clerk Commission   Chairman
                                   J.E. Gunter Com

HUFMAN

DOCKET #1210

CENSUS ROLLS 1835

APPLICANT FOR CHEROKEE CITIZENSHIP

POST OFFICE: Chetopa Kansas   ATTORNEY: A.E. Ivey

No	NAMES	AGE	SEX
1	Sarah E Hufman	45	Female

2	Mary E Hufman	15	"
3	James H Hufman	13	Male
4	Tillman A Hufman	11	"
5	Elroy Hufman	9	"

Ancestor: George Johnson

Office Commission on Citizenship
Cherokee Nation Ind Ter
Tahlequah Sept 13 1889

The above applicant was called three times and no answer and there being no evidence on file in support of the application the Commission decide adversely to claimants Sarah E Hufman age 45 years, Mary E Hufman age 15 years, James H Hufman age 13 years, Tillman A Hufman age 11 years, Elroy Hufman age 9 years. Post Office Chetopa Kansas
Attest

E G Ross
    Clerk Commission

Will.P.Ross
    Chairman
    J.E. Gunter   Com

HUDSPETH

Docket #1211

Census Rolls 1835

Applicant for CHEROKEE CITIZENSHIP

Post Office: Whitesboro Tex   **Attorney:** AE Ivey

No	NAMES	Age	Sex
1	Rufus Hudspeth	64	Male
2	James M Hudspeth	22	"
3	Clarice E Hudspeth	19	Female
4	John W Hudspeth	13	Male
5	William R Hudspeth	11	"

Ancestor: Clancy Coe

Office Commission on Citizenship
Cherokee Nation Ind Ter
Tahlequah Sept 16th 1889

The above case was called three times and no response from applicant or by Attorney and there being no evidence on file in support of claim the

Cherokee Citizenship Commission Docket Books (1880-84, 1887-89) Volume III
Tahlequah, Cherokee Nation

Commission therefore decide that Rufus Hudspeth age 64 years and James M Hudspeth age 22 years, Clarice E Hudspeth age 19 years, *(John)* W Hudspeth age 13 years, and William R Hudspeth age 11 years are not Cherokees by blood. Post Office Whitesboro Texas.

Attest

    E G Ross

        Clerk Commission

Will.P.Ross

    Chairman

J.E. Gunter   Com

HOWARD

DOCKET #1212

CENSUS ROLLS

APPLICANT FOR CHEROKEE CITIZENSHIP

POST OFFICE: Low[sic] Tenn   ATTORNEY: A.E. Ivey

No	NAMES	AGE	SEX
1	N.M. Howard	57	Male
2	Claudia *(Illegible)* Howard	20	Female
3	J.C.P. Howard	18	Male
4	Mary P Howard	15	Female
5	N M Howard	13	Male
6	Garland H Howard	11	"
7	C B Howard	9	"

ANCESTOR: Jack Moton

Office Commission on Citizenship
Cherokee Nation Ind Ter
Tahlequah Sept 14th 1889

    The above case was called three times and no response from applicant or by Attorney and there being no evidence on file in support of the claim the Commission decide that N.M. Howard aged fifty seven years and the following children Claudia Lloyd Howard age 20 years, J.C.P. Howard age 18 years, Mary P Howard age 15 years, N.M. Howard age 13 years, Garland H Howard age 11 years, C.R. Howard age 9 years, are not Cherokees by blood. Post Office Low[sic] Tenn.

Attest

    E G Ross

        Clerk Commission

Will.P. Ross

    Chairman

J.E. Gunter   Com

HILTON

DOCKET #1213

CENSUS ROLLS 1835

APPLICANT FOR CHEROKEE CITIZENSHIP

POST OFFICE: Yeakley Mo   ATTORNEY: A.E. Ivey

No	NAMES	AGE	SEX
1	John Hilton	32	Male
2	Leonard Hilton	7	Male
3	Geo Hilton	5	"
4	Annie Hilton	3	Female
5	Baby Hilton	1 mo	"

ANCESTOR: Silas Hilton

Office Commission on Citizenship
Cherokee Nation Ind Ter
Tahlequah Sept 16th 1889

    The above case was called three times and no response from applicant or by Attorney and there being no evidence on file in support of claim the Commission decide that John Hilton aged 32 years and the following children, Leonard age 7 years, George age 5 years, Annie age 3 years and Baby Hilton age 1 month are not Cherokees by blood.

Will.P. Ross

Attest

        Chairman

    E G Ross   J E Gunter   Com

        Clerk Commission

HOLLIS

DOCKET #1214

CENSUS ROLLS 1835

APPLICANT FOR CHEROKEE CITIZENSHIP

POST OFFICE: Van Buren Ark   ATTORNEY: A.E. Ivey

No	NAMES	AGE	SEX
1	Angeline Hollis	28	Female
2	Frankie Hollis	4	"
3	Mandie Hollis	2	"

ANCESTOR: Nancy Gentry

Cherokee Citizenship Commission Docket Books
(1880-84, 1887-89) Volume III
Tahlequah, Cherokee Nation

Office Commission on Citizenship
Cherokee Nation Ind Ter
Tahlequah Sept 16th 1889

The above case was called three times and no response from applicant or by Attorney and there being no evidence on file in support of the claim the Commission decide that Angeline Hollis age twenty eight years and her children Frankie Hollis age four years and Mandie Hollis age two years are not Cherokees by blood. Post Office Van Buren Ark.

Attest

E G Ross
Clerk Commission

Will.P.Ross
Chairman
J E Gunter   Com

HENSON

DOCKET #1215

CENSUS ROLLS 1835

APPLICANT FOR CHEROKEE CITIZENSHIP

POST OFFICE: Mulberry Ark   ATTORNEY: A E

No	NAMES	AGE	SEX
1	Westley Henson	66	Female[sic]

ANCESTOR: Richard Henson

Office Commission on Citizenship
Cherokee Nation Ind Ter
Tahlequah Sept 13th 1889

The above applicant was called three times and no answer and there being no evidence on file in support of the application the Commission decide that applicant Westley Henson age 66 years is not a Cherokee by blood. P O Mulberry Ark.

Attest

E G Ross
Clerk Commission

Will.P.Ross
Chairman
J E Gunter   Com

Cherokee Citizenship Commission Docket Books
(1880-84, 1887-89) Volume III
Tahlequah, Cherokee Nation

HENSON

DOCKET #1216

CENSUS ROLLS 1835

APPLICANT FOR CHEROKEE CITIZENSHIP

POST OFFICE: Mulberry Ark   ATTORNEY: A E Ivey

No	NAMES	AGE	SEX
1	Jeremiah J Henson	38	Male
2	Sallie A Henson	15	Female
3	John W Henson	13	Male
4	Wm B Henson	11	"
5	Jessie N Henson	7	"
6	J H Henson	5	"
7	Z*(illegible)* L Henson	1	"

ANCESTOR: Richard Henson

Office Commission on Citizenship
Cherokee Nation Ind Ter
Tahlequah   Sept 17th 1889

The above applicant was called three times and no answer and there being no evidence on file in support of the application the Commission decide that applicant Jeremiah J Henson aged thirty eight years and children Sallie A Henson aged fifteen years, John W Henson aged thirteen years, William B Henson aged eleven years, Jesse N Henson aged seven years, J H Henson aged five years Z*(illegible)* L Henson aged one year are not Cherokees by blood. Post Office Mulberry Ark.

Attest   Will.P.Ross

    E G Ross   Chairman

        Clerk Commission   J E Gunter   Com

HENSON

DOCKET #1217

CENSUS ROLLS 1835

APPLICANT FOR CHEROKEE CITIZENSHIP

POST OFFICE: Richard Henson   ATTORNEY: A.E. Ivey

No	NAMES	AGE	SEX
1	Eli Henson	55	Male
2	James Baxter Henson	18	"

ANCESTOR: Richard Henson

Cherokee Citizenship Commission Docket Books (1880-84, 1887-89) Volume III Tahlequah, Cherokee Nation

Office Commission on Citizenship
Cherokee Nation Ind Ter
Tahlequah Sept 17th 1889

The above applicant was called three times and no answer and there being no evidence on file in support of the application the Commission decide that applicant Eli Henson age fifty five years and son James Baxter Henson age *(illegible)* years are not Cherokees by blood. Post Office Mulberry, Ark.
Attest

E G Ross
  Clerk Commission

Will.P.Ross
  Chairman
  J E Gunter   Com

HENSON

DOCKET #1218

CENSUS ROLLS 1835

APPLICANT FOR CHEROKEE CITIZENSHIP

POST OFFICE: Mulberry Ark   ATTORNEY: A E Ivey

No	NAMES	AGE	SEX
1	John Henson	34	Male
2	Wm H Henson	11	"
3	Millie Henson	9	Female
4	M E Henson	7	"
5	Thomas Henson	1	Male

ANCESTOR: Liddia Hopper

Office Commission on Citizenship
Cherokee Nation Ind Ter
Tahlequah   Sept 16th 1889

The above applicant was called three times and no answer and there being no evidence on file in support of the application the Commission decide against applicant John Henson age 34 years and children Wm H Henson age 11 years, Millie Henson age 9 years, M E Henson age 7 years and Thomas Henson age 1 year are not Cherokees by blood and they are hereby rejected.
Attest

E G Ross
  Clerk Commission

Will.P.Ross
  Chairman
  J E Gunter   Com

HENSON

DOCKET #1219

CENSUS ROLLS 1835 to 52

APPLICANT FOR CHEROKEE CITIZENSHIP

POST OFFICE: Dyer Ark   ATTORNEY: A E Ivey

No	NAMES	AGE	SEX
1	George W Henson	27	Male

ANCESTOR: Liddia Hopper

Office Commission on Citizenship
Cherokee Nation Ind Ter
Tahlequah Sept 16th 1889

     The above applicant was called three times and no answer and there being no evidence on file in support of the application the Commission decide that George W Henson is not a Cherokee by blood. Post Office Dyer Ark.
Attest

E G Ross
    Clerk Commission

    Will.P.Ross
       Chairman
    J.E. Gunter   Com

HELTON

DOCKET #1220

CENSUS ROLLS

APPLICANT FOR CHEROKEE CITIZENSHIP

POST OFFICE: Bois d'Arc Mo   ATTORNEY: A E Ivey

No	NAMES	AGE	SEX
1	H F Helton	29	Male
2	Minnie Helton	7	Female
3	Dolly Helton	5	"
4	Romie Helton		

ANCESTOR: Silas Helton

Office Commission on Citizenship
Cherokee Nation Ind Ter
Tahlequah September 17th 1889

269

The above case was called three times and no response from applicant or by Attorney and there being no evidence on file in support of claim the Commission decide that H F Helton age twenty nine years and the following children, Minnie age seven years, Dolly age five years, Romie age three years and Walter Helton age one year are not Cherokees by blood.

Attest

E G Ross

Clerk Commission

Will.P.Ross

Chairman

J E Gunter   Com

HELTON

DOCKET #1221

CENSUS ROLLS 1835

APPLICANT FOR CHEROKEE CITIZENSHIP

POST OFFICE: Bois d'Arc Mo   ATTORNEY: A E Ivey

No	NAMES	AGE	SEX
1	Thomas Helton	22	Male

ANCESTOR: Silas Helton

Office Commission on Citizenship
Cherokee Nation Ind Ter
Tahlequah Sept 16 1889

The above applicant was called three times and no answer and there being no evidence on file in support of the application the Commission decide that applicant Thomas Helton age 22 years is not a Cherokee by blood and he is hereby rejected.

Attest

E G Ross

Clerk Commission

Will.P.Ross

Chairman

J E Gunter   Com

HIGGINS

DOCKET #1222
CENSUS ROLLS 1835 to 52

APPLICANT FOR CHEROKEE CITIZENSHIP

POST OFFICE: *(Illegible)* Creek Ga   ATTORNEY: A E Ivey

No	NAMES	AGE	SEX
1	Rachel Higgins	38	Female
2	Viney Higgins	19	"
3	Sterling V Higgins	16	Male
4	Noah Higgins	14	Male
5	Jane N Higgins	9	"[sic]
6	Rosetta Higgins		Female

ANCESTOR: Nancy Goble

Office Commission on Citizenship
Cherokee Nation Ind Ter
Tahlequah Oct 4th 1889

The above case was submitted by Attorney A E Ivey on the 16th day of March without evidence. The Commission now decide that Rachel Higgins age 38 years and the following children Viney Higgins female 19 years, Sterling V Higgins male 16 years, Noah Higgins male 14 years, Jane N Higgins 9 years and Rossetta[sic] Higgins female ? year are not Cherokees by blood. Post Office *(Illegible)* Creek Ga.

Attest

    E G Ross

      Clerk Commission

Will.P.Ross

      Chairman

    J E Gunter

HELTON

DOCKET #1223
CENSUS ROLLS 1835

APPLICANT FOR CHEROKEE CITIZENSHIP

POST OFFICE: Mo		ATTORNEY: A E Ivey	
No	NAMES	AGE	SEX
1	Arnold Lee Helton	19	Male

ANCESTOR: Silas Helton

Cherokee Citizenship Commission Docket Books
(1880-84, 1887-89) Volume III
Tahlequah, Cherokee Nation

Office Commission on Citizenship
Cherokee Nation Ind Ter
Tahlequah Sept 14th 1889

The above case was called three times and no response from applicant or by Attorney and there being no evidence on file in support of claim the Commission therefore decide that Arnold Lee Helton age nineteen years is not a Cherokee by blood.

Attest

E G Ross
    Clerk Commission

Will.P.Ross
    Chairman
    J E Gunter   Com

HUDSPETH

DOCKET #1224

CENSUS ROLLS 1835

APPLICANT FOR CHEROKEE CITIZENSHIP

POST OFFICE: Whitesboro Texas		ATTORNEY: A.E. Ivey	
NO	**NAMES**	**AGE**	**SEX**
1	J C Hudspeth	32	Male
2	Mary E Hudspeth	3	Female

ANCESTOR: *(Name Illegible)*

Office Commission on Citizenship
Cherokee Nation Ind Ter
Tahlequah Sept 16th 1889

The above applicant was called three times and no answer and there being no evidence on file in support of the application the Commission decide that applicant J C Hudspeth age 32 years and child Mary E Hudspeth age 3 years are not Cherokees by blood. Post Office Whitesboro Texas.

Attest

E G Ross
    Clerk Commission

Will.P.Ross
        Chairman
    J E Gunter   Com

DOCKET #1225   *(All names illegible)*

HODGES

DOCKET #1226
CENSUS ROLLS

APPLICANT FOR CHEROKEE CITIZENSHIP

POST OFFICE: Carter N C		ATTORNEY: L.B. Bell	
NO	NAMES	AGE	SEX
1	Dora E Hodges	26	Female

ANCESTOR: Ana Crews

The Commission decide against claimant. See decision in the case of Andrew Meredith Docket 2180 Book E, Page 26 and John Henly Docket 1250, Book C Page 376.

Will.P.Ross
Chairman
Attest   John E Gunter Com
   DS Williams
   Asst Clk Com

DOCKET #1227   *(All names illegible)*

HILL

DOCKET #1228
CENSUS ROLLS

APPLICANT FOR CHEROKEE CITIZENSHIP

POST OFFICE: Blue Jacket IT		ATTORNEY: L B Bell	
NO	NAMES	AGE	SEX
1	James O Hill		Male

ANCESTOR: Martha Elmore

The Commission decide against claimant. See decision in case Lible J Bogue, Docket 2183, Book E, Page 29.   Will.P.Ross
Attest   Chairman
   DS Williams   J E Gunter   Com
   Asst Clk Com

HUFF

DOCKET #1229

CENSUS ROLLS

APPLICANT FOR CHEROKEE CITIZENSHIP

POST OFFICE: Afton IT		ATTORNEY: L B Bell	
No	NAMES	AGE	SEX
1	E J Huff	66	Male

ANCESTOR:

CHEROKEE NATION, IND. TER.

Tahlequah, August 19th 1889

E.J. Huff

vs

The Cherokee Nation

The Commission against the applicant in the above case for reasons set forth in the aforementioned case of Caleb Hubbard. See Docket 2145, Book D, Page 631. The decision includes the family of said Emily J Huff who at the time of making her declaration the 27th day of February, A.D. 1885 was 63 years of age and her children Rhoda A Woody, Charles L Huff age 35 years, Oliver N Huff age 32 yrs and Atwood H Huff age 26 years. Post Office Afton, Indian Territory.

Will. P. Ross
Chairman
John E Gunter   Com

HARP

DOCKET #1230

CENSUS ROLLS 1835 to 1852

APPLICANT FOR CHEROKEE CITIZENSHIP

POST OFFICE: Carrolton[sic] Ark		ATTORNEY: E.A. Ivey[sic]	
No	NAMES	AGE	SEX
1	Isabell Harp	47	Female

ANCESTOR: Geo Henderson

274

Office Commission on Citizenship
Cherokee Nation Ind Ter
Tahlequah Sept 13th 1889

The above applicant was called three times and no answer and there being no evidence on file in support of the applicant we decide that adversely to claimant Isabell Harp age 47 years. Post Office Carrolton[sic] Ark.
Attest

E G Ross
Clerk Commission

Will.P.Ross
Chairman
J E Gunter   Com

HUBBARD

DOCKET #1231
CENSUS ROLLS

APPLICANT FOR CHEROKEE CITIZENSHIP

POST OFFICE: Afton IT		ATTORNEY: L.B. Bell	
NO	NAMES	AGE	SEX
1	Chas S Hubbard		Male

ANCESTOR: Ana Crews

The Commission decide against claimant. See decision in case of Andrew Meredith Docket 2180 Book E, Page 26 and case John Henly Docket 1250, Book C Page 376.

Will.P.Ross
Chairman
Attest
DS Williams
Asst Clk Com

R. Bunch   Com
J E Gunter   Com

HILLHOUSE

DOCKET #1232
CENSUS ROLLS 1835

APPLICANT FOR CHEROKEE CITIZENSHIP

POST OFFICE: McAlpin Fla		ATTORNEY: A.E. Ivey	
NO	NAMES	AGE	SEX
1	Sam R Hillhouse	26	Male

ANCESTOR: David Morris

Office Commission on Citizenship
Cherokee Nation Ind Ter
Tahlequah Sept 16th 1889

The above case having been called three several times and there being no evidence in support of the allegation as set up by applicant.

The Commission decide that Sam R Hillhouse age twenty six years is not of Cherokee blood and not entitled to Cherokee Citizenship. PO McAlpin Fla. Attest

E G Ross

Clerk Commission

Will.P.Ross

Chairman

JE Gunter   Com

HARLAN

DOCKET #1233

CENSUS ROLLS 1835 to 52

APPLICANT FOR CHEROKEE CITIZENSHIP

POST OFFICE: Echo I.T.		ATTORNEY: L.B. Bell	
No	NAMES	AGE	SEX
1	Samuel L Harlan	19	Male
2	Caroline Harlan	21	Female

ANCESTOR: David Harlan

We the Commission on Citizenship after fully examining into the testimony of the above case as well as the census and pay rolls laid down in the law of Dec. 8th 1886 find that Samuel and Caroline Harlan are the grandchildren of David Harlan whose name appears upon the census and pay rolls of 1851 and 1852, and that Samuel L and Caroline Harlan are Cherokees by blood and are hereby re-admitted to all the rights and privileges of Cherokee Citizens by blood and we do hereby so declare.

J T Adair,   Chairman Commission

H C Barnes   Commissioner

Office Comm on Citizenship
Tahlequah I T Oct 8th 1888

276

Cherokee Citizenship Commission Docket Books
(1880-84, 1887-89) Volume III
Tahlequah, Cherokee Nation

HUBBARD

DOCKET #1234
CENSUS ROLLS

APPLICANT FOR CHEROKEE CITIZENSHIP

POST OFFICE: Albia[sic] Mo		ATTORNEY: L.B. Bell	
NO	NAMES	AGE	SEX
1	James Hubbard	29	Male

ANCESTOR: Ann Crews

The Commission decide against claimant. See decision in the case of Andrew Meredith Docket 2180 Book E, Page 26 and John Henly Docket 1250, Book C Page 376.

Will.P.Ross   Chairman
John E Gunter   Com

Attest
D.S. Williams
Asst Clk Com

DOCKET #1235   *(All names illegible)*

HENSON

DOCKET #1236
CENSUS ROLLS

APPLICANT FOR CHEROKEE CITIZENSHIP

POST OFFICE: Mulberry Ark		ATTORNEY: A.E. Ivey	
NO	NAMES	AGE	SEX
1	James Henson	18	Male

ANCESTOR: *(Name Illegible)*

Office Commission on Citizenship
Tahlequah I T Aug 21st 1889

This case having been submitted by the Attys without evidence the Commission decide that James Henson aged 18 years is not of Cherokee blood. Address Mulberry Ark.

Attest   Will.P.Ross
E G Ross   Chairman
Clerk Commission   J.E. Gunter   Com

DOCKET #1237   *(All names illegible)*

HUBBARD

DOCKET #1238

CENSUS ROLLS

APPLICANT FOR CHEROKEE CITIZENSHIP

POST OFFICE: *(Illegible)*		ATTORNEY: L.B. Bell	
NO	NAMES	AGE	SEX
1	Lillian M Hubbard		

ANCESTOR: Ann Crews

The Commission decide against claimant. See decision in case Andrew Meredith Docket 2180 Book E, Page 26 and case John Henly Docket 1250, Book C Page 376.

Will.P.Ross

Attest   Chairman

E G Ross   John E Gunter   Com

Clerk Com

HUBBARD

DOCKET #1239

CENSUS ROLLS

APPLICANT FOR CHEROKEE CITIZENSHIP

POST OFFICE: Indianapolis Ind		ATTORNEY: L.B. Bell	
NO	NAMES	AGE	SEX
1	Geo M Hubbard	66	Male

ANCESTOR: Ann Crews

The Commission decide against claimant. See decision in case Andrew Meredith Docket 2180 Book E, Page 26 and case John Henly Docket 1250, Book C Page 376.

Will.P.Ross

E G Ross   Chairman

Clerk Com   John E Gunter   Com

HUBBARD

DOCKET #1240
CENSUS ROLLS

APPLICANT FOR CHEROKEE CITIZENSHIP

POST OFFICE: Indianapolis Ind		ATTORNEY: L B Bell	
No	NAMES	AGE	SEX
1	Edwin Hubbard		

ANCESTOR: Anna Crews

The Commission decide against claimant. See decision in case Andrew Meredith Docket 2180 Book E, Page 26 and case John Henly Docket 1250, Book C Page 376.

                              Will.P.Ross
Attest   Chairman
        E G Ross   John E Gunter   Com
            Clerk Com

HUBBARD

DOCKET #1241
CENSUS ROLLS

APPLICANT FOR CHEROKEE CITIZENSHIP

POST OFFICE:		ATTORNEY: L.B. Bell	
No	NAMES	AGE	SEX
1	Robert ? Hubbard		

ANCESTOR: Ann Crews

The Commission decide against claimant. See decision in case Andrew Meredith Docket 2180 Book E, Page 26 and case John Henly Docket 1250, Book C Page 376.

                              Will.P.Ross
Attest   Chairman
        E G Ross   John E Gunter   Com
            Clerk Com

HUBBARD

DOCKET #1242
CENSUS ROLLS

APPLICANT FOR CHEROKEE CITIZENSHIP

POST OFFICE: *(Illegible)*		ATTORNEY: L B Bell	
NO	NAMES	AGE	SEX
1	Chas M Hubbard		Male

ANCESTOR: Ann Crews

The Commission decide against claimant. See decision in case Andrew Meredith Docket 2180 Book E, Page 26 and case John Henly Docket 1250, Book C Page 376.

Will.P.Ross
Chairman

Attest

D S Williams
Asst Clerk Com

John E Gunter   Com

DOCKET #1243   *(All names illegible)*

HUBBARD

DOCKET #1244
CENSUS ROLLS

APPLICANT FOR CHEROKEE CITIZENSHIP

POST OFFICE: *(Illegible)*		ATTORNEY: L B Bell	
NO	NAMES	AGE	SEX
1	William B Hubbard		Male

ANCESTOR: Ann Crews

The Commission decide against claimant. See decision in case Andrew Meredith Docket 2180 Book E, Page 26 and case John Henly Docket 1250, Book C Page 376.

Will.P.Ross
Chairman

Attest

D S Williams
Asst Clerk Com

John E Gunter   Com

HUBBARD

DOCKET #1245
CENSUS ROLLS

APPLICANT FOR CHEROKEE CITIZENSHIP

POST OFFICE: *(Illegible)*		ATTORNEY: L.B. Bell	
No	NAMES	AGE	SEX
1	Emma ? Hubbard		Female

ANCESTOR: Ann Crews

The Commission decide against claimant. See decision in case Andrew Meredith Docket 2180 Book E, Page 26 and case John Henly Docket 1250, Book C Page 376.

J E Gunter   Com

HUBBARD

DOCKET #1246
CENSUS ROLLS

APPLICANT FOR CHEROKEE CITIZENSHIP

POST OFFICE: Broken Bow Neb		ATTORNEY: L.B. Bell	
No	NAMES	AGE	SEX
1	Henry Hubbard		Male

ANCESTOR: Ann Crews

The Commission decide against claimant. See decision in case Andrew Meredith Docket 2180 Book E, Page 26 and case John Henly Docket 1250, Book C Page 376.
Attest

E G Ross   Clerk
Commission

John E Gunter

DOCKET #1247   *(All names illegible)*

281

HENDLEY

DOCKET #1248

CENSUS ROLLS

APPLICANT FOR CHEROKEE CITIZENSHIP

POST OFFICE: Afton I.T.		ATTORNEY: L.B. Bell	
NO	**NAMES**	**AGE**	**SEX**
1	Elvina M Hendley	28	Female

ANCESTOR: Ann Crews

The Commission decide against claimant. See decision in case Andrew Meredith Docket 2180 Book E, Page 26 and case John Henly Docket 1250, Book C Page 376.

Attest

    E G Ross   Clerk

        Commission   John E Gunter   Com

DOCKET #1249   *(All names illegible)*

HUBBARD

DOCKET #1250

CENSUS ROLLS

APPLICANT FOR CHEROKEE CITIZENSHIP

POST OFFICE:		ATTORNEY: L.B. Bell	
NO	**NAMES**	**AGE**	**SEX**
1	Henry H Hubbard	62	Male

ANCESTOR: Ann Crews

The Commission decide against claimant. See decision in case Andrew Meredith Docket 2180 Book E, Page 26 and case John Henly Docket 1250, Book C Page 376.

                      J E Gunter   Com

DOCKET #1250[sic]   *(All names illegible)*

HILL
DOCKET #1251
CENSUS ROLLS

APPLICANT FOR CHEROKEE CITIZENSHIP

POST OFFICE: Afton IT		ATTORNEY: L.B. Bell	
NO	NAMES	AGE	SEX
1	A B Hill	50	Male

ANCESTOR: Ann Crews

The Commission decide against claimant.   See decision in case Andrew Meredith Docket 2180 Book E, Page 26 and case John Henly Docket 1250, Book C Page 376.
Attest

    E G Ross
        Clerk Commission   John E Gunter   Com

DOCKET #1252   *(All names illegible)*

HUBBARD
DOCKET #1253
CENSUS ROLLS

APPLICANT FOR CHEROKEE CITIZENSHIP

POST OFFICE: Afton IT		ATTORNEY: L.B. Bell	
NO	NAMES	AGE	SEX
1	John J Hubbard	33	Male

ANCESTOR: Ann Crews

The Commission decide against claimant.   See decision in case Andrew Meredith Docket 2180 Book E, Page 26 and case John Henly Docket 1250, Book C Page 376.
Attest

    E G Ross
        Clerk Commission   John E Gunter   Com

Cherokee Citizenship Commission Docket Books
(1880-84, 1887-89) Volume III
Tahlequah, Cherokee Nation

DOCKET #1254   *(All names illegible)*

DOCKET #1255   *(All names illegible)*

DOCKET #1256   *(All names illegible)*

HILL

DOCKET #1257

CENSUS ROLLS 1835 to 1852

APPLICANT FOR CHEROKEE CITIZENSHIP

POST OFFICE: *(Illegible)*		ATTORNEY: Boudinot & Rasmus	
NO	**NAMES**	**AGE**	**SEX**
1	John C Hill Sr	48	Male
2	John C Hill Jr	19	"
3	Lilly W Hill	13	Female

ANCESTOR: *(Name Illegible)*

(All information illegible)

DOCKET #1258   *(All names illegible)*

HUBBARD

DOCKET #1259

CENSUS ROLLS

APPLICANT FOR CHEROKEE CITIZENSHIP

POST OFFICE: Afton I T		ATTORNEY: L.B. Bell	
NO	**NAMES**	**AGE**	**SEX**
1	Joseph A Hubbard	36	Male

ANCESTOR: Ann Crews

Rejected July 2nd 1889

Cherokee Citizenship Commission Docket Books
(1880-84, 1887-89) Volume III
Tahlequah, Cherokee Nation

The Commission decide against claimant. See decision in case of Andrew Meredith Docket 2180 Book E, Page 26 and Docket 1250, Book C Page 376 in the John Henly case.

Attest
    D S Williams
Asst Clk Com

DOCKET #1260   *(All names illegible)*

HASKINS

DOCKET #1261
CENSUS ROLLS

APPLICANT FOR CHEROKEE CITIZENSHIP

POST OFFICE: *(Illegible)*		ATTORNEY:	
NO	NAMES	AGE	SEX
1	Stephen M Haskins		Male

ANCESTOR: Ann Crews

The Commission decide against claimant. See decision in the case of Andrew Meredith Docket 2180 Book E, Page 26 and John Henly Docket 1250, Book C Page 376.

          John E Gunter

HALE

DOCKET #1262
CENSUS ROLLS

APPLICANT FOR CHEROKEE CITIZENSHIP

POST OFFICE: *(Illegible)*		ATTORNEY: L.B. Bell	
NO	NAMES	AGE	SEX
1	S H Hale		Male

ANCESTOR: Sarah Elmore

(All information illegible)

HUBBARD

DOCKET #1263

CENSUS ROLLS

APPLICANT FOR CHEROKEE CITIZENSHIP

POST OFFICE: *(Illegible)*		ATTORNEY: L.B. Bell	
NO	NAMES	AGE	SEX
1	W B Hubbard	49	Male

ANCESTOR: Ann Crews

The Commission decide against claimant. See decision in the case of Andrew Meredith Docket 2180 Book E, Page 26 and John Henly Docket 1250, Book C Page 376.

Attest

    E G Ross

        Clerk Commission   John E Gunter Com

DOCKET #1264   *(All names illegible)*

HARBOUR

DOCKET #1265

CENSUS ROLLS 1835 to 1852

APPLICANT FOR CHEROKEE CITIZENSHIP

POST OFFICE: Killian Texas		ATTORNEY: L S Sanders	
NO	NAMES	AGE	SEX
1	Rebecca V Harbour	30	Female
2	Albert Harbour	7	Male
3	Henry Harbour	5	"
4	Mable Harbour	6 mo	Female

ANCESTOR: *(Name Illegible)*

Office Commission on Citizenship
Cherokee Nation Ind Ter
Tahlequah August 14th 1889

There being no evidence in support of the above named case therefore the Commission decide that Rebecca V Harbour age thirty years and the following children Albert age seven years, Henry age five years and Mable Harbour age six months are not Cherokees by blood. Post Office Killen Texas.

Attest

    E G Ross

        Clerk Commission

                           J E Gunter   Com

DOCKET #1266   *(All names illegible)*

DOCKET #1267   *(All names illegible)*

DOCKET #1268   *(All names illegible)*

DOCKET #1269   *(All names illegible)*

DOCKET #1270   *(All names illegible)*

WILLIAMS

DOCKET #1271

CENSUS ROLLS 1835

APPLICANT FOR CHEROKEE CITIZENSHIP

POST OFFICE: *(Illegible)* Ark		ATTORNEY: A E Ivey	
NO	NAMES	AGE	SEX
1	Kizettie Williams	35	Female
2	Bell or Bill "	10	
3	Frank "	2	Male

ANCESTOR: *(Name Illegible)*

The Decission[sic] of the Commission in the above case will be found on page *(illegible)* Book C under the application of Angeline *(Illegible)*

PARTAIN

DOCKET #1272

CENSUS ROLLS 1835 to 52

APPLICANT FOR CHEREKEE CITIZENSHIP

POST OFFICE: Cincinnati Ark		ATTORNEY: L S Sanders	
No	NAMES	AGE	SEX
1	Virginia K Partain	30	Female
2	Lewis W "	6	Male
3	Laura M "	4	Female
4	Joe Otis "	1	Male

ANCESTOR: Harris England

Office Commission on Citizenship
Tahlequah I T Aug 14th 1889

There being no evidence in support of the above named case the Commission therefore decide that Virginia K Partain aged 30 years and the following children Lewis W age 6 years, Laura M age 4 years, Joe Otis Partain age 1 year are not Cherokees by blood. Post Office Cincinnati Ark.
Attest

E G Ross
Clerk Commission

J E Gunter Com

PRAGUE

DOCKET #1273

CENSUS ROLLS 1852

APPLICANT FOR CHEROKEE CITIZENSHIP

POST OFFICE: Union Town Ark		ATTORNEY: A E Ivey	
No	NAMES	AGE	SEX
1	S A M J Prague	27	Female
2	Lillie M Branson	7	"

ANCESTOR: Elizabeth *(Illegible)*

Office Commission on Citizenship
Cherokee Nation Ind Ter
Tahlequah Aug 14th 1889

288

There being no evidence in support of the above named case the Commission decide that S.A.M.J. Prague age 27 years and Lillian M Branson female age 7 years are not Cherokees by blood. Post Office Union Town Ark. Attest

E G Ross
> Clerk Commission

> > J E Gunter   Com

DOCKET #1274   *(All names illegible)*

PRICE

DOCKET #1275

CENSUS ROLLS 1835 to 1852

APPLICANT FOR CHEROKEE CITIZENSHIP

POST OFFICE: Gonzallis[sic] Tex		ATTORNEY: Boudinot and Rasmus	
NO	**NAMES**	**AGE**	**SEX**
1	Monty Price	36	Male

ANCESTOR: Jane Coody nee Ross

Now on this the 27th day of June 1888, comes the above case up for final hearing, and the Commission says; "We the Commission on Citizenship after examining the evidence and also the Old Settler pay rolls taken in the year 1851 find that the above applicant, Monty Price is a Cherokee by blood and is hereby re admitted to all the rights and privileges of a Cherokee citizen by blood, which is based upon an Act of the National Council dated Febry 7th 1888".

> > J.T. Adair   Chairman Commission
> > D.W. Lipe   Commissioner

PRICE

DOCKET #1276

CENSUS ROLLS 1835, 1851 & 2

APPLICANT FOR CHEROKEE CITIZENSHIP

POST OFFICE: Gonzallis Tex		ATTORNEY: Boudinot & Rasmus	
NO	**NAMES**	**AGE**	**SEX**
1	Letitia Price	70	Female

ANCESTOR: Jane Coody nee Ross

Now on this the 27th day of June 1888, comes the above case up for final hearing, and the Commission says; "We the Commission on Citizenship after examining the testimony in the above case and also the Old Settler rolls taken in the year 1851 find that the above applicant, Letitia Price is a Cherokee by blood and is hereby re-admitted to all the rights and privileges of a Cherokee citizen by blood, which is in compliance with an Act of the National Council dated Febry 7th 1888, to determine the rights of citizenship".

J.T. Adair   Chairman Commission

D.W. Lipe   Commissioner

PRICE

DOCKET #1277

CENSUS ROLLS 1835-1852 & 2

APPLICANT FOR CHEROKEE CITIZENSHIP

POST OFFICE: Gonzallis[sic] Tex		ATTORNEY: Boudinot & Rasmus	
NO	**NAMES**	**AGE**	**SEX**
1	George Price	30	Male

ANCESTOR: Jane Coody nee Ross

Now on this the 27th day of June 1888, comes the above case up for final hearing, and the Commission says; "We the Commission on Citizenship after examining the evidence and also the Old Settler pay rolls taken in the year 1851 find that the above applicant, George Price is a Cherokee by blood and is hereby re admitted to all the rights and privileges of a Cherokee citizen by blood, which is in compliance with an Act of the National Council dated Febry 7th 1888".

J.T. Adair   Chairman Commission

D.W. Lipe   Commissioner

DOCKET #1278   *(All names illegible)*

Cherokee Citizenship Commission Docket Books
(1880-84, 1887-89) Volume III
Tahlequah, Cherokee Nation

PITTS

DOCKET #1279
CENSUS ROLLS

APPLICANT FOR CHEROKEE CITIZENSHIP

POST OFFICE: Richmond Ind		ATTORNEY: L.B. Bell	
NO	**NAMES**	**AGE**	**SEX**
1	Martha Pitts	45	Female

ANCESTOR: Mary Crews

The Commission decide against claimant. See decision in the case of Andrew Meredith Docket 2180 Book E, Page 26 and John Henly Docket 1250, Book C Page 376.

J.E. Gunter   Com

DOCKET #1280   *(All names illegible)*

PHILLIPS

DOCKET #1281
CENSUS ROLLS 1835

APPLICANT FOR CHEROKEE CITIZENSHIP

POST OFFICE: Lead Hill Ark		ATTORNEY: C.H. Taylor	
NO	**NAMES**	**AGE**	**SEX**
1	Martha Phillips	43	Female

ANCESTOR: Lela Brown

Office Commission on Citizenship
Cherokee Nation Ind Ter
Tahlequah Aug 14th 1889

There being no evidence in support of the above case the Commission therefore decide that Martha Phillips age 43 years is not a Cherokee by blood. Post Office Lead Hill Ark.
Attest

E G Ross
Clerk Commission

J E Gunter   Com

PERRY

DOCKET #1282

CENSUS ROLLS

APPLICANT FOR CHEROKEE CITIZENSHIP

POST OFFICE: Lead Hill Ark		ATTORNEY: C H Taylor	
No	NAMES	AGE	SEX
1	Rebecca Perry	34	Female

ANCESTOR: Lela Brown

Office Commission on Citizenship
Cherokee Nation Ind Ter
Tahlequah Aug 14th 1889

There being no evidence in support of the above case the Commission therefore decide that Rebecca Perry age 34 years is not a Cherokee by blood. Post Office Lead Hill Ark.

Attest

E G Ross
Clerk Commission

JE Gunter   Com

PARKER

DOCKET #1283

CENSUS ROLLS 1835

APPLICANT FOR CHEROKEE CITIZENSHIP

POST OFFICE: Huntsville Ark		ATTORNEY: C H Taylor	
No	NAMES	AGE	SEX
1	Julia A B Parker	18	Female
2	Odie "	1	"

ANCESTOR: *(Illegible)* Vaughn

Office Commission on Citizenship
Cherokee Nation July 2nd 1889

There being no evidence in support of the above named case the Commission decide that Julia A B Parker age 18 years and child Odie Parker female age 1 yr are not Cherokees by blood. Post Office Huntsville Ark.

D S Williams
Clerk Commission

J E Gunter   Com

PARKER

DOCKET #1284
CENSUS ROLLS 1835

APPLICANT FOR CHEROKEE CITIZENSHIP

POST OFFICE: Whitmore Ark		ATTORNEY: C.H. Taylor	
NO	**NAMES**	**AGE**	**SEX**
1	Nancy A Parker	31	Female
2	Andrew J Sanders	14	Male
3	Samuel D "	7	"
4	*(Illegible)* S Parker	4	"
5	A*(illegible)* "	1	Female

ANCESTOR: *(Illegible)* Vaughn

Office Commission on Citizenship
Cherokee Nation Ind Ter
Tahlequah July 2nd 1889

There being no evidence in support of the above named case the Commission decide that Nancy A Parker age 31 yrs and the following children Andrew J Sanders male age 14 yrs, Samuel D male age 7 yrs, *(Illegible)* S Parker male age 4 yrs and *(Illegible)* Parker female age 1 yr are not Cherokees by blood. Post Office Whitmore Ark.

Attest
    D S Williams
Asst Clerk Commission

J E Gunter   Com

PARKER

DOCKET #1285
CENSUS ROLLS

APPLICANT FOR CHEROKEE CITIZENSHIP

POST OFFICE: New London Ind		ATTORNEY: L.B. Bell	
NO	**NAMES**	**AGE**	**SEX**
1	Anna Parker	26	Female

ANCESTOR: Ann Crews

293

The Commission decide against claimant. See decision in the case of Andrew Meredith Docket 2180 Book E, Page 26 and John Henly Docket 1250, Book C Page 376.

J. E. Gunter   Com

DOCKET #1286   *(All names illegible)*

LYLE

DOCKET #1287
CENSUS ROLLS

APPLICANT FOR CHEROKEE CITIZENSHIP

	POST OFFICE: Afton IT		ATTORNEY: L B Bell	
No	**NAMES**		**AGE**	**SEX**
1	Sarah Emma Lyle		29	Female

ANCESTOR: Ann Crews

The Commission decide against claimant. See decision in the case of Andrew Meredith Docket 2180 Book E, Page 26 and John Henly Docket 1250, Book C Page 376.

J E Gunter   Com

PARKER

DOCKET #1288
CENSUS ROLLS 1835-48-51-2

APPLICANT FOR CHEROKEE CITIZENSHIP

	POST OFFICE: Talking Rock Ga		ATTORNEY: Boudinot & Rasmus	
No	**NAMES**		**AGE**	**SEX**
1	Caroline Parker		38	Female

ANCESTOR: Sallie Langley & others

Office Commission on Citizenship
Cherokee Nation Ind Ter
Tahlequah Sept 28th 1889

(Illegible...) Sally Langley *(illegible...)* on the Roll of Cherokee Indians by blood taken by the United States *(illegible...)* is hereby readmitted *(remaining illegible)* Post Office Talking Rock Ga.

Attest

    E G Ross

        Clerk Commission   JE Gunter Com

PAIN

DOCKET #1289

CENSUS ROLLS 1835 & 52

APPLICANT FOR CHEROKEE CITIZENSHIP

POST OFFICE: Grape Creek NC		ATTORNEY: C H Taylor	
NO	NAMES	AGE	SEX
1	Martha Pain	35	Female

ANCESTOR: Catherine McDaniel

Office Commission on Citizenship
Cherokee Nation Ind Ter
Tahlequah Aug 14th 1889

There being no evidence in support of the above named case the Commission therefore decide that Martha Pain age 35 years is not a Cherokee by blood. Post Office Grape Creek N C

Attest

    E G Ross

        Clerk Commission

                J E Gunter Com

PORTER

DOCKET #1290

CENSUS ROLLS 1835

APPLICANT FOR CHEROKEE CITIZENSHIP

POST OFFICE: Indianapolis Ind		ATTORNEY: C H Taylor	
NO	NAMES	AGE	SEX
1	Wm M Porter		Male

ANCESTOR: Morning Jeffries Porter

Rejected April 18, 1889

Now on this the 10th day of April 1889, comes the above case of Wm M Porter v.s. Cherokee Nation for final hearing. The applicant bases his application for readmission to citizenship in the Cherokee Nation upon the ground of his descent from Morning Jeffries Porter nee Morning Jeffries, a full blood Cherokee whose name is entered on the roll of Cherokees by blood taken in 1835. His *(illegible)* as a descendant of William Porter who was the son of Morning Jeffries Porter is supported exclusively by exparte affidavits taken by the clerk of the District Court of the United States for the state of Indiana at Indianapolis in 1884, which alleges that Morning Jeffries Porter was born in the Cherokee reservation in 1779 and died in Randolph County North Carolina in 1840 and that Wm Porter was born in Guilford County NC. in 1796 and died in *(Illegible)* County Indiana in 1850. The applicant alleges that he was 47 yrs old in 1884 and yet the names of neither Morning Jeffries Porter nor Wm M Porter appears on the roll of Cherokees by blood taken in *(illegible)* or any other roll specified in section 7 of the act of December 1886 and *(illegible)* acts, on citizenship under which the Commission is acting. It is therefore adjudged and decreed that William M Porter whose Post Office address is Indianapolis Indiana, is not entitled to readmission to citizenship in the Cherokee Nation as a Cherokee Indian by blood. Will.P.Ross   Chairman

John E Gunter   Com

Attest

DS Williams   Clerk Com

PARSLEY

DOCKET #1291

CENSUS ROLLS 1835 – 52

APPLICANT FOR CHEROKEE CITIZENSHIP

POST OFFICE: Webbers Falls IT		ATTORNEY: LS Sanders	
NO	NAMES	AGE	SEX
1	Alice Jane Parsley	32	Female
2	Harry Preston "	11	Male
3	James Walter "	7	"
4	Ada Bell "	6	Female

ANCESTOR: Emaline Boatright

Office Commission on Citizenship
Cherokee Nation Ind Ter
Tahlequah Aug 15th 1889

The application in the above case is supported by no evidence. The Commission therefore decide against the applicant Alice Jane Parsley age thirty two years and her son Harry Preston age eleven years, James Walter age seven years and daughter Ada Bell age six months. Post Office Webbers Falls Indian Territory.

Attest

    E G Ross

        Clerk Commission

                J E Gunter Com

PARSLEY

DOCKET #1292

CENSUS ROLLS 1835 – 52

APPLICANT FOR CHEROKEE CITIZENSHIP

POST OFFICE: *(Illegible)* Tex		ATTORNEY: L.S. Sanders	
NO	**NAMES**	**AGE**	**SEX**
1	Martha A E Parsley	33	Female
2	Henry *(Illegible)* "	15	Male
3	William F "	13	"
4	*(Illegible)* "	9	Female
5	Marion F "	7	Male
6	Etta Lee "	6	Female
7	Esther Arbella "	4	"

ANCESTOR: Emaline Boatright

        Office Commission on Citizenship

          Cherokee Nation Ind Ter

           Tahlequah Aug 18th 1889

        The application in the above case is supported by no evidence and having been called three several times without answer at intervals of not less than one hour, the Commission decide that Martha Ann E Parsley age 33 years and sons Henry *(Illegible)* age 15 years, William F. aged 13 years, Marion F aged 7 years and daughters *(Illegible)* 9 years, Etta Lee 6 years and Esther Arbella Parsley 4 years are not of Cherokee blood. Post Office *(Illegible)* Texas.

Attest

    E G Ross

        Clerk Commission   J E Gunter Com

PARKS

DOCKET #1293

CENSUS ROLLS 1835, 1851-2

APPLICANT FOR CHEROKEE CITIZENSHIP

POST OFFICE: *(Illegible)* Ark		ATTORNEY: Boudinot & Rasmus	
NO	NAMES	AGE	SEX
1	Margaret L Parks	24	Female

ANCESTOR: Andrew Miller

Now on this the 14th day of May 1889, comes the above case for a final hearing, the same having been submitted by Attorneys for both parties. The application which was filed 5th Oct 1887 *(illegible)* not sustained by any evidence the Commission decides that the applicant Margaret L Parks age 24 years together with children are not entitled to readmission to citizenship in the Cherokee Nation by virtue of having Cherokee blood and the Commission declare them to be intruders within the limits of the Cherokee Nation.

     Attest

        E G Ross

          Clerk Commission

                        J E Gunter   Com

PRATER

DOCKET #1294

CENSUS ROLLS 1835-52

APPLICANT FOR CHEROKEE CITIZENSHIP

POST OFFICE: Evansville Ark		ATTORNEY:	
NO	NAMES	AGE	SEX
1	Drunnette Prater	29	Female
2	Oscar "	7	Male
3	Elizabeth "	5	Female
4	Lafayette "	3	Male
5	Maud "	5	Female

ANCESTOR: William Lee

               Office Commission on Citizenship
                  Cherokee Nation Ind Ter
                    Tahlequah Aug 15th 1889

Cherokee Citizenship Commission Docket Books
(1880-84, 1887-89) Volume III
Tahlequah, Cherokee Nation

The above applicant claims admission to citizenship in the Cherokee Nation because she is the Grand daughter of one William Lee whose name she believes was enrolled on the census rolls of Cherokees by blood taken and made by the United States in the year 1835 to 52, no evidence accompanies the case. The Commission therefore decide that Drunnette Prater age 29 years and her children Oscar aged seven years, Elizabeth aged 5 years, Lafayette aged 3 years and Maud age 5 months are not of Cherokee blood. Post Office Evansville Ark.
Attest

    E G Ross

        Clerk Commission

                        J E Gunter   Com

PEARSON

DOCKET #1295

CENSUS ROLLS 1835, 48, 51-52

APPLICANT FOR CHEROKEE CITIZENSHIP

POST OFFICE: Clarksville Ark		ATTORNEY: Boudinot & Rasmus	
NO	NAMES	AGE	SEX
1	Rebecca J Pearson	51	Female
2	Andrew J "	15	Male
3	Mary J "	9	Female

ANCESTOR: Basheba Goodrich

Office Commission on Citizenship
Cherokee Nation Ind Ter
Tahlequah Aug 15th 1889

There being no evidence in support of this case the Commission therefore decide that Rebecca J Pearson age fifty one years and son Andrew J Pearson age fifteen years and daughter Mary J Pearson age nine years are not of Cherokee blood. Post Office Clarksville Arkansas.
Attest

    E G Ross

        Clerk Commission

                        J E Gunter   Com

PEARSON

DOCKET #1296

CENSUS ROLLS 1835

APPLICANT FOR CHEROKEE CITIZENSHIP

POST OFFICE: Clarksville Ark	ATTORNEY: Boudinot & Rasmus		
No	NAMES	AGE	SEX
1	James M Pearson	25	Male

ANCESTOR: Basheba Goodrich

Office Commission on Citizenship
Cherokee Nation Ind Ter
Tahlequah August 15th 1889

The application in the above case being supported by no evidence the Commission decide against the applicant Jams M Pearson aged twenty five years and whose Post Office address is Clarksville Ark.

Attest

E G Ross

Clerk Commission

J E Gunter   Com

PARKS

DOCKET #1297

CENSUS ROLLS 1835

APPLICANT FOR CHEROKEE CITIZENSHIP

POST OFFICE: Mayesville[sic] Ark	ATTORNEY: C H Taylor		
No	NAMES	AGE	SEX
1	R E Parks	53	Male

ANCESTOR: Samuel Parks

Office Commission on Citizenship
Cherokee Nation Ind Ter
Tahlequah Aug 25th 1889

There being no evidence in support of the above case the Commission decide that R E Parks age 53 years is not a Cherokee by blood.

Attest

E G Ross

Clerk Commission   J E Gunter   Com

300

Cherokee Citizenship Commission Docket Books
(1880-84, 1887-89) Volume III
Tahlequah, Cherokee Nation

PILGRIM

DOCKET #1298
CENSUS ROLLS 51-52

APPLICANT FOR CHEROKEE CITIZENSHIP

POST OFFICE: Dalton Ga		ATTORNEY: H C Rogers	
NO	**NAMES**	**AGE**	**SEX**
1	Elma Pilgrim		Male[sic]

ANCESTOR: *(Name Illegible)*

Office Commission on Citizenship
Cherokee Nation Ind Ter
Tahlequah Aug 13th 1889

In this case there is no regular application. Ellma Pillgram[sic] being only five months old on the 26th of September 1887. The *(illegible)* is one *(illegible)* presented to the Commission by the sworn certificate of W.R. Rogers, who states that Ellma Pillgram to the best of his knowledge and belief is his son and the statement of Henry C. Rogers before the Commission on citizenship Oct. 7th 1887, who swears that applicant is said to be the son of W.R. Rogers, who is the son of *(illegible)* Jack Rogers and grand son of Sarah Cordery, and if so is a Cherokee by blood but that he was *(illegible)* out of wedlock. The testimony in the opinion of the Commission does not establish the Cherokee blood of said Pillgram and the Commission decide that he is not of Cherokee blood.

Attest
    D.S. Williams
    Asst Clk Com

                         J E Gunter   Com

PARKER

DOCKET #1299
CENSUS ROLLS 1835 to 52

APPLICANT FOR CHEROKEE CITIZENSHIP

POST OFFICE: Van Alstyne Tex		ATTORNEY: A E Ivey	
NO	**NAMES**	**AGE**	**SEX**
1	M L Parker	19	Male

ANCESTOR: Job Parker

Cherokee Citizenship Commission Docket Books
(1880-84, 1887-89) Volume III
Tahlequah, Cherokee Nation

Office Commission on Citizenship
Tahlequah Aug 15th 1889

The applicant alleges that he is the son of one Job Parker whose name would be found on the census rolls of Cherokees by blood taken and made in the years 1835 and 1852. There is no evidence however in the case and the Commission decide against the applicant who was nineteen years of age and whose Post Office at the time of filing his application Oct. 4th 1887 was Van Alstyne Texas.

Attest

E G Ross

Clerk Commission

J E Gunter   Com

POLLOCK

DOCKET #1300

CENSUS ROLLS 1835-52

APPLICANT FOR CHEROKEE CITIZENSHIP

POST OFFICE: Savannah Ga		ATTORNEY: A E Ivey	
NO	NAMES	AGE	SEX
1	Ellen B Pollock	4	Female

ANCESTOR: Lawrence Slaughter

Office Commission on Citizenship
Cherokee Nation Ind Ter
Tahlequah Aug 15th 1889

The applicant in the above case is *(illegible...)* as four years of age in October 1887 but there is no evidence in support of her declaration. The Commission decide against her. Post Office Savannah.

Attest

E G Ross

Clerk Commission

J E Gunter Com

Cherokee Citizenship Commission Docket Books
(1880-84, 1887-89) Volume III
Tahlequah, Cherokee Nation

PARKER

DOCKET #1301

CENSUS ROLLS 1835 to 52

APPLICANT FOR CHEROKEE CITIZENSHIP

POST OFFICE: Dahlonega Ga	ATTORNEY: A E Ivey & J M Bell		
No	NAMES	AGE	SEX
1	Joseph A Parker	29	Male

ANCESTOR: John A Parker

(All information illegible)

PARKER

DOCKET #1302

CENSUS ROLLS 1835 – 52

APPLICANT FOR CHEROKEE CITIZENSHIP

POST OFFICE: Dahlonega	ATTORNEY: A E Ivey & J.M. Bell		
No	NAMES	AGE	SEX
1	John A Parker	67	Male
2	William E "	20	"

ANCESTOR: Anny Blythe

See decision in this case in that of George W Parker in Book "A" page 119. Adverse to claimant.

Cornell Rogers
Clerk Com. on Citizenship

Office Com on Citizenship
Tahlequah I T   Sept 25th 1888

PULLEAM

DOCKET #1303

CENSUS ROLLS 1835-51-52

APPLICANT FOR CHEROKEE CITIZENSHIP

POST OFFICE: Chester Ark	ATTORNEY: A E Ivey		
No	NAMES	AGE	SEX
1	Maddie S Pulleam	38	Female
2	Ophelia S Rushing	17	"
3	Walter Lawrence Rushing	15	Male
4	George W Rushing	13	"

5	Samuel W Pulleam	6	"

ANCESTOR: Lawrence Slaughter

Office Commission on Citizenship
Cherokee Nation Ind Ter
Tahlequah Aug 15th 1889

There being no evidence in this case and the parties having been called three several times without answer, the Commission decide against applicant Maddie S Pulleam age 38 years and her daughter Orphelia[sic] S Rushing age 17 years and sons Walter Lawrence Rushing aged 15 years, and George W Rushing aged 13 years by her first husband (Rushing) and her son Samuel W Pulleam by her second husband. Post Office Chester Ark.

Attest

E G Ross
Clerk Commission

J E Gunter   Com

PHILLIPS

DOCKET #1304
CENSUS ROLLS 1835

APPLICANT FOR CHEREE CITIZENSHIP

POST OFFICE: Van Buren Ark		ATTORNEY: A E Ivey	
No	**NAMES**	**AGE**	**SEX**
1	Cynthia R Phillips	33	Female
2	William J "	14	Male
3	Francis L "	8	Female
4	Nevada B "	4	"
5	Virgil "	3	Male
6	Maud "	1	Female

ANCESTOR: Mrs Mitchel

Office Commission on Citizenship
Cherokee Nation Ind Ter
Tahlequah   Aug 15th 1889

The application in this case is supported by no evidence and having been called three several times without answer the Commission decide against applicant Cynthia R Phillips age 34 years and son William J Phillips age 14 years, Frances L age 8 years, Virgil 3 years and daughters Nevada B 4 years and Maud Phillips one year. Post Office Van Buren Ark.

Attest

    E G Ross

        Clerk Commission

                     J E Gunter   Com

PARKER

DOCKET #1305

CENSUS ROLLS 1835 & 52

APPLICANT FOR CHEROKEE CITIZENSHIP

POST OFFICE: *(Illegible)*		ATTORNEY: A E Ivey	
NO	**NAMES**	**AGE**	**SEX**
1	Joseph P Parker	49	Male

ANCESTOR: Annie Barnes

See decision in this case in that of George W Parker in Book "A" page 119. Adverse to claimant.

                     Cornell Rogers

                     Clerk Com. on Citizenship

Office Com on Citizenship

Tahlequah I T   Sept 25th 1888

PARKER

DOCKET #1306

CENSUS ROLLS

APPLICANT FOR CHEROKEE CITIZENSHIP

POST OFFICE: Dalonega[sic] Ga		ATTORNEY: A E Ivey	
NO	**NAMES**	**AGE**	**SEX**
1	Joseph P Parker	50	Male
2	Frank "	17	"
3	Willie A "	10	"
4	Fannie L "	7	Female
5	Lucy M "	5	"
6	James G "	2	Male

ANCESTOR: Leoma Parker

See decision in this case in that of George W Parker in Book "A" page 119. Adverse to claimant.

Cornell Rogers
Clerk Com. on Citizenship

Office Com on Citizenship
Tahlequah IT   Sept 25th 1888

PARKER

DOCKET #1307

CENSUS ROLLS 1835-48-52

APPLICANT FOR CHEROKEE CITIZENSHIP

POST OFFICE:		ATTORNEY: A E Ivey	
No	NAMES	AGE	SEX
1	Wm A Parker		

ANCESTOR: *(Illegible)* Parker

See decision in this case in that of George W Parker in Book "A" page 119. Adverse to claimant.

Cornell Rogers
Clerk Com. on Citizenship

Office Com on Citizenship
Tahlequah I T   Sept 25th 1888

PUFFER

DOCKET #1308

CENSUS ROLLS 1835 and Old Settler Roll of Cherokees

APPLICANT FOR CHEROKEE CITIZENSHIP

POST OFFICE: Chetopa Kansas		ATTORNEY: ~~A E Ivey~~ C.H. Taylor	
No	NAMES	AGE	SEX
1	Margaret A Puffer	45	Female
2	*(Illegible)* M "	24	Male
3	Andy S "	22	"
4	Geo W "	19	"

ANCESTOR: James Smith and Annie Shoemake

Office Commission on Citizenship.

Tahlequah, Ind. Ter. Sept 24ᵗʰ 1888

Margaret A Puffer, Et. al.
Mary Harman
Vicy J Brown
John A Smith
Harvey Smith
W W McDonald
Thomas K McDonald
Sarah Stewart & Son William
and
Rosa Smith

Applicants for
Cherokee Citizenship
before the Commission
now Sitting Judge
I.J. Adair Chairman

In the matter of the above applicants for Cherokee citizenship, we have carefully taken up the several affidavits in this case, and from the affidavit of Mary Harman, states she was born in Overton County Tenn, and that her father James Smith sometimes called "Buck" was her father and the ancestor of all the above applicants and they all claim their Cherokee blood from him. All the testimony before this Commission is documentary and exparte and the parties testifying in their own behalf, with the exception of William Baily who claims he is not related and has no interest in the matter, he states he first became acquainted with James or Buck Smith in 1824 in the state of Tennessee, his last *(illegible)* of him was in 1832, don't say whether he remained there or came to this country. We have examined all the rolls and fail to find the name of James or Buck Smith on any of them ~~rolls~~ taken by the U.S. government, the law creating this Commission dated Dec. 8ᵗʰ 1886, especially the 7ᵗʰ Sec. of said Act, *(illegible)* states that any person making application for citizenship must name an ancestor on some one of the several rolls, we have examined carefully and find no such ancestor. Therefore we the Commission unanimously agree that the said, Margaret A Puffer, Henry M – Andy M & George Puffer – Mary Harman, Vicy J. Brown – John A Smith – Harvey Smith – W.W. McDonald – Thomas K McDonald – Sarah J Stewart and her son William Stewart and Rosa Smith, are not Cherokee by blood and are hereby rejected and are intruders upon the public domain of the Cherokee Nation, and not entitled to any rights and privileges of the Nation.

J.T. Adair   Chairman of Commission
D.W. Lipe   Commissioner
H.C. Barnes   Commissioner

307

PENINGTON

DOCKET #1309

CENSUS ROLLS 1835 – 52

APPLICANT FOR CHEROKEE CITIZENSHIP

POST OFFICE:			ATTORNEY: A E Ivey	
NO	**NAMES**		**AGE**	**SEX**
1	John G Penington		48	Male
2	Jos W "		20	"
3	Mary E "		17	Female
4	George R "		12	Male
5	Gertrud "		2	Female

ANCESTOR: Caswell Edwards

Now on this the 9th day of January 1889, comes the above case up for final hearing, the applicant having made application pursuant to the provisions of an Act of the National Council approved December 8th 1886, and all the evidence being fully considered in the Mary A. Couch case it having been made a list one in ~~which~~ governing all cases claiming a direct lineage from the same ancestor, Mima Edwards, it is adjudged and determined by the Commission that and determined by the Commission that John G Penington – Jos W – Mary E. – George R. – and Gertrud Penington are not Cherokees by blood, and in consequence no entitled to the rights of such.

The decision of the Mary A Couch case, found on page 100 of Docket "A" *(remainder illegible)*.

     J T Adair Chairman Commission
     D. W. Lipe Commissioner
            Commissioner

Attest

  C C Lipe
    Clerk Com

Cherokee Citizenship Commission Docket Books
(1880-84, 1887-89) Volume III
Tahlequah, Cherokee Nation

PATTON

DOCKET #1310

CENSUS ROLLS 1835 – 52

APPLICANT FOR CHEROKEE CITIZENSHIP

POST OFFICE: Curtis Texas		ATTORNEY: A.E. Ivey	
NO	NAMES	AGE	SEX
1	George R Patton	50	Male

ANCESTOR: Thomas Patton

Office Commission on Citizenship
Cherokee Nation Ind Ter
Tahlequah Aug 13th 1889

There is no evidence presented in the above *(illegible...)* the Commission therefore decide against the applicant George R Patton aged 50 years and whose Post Office address is Curtis Texas.

J.E. Gunter   Com

PARKER

DOCKET #1311

CENSUS ROLLS

APPLICANT FOR CHEROKEE CITIZENSHIP

POST OFFICE: Delonega[sic] Ga		ATTORNEY: A.E. Ivey	
NO	NAMES	AGE	SEX
1	Joseph A Parker	30	Male

ANCESTOR: John A. Parker

See decision in this case in that of George W Parker in Book "A" page 119. Adverse to claimant.

Cornell Rogers
Clerk Com. on Citizenship

Office Com on Citizenship
Tahlequah I T   Sept 25th 1888

PITTS

DOCKET #1312

CENSUS ROLLS 1835 – 52

APPLICANT FOR CHEROKEE CITIZENSHIP

POST OFFICE: Red Bridge Ind		ATTORNEY: L B Bell	
NO	NAMES	AGE	SEX
1	David Pitts	62	Male

ANCESTOR: John Meridith[sic]

Commission on Citizenship
Cherokee Nation Ind Ter
Tahlequah   July 2nd 1889

Application for Cherokee Citizenship

The Commission de*(illegible)* against the claimant for Cherokee Citizenship in above case because by the want of evidence in this case of Andrew Meredith Docket 2180 B.E. Page 26 P.O. Red Bridge Indiana.

Attest

D.S. Williams   J.E. Gunter   Com
Asst. Clk Com.

PERRYMAN

DOCKET #1313

CENSUS ROLLS 1835-52

APPLICANT FOR CHEROKEE CITIZENSHIP

POST OFFICE: Morrison Bluff Ark		ATTORNEY: A E Ivey	
NO	NAMES	AGE	SEX
1	Mary J Perryman	33	Female
2	Edner M "	9	"
3	Thos F "	6	Male
4	Mollie M "	3	Female
5	Earl G "	1	"[sic]

ANCESTOR: James Parker

Office Commission on Citizenship
Tahlequah I T August 16th 1889

There being no evidence in support of this case the Commission decide that Mary J Perryman age thirty three years, Edner M female age nine years,

Thomas F male age sic years, Mollie M female age three years and Ear G Perryman, are not Cherokees by blood. Post Office Mirrosson[sic] Bluff Ark. Attest

E G Ross

Clerk Commission

J.E. Gunter   Com

DOCKET #1314   *(All names illegible)*

DOCKET #1315   *(All names illegible)*

PRICE

DOCKET #1316

CENSUS ROLLS

APPLICANT FOR CHEROKEE CITIZENSHIP

POST OFFICE: Whitesboro Tex		ATTORNEY: A E Ivey	
NO	NAMES	AGE	SEX
1	William Price	25	Male

ANCESTOR:

Office Commission on Citizenship
Cherokee Nation Ind Ter
Tahlequah Aug 16 1889

There being no evidence in support of the above case the Commission decide that William Price age twenty five is not a Cherokee by blood. Post Office Whitesboro Texas.

Attest

E G Ross

Clerk Commission

J E Gunter   Com

Cherokee Citizenship Commission Docket Books
(1880-84, 1887-89) Volume III
Tahlequah, Cherokee Nation

PRICE

DOCKET #1317

CENSUS ROLLS 1835 – 52

APPLICANT FOR CHEROKEE CITIZENSHIP

POST OFFICE: Van Buren Ark		ATTORNEY: A E Ivey	
No	**NAMES**	**AGE**	**SEX**
1	Mrs. Margaret Price	52	Female

ANCESTOR: *(Illegible Name)*

Office Commission on Citizenship
Cherokee Nation Ind Ter
Tahlequah Aug 16th 1889

There being no evidence in support of this case the Commission decide that Margaret Price age 52 years is not a Cherokee by blood. Post Office Van Buren Ark.

Attest

E G Ross
Clerk Commission

J E Gunter   Com

DOCKET #1318   *(All names illegible)*

PINION

DOCKET #1319

CENSUS ROLLS 1851

APPLICANT FOR CHEROKEE CITIZENSHIP

POST OFFICE: Jasper Ark		ATTORNEY: A E Ivey	
No	**NAMES**	**AGE**	**SEX**
1	William Pinion	65	Male
2	Dovey M "	30	Female

ANCESTOR: Nancy Talley

Now on this the 17th day of May 1889, comes the above case up for final hearing, and the Commission says, "We the Commission on citizenship after examining the evidence in the above case, and also the rolls of 1851, find that the above applicant, William Pinion and his daughter Dovey M Pinion are not Cherokees by blood. They claim as their ancestor one Nancy Talley, whose name does not appear on any of the rolls as alleged. The testimony of G.W. Morris, who at one time resided in the locality where they live, *(illegible)* that they were not recognized as Cherokees by blood, but were looked upon as being of Cawtaba[sic] Indian blood.

Therefore the Commission decide that William Pinion and his daughter Dovey M. Pinion are not entitled to any rights and privileges of the Cherokee nation, and are hereby rejected.

J.T. Adair   Chairman Commission
D.W. Lipe   Commissioner

DOCKET #1320   *(All names illegible)*

PHILLIPS

DOCKET #1321
CENSUS ROLLS 1835-48-51-2

APPLICANT FOR CHEROKEE CITIZENSHIP

POST OFFICE: Spava[sic] Ark		ATTORNEY: Boudinot & Rasmus	
NO	**NAMES**	**AGE**	**SEX**
1	Missouri F Phillips	26	Female
2	William F "	5	Male
3	Cassie M "	3	Female
4	Amanda L "	1	"

ANCESTOR: Nancy Reeves

Office Commission on Citizenship
Cherokee Nation
Tahlequah June 20th 1889

There being no evidence in support of the above named case the Commission decide that Missouri F Phillips age 26 years and the following named children William F male age 5 years, Cassie M Female age 3 years and Amanda L Phillips age 1 year are not Cherokees by blood. Post Office Spava Ark.

Attest
        D S Williams
        Asst Clk Com

                              J E Gunter   Com

313

Cherokee Citizenship Commission Docket Books
(1880-84, 1887-89) Volume III
Tahlequah, Cherokee Nation

DOCKET #1322   *(All names illegible)*

DOCKET #1323   *(All names illegible)*

MORTON

DOCKET #1324

CENSUS ROLLS 1835 to 52

APPLICANT FOR CHEROKEE CITIZENSHIP

POST OFFICE: Alma Ark		ATTORNEY: A E Ivey	
NO	NAMES	AGE	SEX
1	Samuel E Morton	35	Male
2	Sarah "	11	Female
3	Joseph "	8	Male

ANCESTOR: Samuel Morton

Office Commission on Citizenship
Cherokee Nation Ind Ter
Tahlequah Aug 16th 1889

There being no evidence in support of this case the Commission decide that Samuel E Morton age 35 yrs and the following named children Sarah Morton Female 11 yrs and Joseph Morton male age 8 yrs are not Cherokees by blood. Post Office Alma Ark.

Attest
      D.S. Williams
      Asst Clk Com

                              J E Gunter   Com

MARTIN

DOCKET #1325

CENSUS ROLLS 1835

APPLICANT FOR CHEROKEE CITIZENSHIP

POST OFFICE: Fort Graham Tex		ATTORNEY: A E Ivey	
NO	NAMES	AGE	SEX
1	Mrs. Adaline Martin	26	Female

314

2	M N "	9	"
3	M F "	7	"
4	W W "	5	Male
5	L O "	3	"
6	A O "	1	Female

ANCESTOR: David Cline

Rejected Aug 16th 1889

Office Commission on Citizenship
Cherokee Nation Ind Ter
Tahlequah Aug 16th 1889

There being no evidence in support of this case the Commission decide that Adaline Martin age 26 yrs and the following children, M N Martin female age 9 yrs, M F Martin Female 7 yrs, W W Martin male 5 yrs, L O Martin male 3 yrs and A O Martin Female age 1 year are not Cherokees by blood. Post Office Fort Graham Tex.

Attest
    D S Williams
Asst Clk Com

                                J E Gunter   Com

DOCKET #1326   *(All names illegible)*

MORTON

DOCKET #1327

CENSUS ROLLS 1835 to 1852

APPLICANT FOR CHEROKEE CITIZENSHIP

POST OFFICE: Union Town Ark		ATTORNEY: A E Ivey	
NO	**NAMES**	**AGE**	**SEX**
1	J F Morton	52	Male
2	Lucy A "	17	Female
3	Amanda "	15	"
4	Louana "	12	"
5	Joe Aggie "	9	"
6	Thomas "	6	Male

ANCESTOR: Samuel Morton

Cherokee Citizenship Commission Docket Books
(1880-84, 1887-89) Volume III
Tahlequah, Cherokee Nation

Office Commission on Citizenship
Cherokee Nation Ind Ter
Tahlequah August 16th 1889

There being no evidence in support of this case the Commission decide that J. F. Morton age 52 years and the following named children, Lucy A age 17 years, Amanda age 15 years, Louana age 12 years, Joe Aggie age 9 years, Thomas Morton age 6 years are not Cherokees by blood.

Attest

  E G Ross
   Clerk Commission

       J E Gunter   Com

MORTON

DOCKET #1328

CENSUS ROLLS 1835 to 1852

APPLICANT FOR CHEROKEE CITIZENSHIP

POST OFFICE: Union Town Ark		ATTORNEY: A E Ivey	
NO	**NAMES**	**AGE**	**SEX**
1	Joseph Morton	37	Male

ANCESTOR: Samuel Morton

Office Commission on Citizenship
Cherokee Nation Ind Ter
Tahlequah Aug 16th 1889

There being no evidence in support of this case the Commission decide that Josephine[sic] Morton age *(blank)* yrs. is not a Cherokee by blood

Post Office Union Town, Ark.

Attest

  D S Williams

Asst   Clk Com   J E Gunter   Com

MILLER

DOCKET #1329

CENSUS ROLLS 1835 to 1852

APPLICANT FOR CHEROKEE CITIZENSHIP

POST OFFICE: Union Town Ark		ATTORNEY: A E Ivey	
No	**NAMES**	**AGE**	**SEX**
1	Mary E Miller	21	Female

ANCESTOR: Samuel Morton

Office Commission on Citizenship
Cherokee Nation Ind Ter
Tahlequah Aug 16th 1889

There being no evidence in support of this case the Commission decide that Mary E Miller age 21 yrs is not a Cherokee by blood and is not entitled to Cherokee Citizenship in the Cherokee Nation.

Attest
    D S Williams
Asst   Clk Com

        J E Gunter Com

MILLER

DOCKET #1330

CENSUS ROLLS 1835

APPLICANT FOR CHEROKEE CITIZENSHIP

POST OFFICE: Lancaster Ark		ATTORNEY: A E Ivey	
No	**NAMES**	**AGE**	**SEX**
1	Charles B Miller	51	Male
2	Henry E "	19	"
3	Sabra E "	14	Female

ANCESTOR: Mary Blair

Rejected Aug 16th 1889

Office Commission on Citizenship
Cherokee Nation Ind Ter
Tahlequah Aug 16th 1889

317

There being no evidence in support of this case the Commission decide that Charles B Miller and the following children Henry E Miller male age 19 yrs and Sabra E Miller Female age 14 yrs are not Cherokees by blood.
Post Office Lancaster Ark

Attest
> D S Williams   J E Gunter Com
> Asst Clk Com

MORTON

DOCKET #1331

CENSUS ROLLS 1835 to 1852

APPLICANT FOR CHEROKEE CITIZENSHIP

POST OFFICE: Webbers Falls IT		ATTORNEY: A E Ivey	
No	**NAMES**	**AGE**	**SEX**
1	Sherard Morton	30	Male
2	George "	10	"
3	Siss*(illegible)* "	8	Female
4	Julia "	4	"
5	William "	2	Male
6	Pig "	1	"

ANCESTOR: Alice Beaty

See decision in the Wm Morton case in Book "B" page 278, Docket *(Illegible)*. Adverse to the claimant.

> D W Lipe
> *(Illegible)*

Office Commission on
Citizenship
> Tahlequah IT
> Oct ? 1888

MARTIN

DOCKET #1332
CENSUS ROLLS

APPLICANT FOR CHEROKEE CITIZENSHIP

POST OFFICE: Bartlesville IT		ATTORNEY: A E Ivey	
NO	**NAMES**	**AGE**	**SEX**
1	Benj L Martin		Male
2	Callie J "	17	Female
3	Wm H "	15	Male
4	Berlton "	11	"
5	J S "	9	"
6	Cora "	4	Female

ANCESTOR: Hanson James

Office Commission on Citizenship
Cherokee Nation Ind Ter
Tahlequah August 16th 1889

There being no evidence in support of this case the Commission decide that Benjamin L Martin and children Callie J Martin age 17 years, William A[sic] Martin age 15 years, Berlton Martin age 11 years, J S Martin age 4[sic] years and Cora Martin age 4 years are not Cherokees by blood.
Attest

E G Ross
Clerk Commission

J E Gunter   Com

MOORE

DOCKET #1333
CENSUS ROLLS 1835

APPLICANT FOR CHEROKEE CITIZENSHIP

POST OFFICE: Tahlequah CN		ATTORNEY: A E Ivey	
NO	**NAMES**	**AGE**	**SEX**
1	Joseph S Moore	23	Male

ANCESTOR: William Moore

Office Commission on Citizenship
Tahlequah TI Aug 16th 1889

319

There being no evidence in support of this case the Commission decide that Joseph S Moore age 23years is not a Cherokee by blood. Post Office Tahlequah CN

Attest

E G Ross

Clerk Commission

J E Gunter   Com

MURPHY

DOCKET #1334

CENSUS ROLLS 1835 or 51 or 52

APPLICANT FOR CHEROKEE CITIZENSHIP

POST OFFICE: McKinney Tex		ATTORNEY: W A Thompson	
NO	NAMES	AGE	SEX
1	Martha Ann Murphy	17	Female

ANCESTOR: John Rich

Office Commission on Citizenship
Cherokee Nation
July 3rd 1889

There being no evidence in support of the above named case the Commission decide that Martha Ann Murphy age 17 yrs is not a Cherokee by blood. Post Office McKiney[sic] Tex

Attest

D S Williams
Asst Clk Com

J E Gunter   Com

MERIDITH[SIC][sic]

DOCKET #1335

CENSUS ROLLS

APPLICANT FOR CHEROKEE CITIZENSHIP

POST OFFICE: Afton IT		ATTORNEY: L B Bell	
NO	NAMES	AGE	SEX
1	John C Meridith[sic]		Male

ANCESTOR: Mary Crews

The Commission decide against claimant. See decision in the case of Andrew Meridith[sic] Docket 2180 Book E, Page 26 and John Henly Docket 1250, Book C Page 376.

J E Gunter   Commis

MITCHEL

DOCKET #1336

CENSUS ROLLS 1835

APPLICANT FOR CHEROKEE CITIZENSHIP

POST OFFICE: Van Buren Ark		ATTORNEY: A E Ivey	
No	NAMES	AGE	SEX
1	Jesse Mitchel	59	Male
2	Martha Ann Mitchel		Female

ANCESTOR: Mrs Mitchel

Rejected August 16th 1889

Office Commission on Citizenship
Cherokee Nation Ind Ter
Tahlequah Aug 16th 1889

There being no evidence in support of this case the Commission decide that Jesse Mitchell[sic] age 59 years and his family Martha Ann Mitchell his wife, Mary E Miller daughter, John S Mitchell Son, William A Mitchell Son, Cynthia R Phillips daughter, Adely J Arnold daughter are not Cherokees by blood and are not entitled to Cherokee citizenship in the Cherokee Nation.
Post Office Van Buren Ark.

Attest
    D S Williams
    Asst Clk Com

J E Gunter   Com

MARTIN

DOCKET #1337

CENSUS ROLLS 1835

APPLICANT FOR CHEROKEE CITIZENSHIP

POST OFFICE:		ATTORNEY: A E Ivey	
No	NAMES	AGE	SEX
1	Mary G Martin	35	Female

2	Georgia O "	12	"
3	Octave A "	10	"
4	Maggie L "	7	"
5	Flora L "	1	"

ANCESTOR: Dinah Carnes

Now on this the 30th day of May 1889, comes the above case up *(illegible...)* are hereby re-admitted to all the rights and privileges of Cherokee citizens by blood.

J T Adair   Chairman Commission
John E Gunter   Commissioner
D W Lipe   Commissioner

MARTIN

DOCKET #1338
CENSUS ROLLS 1851

APPLICANT FOR CHEROKEE CITIZENSHIP

POST OFFICE: Ophir Ga		ATTORNEY: A E Ivey	
NO	NAMES	AGE	SEX
1	Margaret A Martin	37	Female
2	Ada A "	13	"

ANCESTOR: Dinah Carnes

Now on this the 30th day of May 1889, comes the above case up *(illegible...)* are hereby re-admitted to all the rights and privileges of Cherokee citizens by blood.

J T Adair   Chairman Commission
John E Gunter   Commissioner
D W Lipe   Commissioner

Cherokee Citizenship Commission Docket Books
(1880-84, 1887-89) Volume III
Tahlequah, Cherokee Nation

McCOY

DOCKET #1339

CENSUS ROLLS 1851

APPLICANT FOR CHEROKEE CITIZENSHIP

POST OFFICE: Mineral Springs Ga		ATTORNEY: A.E. Ivey	
No	NAMES	AGE	SEX
1	George W McCoy	30	Male
2	Lela A "	2	Female

ANCESTOR: Rosanah McCoy

Now on this the 13th day of June 1889, comes the above case up for final hearing, and the Commission says "We the Commission on Citizenship after examining the evidence in the above case and also the rolls of 1852 find the applicants are Cherokees by blood and the said George W. McCoy & his daughter Lela A McCoy are hereby re-admitted to all the rights and privileges of Cherokee citizens by blood.

J T Adair   Chairman Commission

John E Gunter   Commissioner

D W Lipe   Commissioner

MILLIKEN

DOCKET #1340

CENSUS ROLLS 1835 & 1852

APPLICANT FOR CHEROKEE CITIZENSHIP

POST OFFICE: Lewisville Tex		ATTORNEY: A E Ivey	
No	NAMES	AGE	SEX
1	Nannie B Milliken	26	Female
2	Nannie L "	4	Male[sic]
3	Ada "	6 mo	Female

ANCESTOR: Ward

Office Commission on Citizenship
Cherokee Nation Ind Ter
Tahlequah Aug 16th 1889

There being no evidence in support of this case the Commission decide that Nannie B Milliken age 26 yrs and the following children Nannie L male age 4 yrs and Ada Milliken Female age 6 months are not Cherokees by blood. Post Office Lewisville Tex.

Cherokee Citizenship Commission Docket Books
(1880-84, 1887-89) Volume III
Tahlequah, Cherokee Nation

Attest

D S Williams

Asst Clk Com

John E Gunter

Commissioner

MITCHEL

DOCKET #1341

CENSUS ROLLS 1835

APPLICANT FOR CHEROKEE CITIZENSHIP

POST OFFICE: Van Buren Ark		ATTORNEY: A E Ivey	
NO	**NAMES**	**AGE**	**SEX**
1	John T Mitchel	36	Male
2	Martha C "	12	Female
3	Jesse E "	7	Male
4	Ruth Lanora "	5	Female
5	Sidney V "	1	Male

ANCESTOR: Jesse Mitchel

Office Commission on Citizenship

Tahlequah I.T. August 16th 1889

There being no evidence in support of this case the Commission decide that John T. Mitchel age 36 years and the following named children Martha C Mitchel age 12 years, Jesse E aged 7 years, Ruth Lanora age 5 years and Sidney V Mitchel age 1 year are not Cherokees by blood.

Attest

E G Ross

Clerk Commission

J E Gunter   Com

MILLIKIN

DOCKET #1342

CENSUS ROLLS 1835 & 1852

APPLICANT FOR CHEROKEE CITIZENSHIP

POST OFFICE: Lewisville Tex		ATTORNEY: A E Ivey	
NO	**NAMES**	**AGE**	**SEX**
1	Maggie C Millikin	36	Female
2	William D "	12	Male
3	Sam "	8	"

324

4	Thos G "	6	"
5	Martin H "	4	"
6	Maggie B "	2	Female
7	Charles G "	2 mon	Male

ANCESTOR: Ward

Office Commission on Citizenship
Cherokee Nation Ind Ter
Tahlequah Aug 16th 1889

There being no evidence in support of this case the Commission decide that Maggie C Millikin 36 years and the following named children Will D age 12 years, Sam age 8 years, Thomas G age 6 years, Martin H age 4 years, Maggie B age 1 years and Charles G Millikin age 2 months are not Cherokees by blood. Attest

E G Ross
Clerk Commission

J E Gunter   Com

MABRY

DOCKET #1343

CENSUS ROLLS 1835 & 1852

APPLICANT FOR CHEROKEE CITIZENSHIP

POST OFFICE: *(Illegible)* IT		ATTORNEY:	
No	**NAMES**	**AGE**	**SEX**
1	Belle Mabry	23	Female
2	Ida "	5	"
3	Lizzie E "	1	"

ANCESTOR: Uriah Wilkerson

Rejected Jan 29th 1889

Now on this the 29th day of January comes this case for final hearing the same having been submitted to the Commission on citizenship created by Act of December 8th 1886 by the attorneys for the Plaintiff and the defendant with the evidence on this 29th day of September 1888, but not decided by said Commission under the provisions of the Act of December 4th 1888 creating a commission on citizenship it is made the duty of this Commission to determine all cases not decided by the Commission created by the Act of December 8th 1886. In obedience to this requirement the under signed Commissioners having taken into consideration all the evidence submitted directly or by reference have failed to find the name of Uriah Wilkerson on the rolls of either 1835 or 1852 or any other roll named in the 7th Section of the before named Act of 1886, nor do they find the name of the mother of George W Wilkerson on the roll of 1851. *(Illegible)* this the evidence submitted fails in the opinion of the Commission to establish the identity of George W Wilkerson the Father of Plaintiff Belle Mabry or the son of the before named Uriah Wilkerson. It is adjudged and determined by the Commission that therefore by this Commission that Belle Mabry is not a Cherokee by blood and is hereby rejected and declared to be an intruder.

Will P Ross   Chair Com

This Jan 29th 1889
DS Williams   Asst Clerk Com